KLAUS BARBIE

THE BUTCHER OF LYONS

Also by Tom Bower
The Pledge Betrayed

KLAUS BARBIE

THE BUTCHER OF LYONS

B Y

TOM BOWER

PANTHEON BOOKS   NEW YORK

Library of Congress Cataloging in Publication Data
Bower, Tom.
Klaus Barbie: the Butcher of Lyons
Bibliography: p.
1. World War II, 1939-1945—Atrocities. 2. Barbie,
Klaus, 1913-   . 3. War criminals—Germany—
Biography. I. Title.
D804.G4B68 1984   940.54′05   83-21995
ISBN 0-394-53359-3

Manufactured in the United States of America
First American Edition

CONTENTS

LIST OF ILLUSTRATIONS

Section one   *(Between pages 96 and 97)*

Klaus Barbie with his wife and children (*Klarsfeld*)
Barbie with the SS team (*Klarsfeld*)
SS officers based in Lyons: Erich Bartelmus, Werner Knab and
    August Moritz
Resistance leaders captured by Barbie in 1943: Jean Moulin
    (*Sygma*) and Raymond and Lucie Aubrac (*France Soir*)
Moulin's alleged betrayer René Hardy (*Sygma*). SOE agent Henry
    Newton with Resistance radio operator André Courvoisier
    (*Kentish Gazette*)
Izieu: the Halaunbrenner family, the Jewish schoolchildren
    deported to Auschwitz, and the plaque which commemorates
    the tragedy (*Klarsfeld*)
The SOE and the Maquis de l'Ain: Richard 'Xavier' Heslop, Paul
    Johnson, Julien and Marius Roche, and Albert 'Didier'
    Chambonnet
The Klarsfeld family (*Klarsfeld*)

Section two   *(Between pages 192 and 193)*

Barbie's American handlers: Herbert Bechtold (*Bower*),
    Eugene Kolb (*Bower*), Erhard Dabringhaus (*UPI*), Earl
    Browning (*Bower*) and Dale Garvey (*Bower*)
Barbie in 1948, when he was interrogated by US Army
    Intelligence (*Klarsfeld*). The 'Rat Line' organisers: George
    Neagoy and Jim Milano (*Bower*)
The 'Rat Line' documents used by Barbie and his family for their
    passage through Italy and into Bolivia (*McFarren*)
Barbie under American protection: with his wife, children, and
    Herbert Bechtold in the garden of their house in Augsburg
Klaus Barbie in 1969, as managing director of the Transmaritima
    Shipping Corporation (*Sygma*). Beate Klarsfeld demonstrating
    in La Paz in 1972 (*Gamma*)

7

The 1972/3 attempt to kidnap Barbie (*Klarsfeld*). Regis Debray
who helped in the attempt. Barbie released from prison in 1972
(*AP/Wide World*) and with his permanent bodyguard, Alvaro
de Castro (*McFarren*)

The Fiebelkorn Gang in 1982 (*McFarren*). Barbie en route from
La Paz to Montluc prison, February 1983 (*McFarren*)

Justice and investigation: Allan Ryan, US Special Investigator
(*UPI*), Christian Riss, the Lyons examining magistrate (*UPI*),
and Alain de la Servette, Barbie's first defence lawyer, with Ute
Messner (*Gamma*)

All photographs not credited are from private sources

GLOSSARY

BND	Bundesnachrichtendienst, the West German secret service
CDU	Christian Democratic Union, the largest conservative party in West Germany
CIA	Central Intelligence Agency
CIC	Counter Intelligence Corps, US Army
CID	Criminal Investigation Department
CNR	Conseil National de la Résistance, the co-ordinating committee of the Resistance established by Moulin
CROWCASS	Central Registry of War Criminals and Security Suspects, based in Paris
DGER	Direction Générale des Etudes et Recherches, French organisation investigating Nazi war crimes
DGSE	Diréction Générale de la Sureté Extérieure, the external security service of the French police
DST	Direction de la Sureté du Territoire, the French equivalent of MI5
EUCOM	European command, the US military occupation authority in the US zone
FSM	French Security (Military), based in Baden-Baden in the French zone
HICOG	American High Commission for Germany, which replaced OMGUS, military government in the US zone
JAG	Judge Advocate General, the British/American army legal service
KPD	Kommunistische Partei Deutschlands, the West German Communist Party
MNAT	Mouvement National Anti-Terroriste, anti-Resistance organisation set up by the Vichy government
MNR	Movimiento Nationalista Revolucionario, a

	Bolivian pro-Nazi party which has swung towards the centre in recent years
MUR	Mouvement Unis de la Résistance
OMGUS	Office of Military Government (US), replaced by HICOG in September 1949
OSS	Office of Strategic Services, the American wartime foreign intelligence agency
PPF	Parti Populaire Français, the French wartime Fascist party
RSHA	Reichsicherheitshauptamt, Himmler's head office
SD	Sicherheitsdienst, an elite organisation responsible for the Nazi Party's intelligence and security service
SDECE	Service de Documentation et de Contre-Espionage, the French equivalent of MI6
SED	Sozialistische Einheitspartei Deutschlands, the East German Communist party
SHAEF	Supreme Headquarters, Allied Expeditionary Force
SOE	Special Operations Executive, which co-ordinated British support for the Resistance
SOL	Service d'Ordre Légionnaire, a system of conscripted labour organised by the Germans in France
SS	Schutzstaffel, the guardians of the Nazi party
UGIF	Union Générale des Israelites de France, the Jewish federation established by the Germans in France
UNWCC	United Nations War Crimes Commission

PREFACE AND ACKNOWLEDGEMENTS

For fifty years Klaus Barbie has worked for governments – both officially and unofficially. He has served both democracy and dictatorship. The governments which hired him for his skills were never disappointed. Manipulation, interrogation, extraction, torture and murder were the services he offered, and they were purchased in the full knowledge that Barbie had considerable experience of his trade. Invariably, it is the same kind of politicians and officials as those who hired him, who now pay sanctimonious homage in mighty-sounding phrases to the cause of justice. Yet, since the end of the Second World War, they have, both implicitly and explicitly, protected him.

The return of Klaus Barbie to France on 5 February 1983 to be tried for his wartime crimes was the victorious culmination of an extraordinary campaign by Serge and Beate Klarsfeld against sceptical, lethargic and downright hostile government officials and politicians. With enormous effort, Serge Klarsfeld discovered many vital documents and eyewitnesses which revealed Barbie's miserable career and which convinced governments finally that his continued freedom insulted too many people and ideals. Beate Klarsfeld devoted months, despite discomfort and hardship, to protest against what they both saw as the immorality of protecting a notorious criminal. Whether the course of justice will reward that effort remains to be seen. In writing this book, I am very grateful for all the help they have given me.

My investigation of the postwar treatment of Nazi war criminals began in 1978, when Christopher Capron, then editor of BBC Television's *Panorama* programme, encouraged me to pursue what proved to be an unexplored area. The result has been several programmes on the subject which have been shown in more than twenty-five countries. He is now the head of the BBC's Current Affairs group and generously gave me permission to pursue this present saga. With equal goodwill, George Carey, then editor of *Panorama*, allowed me the time and gave me the necessary

11

support to make two programmes about Barbie. The second (first broadcast in July 1983), revealing his American connections, was reported by Margaret Jay. She gave me important help and good advice. To all three, and to many other colleagues in Lime Grove, I am very indebted.

This type of book cannot be written without the friendship, help and unqualified generosity of many people. It is their professionalism and enthusiasm which has made this report possible. Foremost is Bob Fink in Washington, whose extraordinarily meticulous research has won him not only my gratitude but the respect of many American officials and former US intelligence agents. In France, I owe a special debt to Janet Thorpe; in Germany to Stefan Aust; in South America to Peter McFarren and Jan Rocha; in London to Caroline Wolfe and Isobelle Daudy, who helped me full time on all aspects of the project.

Others who helped me at various stages are David Bernouw at the Dutch Institute for War Documents, Hero Buss, Phillipe Daudy, Professor James Dunkerley, Jean-Claude Gallo, Elke Gerdener, Dr Josef Henke at the Federal archives in Koblenz, Dr M. Koenigsberg, Fred Kufferman, John Loftus, Henri Nogueres, David Pryce-Jones, Marcel Ruby, Jacques de la Rue, Fay Sharman, Daniel Simon at the Berlin Document Center, Tulla Skari, Lucien Steinberg, Paul Tarr, and Dr Hans Umbreit at the Federal archives in Freiburg. A special thanks also to Chris Bates who rapidly taught me the delights of a word processor.

More than two hundred people were interviewed in the course of research for this book. I am grateful to all those who are quoted, but also to those who have had to remain anonymous. Much of the material in this book has come either from classified government archives or from government officials who wanted an authoritative version told, but could not be quoted. I am naturally very grateful to them all. The editing and production of the book was managed at record speed thanks to the hard work and skill of my editors.

Finally I owe a special debt to my parents for their support and friendship, and to Nicholas and Oliver, who were always interested but, more important, always patient.

THE CONSPIRACY

Lawyers do not usually contemplate murder, but this was a special case. For eleven years, Parisian lawyer Serge Klarsfeld and his German wife Beate had battled in vain to bring a vicious Nazi torturer and mass murderer back to Europe to face his victims. With guile and contempt he had frustrated their most dedicated efforts. Ever since he had been discovered hiding in Bolivia in 1971, Klaus Barbie had boasted provocatively about his love for Adolf Hitler, his undying devotion to Nazism, and how he had humiliated the French Resistance in Lyons. His scornful defiance of the French had wounded his surviving victims and the Klarsfelds were determined on revenge.

In late summer 1982, the Klarsfelds feared that he was about to disappear forever into the impenetrable South American under-world of fugitive Nazis, that haven which had nourished and protected so many of the architects and executioners of Hitler's Reich. They were, quite simply, determined that 'The Butcher of Lyons' was not going to have the pleasure of joining them. Their options were crude, perhaps, but were, they felt, inevitable. If Barbie could not be brought back to Europe alive to stand trial for his massive crimes as Gestapo chief of Lyons during the Occupation, he would have to be killed.

Seven thousand miles away, on the high plateau of the Andean mountains, Bolivian politicians and generals were struggling through a more than usually turbulent political crisis to settle the fate of the country's 191st president. Waiting in exile to become the country's next leader was the liberal president-elect, Hernán Siles Zuazo. In July 1982, Zuazo had told reporters that the protection and friendship which Klaus Barbie and his family had enjoyed from Bolivian generals since 1951 would end once he took over in La Paz. Zuazo did not explain his intentions, but no-one missed the important new ingredient: this was the first time that any Bolivian politician had even suggested that Barbie was not a fully protected Bolivian citizen. Yet, Zuazo's statement contrasted sharply with

13

events in the capital: at that very moment, the grey-haired tubby figure of Klaus Barbie was seen emerging from the presidential palace. He had just spent one hour paying his compliments to his good friend, the new President. The significance of that visit was clear. Klaus Barbie was the first civilian to be received by the new President since taking office – confirmation, if it were needed, of his importance in the country.

In Paris, the Klarsfelds warily monitored developments. Although experienced and successful Nazi-hunters, they could not predict his tactics on this occasion. In such a volatile climate they could only guess at their prey's reactions to political change. At the beginning of October, Bolivia was reported to be preparing itself for yet another president. Siles Zuazo was finally sworn in on 10 October and now the Klarsfelds feared that Barbie would flee the country. Exactly three days later, Serge Klarsfeld bought a one-way ticket for a young Bolivian to fly to La Paz (via Barcelona and Buenos Aires, 'so as not to raise suspicion') to see if Barbie was preparing to escape. Beate Klarsfeld is unashamedly honest about their intentions and motives had the report been positive:

> Barbie would have been killed. Serge and I felt responsible for the mothers of the children he had murdered. It was inconceivable to us that the mothers would one day die, having suffered terrible anguish for forty years, and Barbie would still be enjoying life. We always told the mothers that killing would be an act of despair, a defeat, but that we had to be prepared to kill him if we couldn't find a legal solution. It would still have been a success.

The Klarsfelds' agent reported from La Paz that, posing as a businessman, he had actually met and spoken with Barbie and there was no immediate indication that the German was planning a swift escape. Instead, he was sticking to his regular routine of drinking coffee in his favourite bar, the *Confiteria La Paz*, and visiting his dying wife in hospital. His faithful Bolivian bodyguard, Alvaro de Castro, was by his side, but then Barbie had been protected thus for ten years. Asked by a journalist a few days after Zuazo became President whether he feared extradition, Barbie replied, 'I doubt if President Zuazo will extradite me. The war has been over for thirty-seven years. I was doing nothing but defending my people when Germany and France were at war.' The only outward sign of the Nazi fugitive's concern about his safety, was that he had relinquished his favourite table in the middle of the café and now sat at the side, with his back to the wall. Serge Klarsfeld asked his associate to keep Barbie under observation and decided to see whether the French government was prepared to renew its 1972 request for Barbie's extradition. He telephoned an old friend at the Elysée Palace, Régis Debray, a special assistant to President Mitterrand. Debray had more than a passing interest in both Bolivia and Barbie.

In 1967, Debray had become internationally famous as a French Marxist and journalist. He had joined the legendary Cuban guerrilla leader, Che Guevara, on his historic but futile attempt to encourage the Bolivian peasants to revolt against the country's dictatorial landowners and generals. Guevara was soon killed and Debray arrested. In the late Sixties, the young Frenchman became a martyr. His whole cause – books, the trial, and the imprisonment – aroused passionate sympathy among student radicals around the world who were demonstrating against the Vietnam war. In 1970, with the help of President de Gaulle, he was reprieved of his thirty-year sentence. Inevitably, on his return to France, his anger against the repressive and murderous Bolivian juntas and their 'security advisers' had not disappeared. Klaus Barbie was one of those advisers. In early 1972, the Klarsfelds had masterminded an aggressive international campaign to force Barbie's extradition from Bolivia, but it had failed. Bitterly disappointed, the Klarsfelds immediately recruited Debray into an audacious plot.

Using a false passport, Serge Klarsfeld flew to Chile in December 1972 to meet Debray, who at the time was living in the capital. Renting a small plane, they flew together from Santiago to Chile's north-eastern border with Bolivia for a prearranged meeting with Bolivian guerrillas who were keeping Guevara's cause alive. The Frenchmen's plan was for the guerrillas to kidnap Barbie and bring him, drugged, across the border, whence he would be flown down to Santiago and loaded onto a ship bound for France. The plan agreed, Klarsfeld returned to France, leaving the guerrillas to arrange the safe houses, cars and other necessary ingredients of a kidnap. Their plan depended on the sympathetic cooperation of Chile's Marxist President, Salvador Allende. But in early 1973, the CIA's sudden destabilisation of the Allende government plunged Chile into crisis.

After weeks of planning, there was no alternative but for Klarsfeld and Debray to abort their mission.

They had kept in touch over the next decade, so when Serge called Debray at the Elysée Palace on 26 October 1982, asking to see him urgently, he was given an appointment the following afternoon. For an hour, Klarsfeld and Debray discussed the new conditions in Bolivia and the chances of a successful request for Barbie's extradition. The legal hurdles seemed, as ever, insurmountable: Barbie had Bolivian nationality, he seemed to be an intimate friend of many important Bolivians, and France had no extradition treaty with Bolivia. Yet Klarsfeld and Debray agreed that they could never hope for better conditions. Bolivia's new President was a socialist, very friendly towards France and a personal friend of several French cabinet ministers. He was also anxious to improve Bolivia's image and wanted French help. A week earlier he had told the *New York Times* that he favoured Barbie's extradition. When the French ambassador in La Paz read the report, he had discreetly reminded the new President that the West German government had officially requested the Nazi's extradition the previous May. To ensure Zuazo's complete cooperation, Klarsfeld and Debray agreed that they now needed the personal prestige and authority of the French President.

There was a strong Jewish contingent in President Mitterrand's cabinet and many of their fathers, including the President's, had been members of the French Resistance. Mitterrand's and Klarsfeld's fathers had been members of the same Resistance group. Everyone knew that President Mitterrand was always anxious to ennoble the memory of the Resistance. To emphasise that commitment, the President had on the day of his inauguration, paid a special solemn visit to the tomb of the Resistance leader, Jean Moulin, in the Pantheon, the resting place of many French heroes. Moulin had been tortured to death by Barbie and the fortieth anniversary of his death was approaching. The catalogue of Barbie's other alleged crimes in Lyons would make the prospect of his arrest, in Debray's view, very attractive to the government. It would be a national homage to his victims – 4,342 murdered, 7,591 deported to German concentration camps and 14,311 arrested.

Debray had good access to the President and had soon explained the chances of extracting Barbie from South America. Predictably, the President was immediately interested, and not just to satisfy his own feelings. It is in the nature of politics that governments seek any device to increase their popularity: Mitterrand was not averse to a project which might cost little but produce so much. His government had won a spectacular election victory in May 1981 but it was already under pressure to compromise and sacrifice many of its election promises. The opinion polls showed that support for France's first socialist government to be elected since 1936 had declined sharply. Any opportunity of winning overwhelming national approval and boosting the government's prestige was not to be missed.

Mitterrand cautioned Debray about the need for utmost secrecy, not only to avoid alarming Barbie, but also to protect the government in the event of failure. Both men knew that success depended on a sensitive approach and on delicate negotiations with both West Germany and Bolivia. The West Germans had to be consulted because, since 1975, they were empowered to prosecute Germans who had committed war crimes in France. President Zuazo had to be convinced that he should accept Germany's recent request for Barbie's extradition. There was no doubt in the President's mind that Bonn would be agreeable, and France, which had always prided itself on its special understanding of Latin America, could help diplomatically.

Not all the news from La Paz in early November was encouraging. Barbie was reported suddenly to have disappeared, probably to another country. Paraguay, the reputed refuge of Josef Mengele, the infamous Auschwitz 'doctor', was mentioned as his likeliest destination. The Elysée was not deterred. Common sense dictated that even Nazi murderers do not abandon their dying wives. Quietly, the operation was launched. Only a handful of ministers and officials with a 'need-to-know' were to be alerted and included in the special team which was to be masterminded by Jean Louis Bianco, the head of the President's personal staff. Others in the select group were the Foreign Minister, Claude Cheysson, a courageous Resistance veteran, and the Minister of Justice, Robert Badinter, whose father had been arrested in Lyons by Barbie personally in 1943, and had never returned from Auschwitz.

The first to leave for Bolivia was Antoine Blanca, France's roving ambassador on the continent. When he arrived at the end of

17

November, his access to Zuazo was guaranteed: the French ambassador in La Paz, Raymond Césaire, had given the Bolivian President sanctuary when his life was in danger during a coup in 1980. Blanca was immediately assured of Zuazo's sympathy but cautioned that there were many problems. Zuazo's reaction was telexed to the Elysée.

In Lyons, a town covered with plaques and statues commemorating the victims of Barbie's reign of terror, Christian Riss, a thirty-six-year-old examining magistrate, had been slowly sifting through the Barbie files since February. Serge Klarsfeld had discovered, to his astonishment, in late 1981, that, because of bureaucratic incompetence, there were neither charges nor a warrant outstanding against Barbie in France. As the Elysée prepared its Barbie operation, Robert Badinter advised Riss to find, discreetly but urgently, a list of new charges and formally issue a warrant for Barbie's arrest.

At the beginning of December, the French ambassador in Bonn called at the West German Foreign Ministry. After briefing senior officials about the French government's assessment of the new situation in Zuazo's Bolivia, and of its strong interest in securing Barbie's extradition, he asked the German government to press their case immediately in La Paz. Neither he nor his government in Paris was prepared for the reply. With the authority of Hans-Dietrich Genscher, the Foreign Minister, the German officials explained that, although they had requested Barbie's extradition, Germany felt distinctly lukewarm about his return and a trial. According to one of the French ministers, 'When we heard the news from Bonn, we were very surprised, but when Zuazo heard about it in Bolivia, he was stunned and embarrassed. He wanted to get rid of Barbie; but it was a new, democratic government, and he wanted it done legally. Unless the Germans changed their minds, it was going to be very difficult.'

Barbie had just celebrated his sixty-ninth birthday. If he was brought back to Europe, the worst he could expect was life imprisonment. Germany had abolished the death penalty after the war and President Mitterrand's own government had just passed the unpopular legislation dismantling the guillotine. When Barbie finally returned, outraged, to Europe, he protested not at his unjust imprisonment but at his illegal expulsion from Bolivia. After nearly fifty years of serving tyranny, the outlaw was criticising democratic governments for failing to obey the letter of international law.

THE NAZI

Nikolaus 'Klaus' Barbie was born on 25 October 1913 in Bad Godesberg, a small quiet town next to the Rhine, just south of Bonn. Although both his parents were Catholic, they did not marry until three months after his birth. The ceremony was held in Merzig, in the Saar, where the Barbie family had lived since the French Revolution. According to Barbie himself, his forefathers were probably called Barbier, and left France as refugees during the reign of Louis XIV.

His father, also called Nikolaus, was first an office worker and later a primary school teacher at the Noder school where Barbie himself was a pupil until the age of eleven; he died in 1933, aged forty-five, the late victim of a First World War bullet wound. Barbie claimed that his father was wounded at Verdun and, in anger at French occupation of the Rhineland, had joined the German resistance movement. Naturally, he claimed that his father's activities were, unlike those of the French Resistance, both legal and justified. That occupation undoubtedly coloured his feelings about the French. Those who knew Barbie after the war say that he was very fond of his mother, Anna Hees. Her second son had died at eighteen, of a heart disease, and she was proud of her surviving son's distinction although probably quite ignorant of his activities.

Barbie's relations with his father were very strained. A heavy drinker, whose developing illness was sharply cutting into his income, his father increasingly subjected his young son to disciplinarian tirades which Barbie himself admits had a very detrimental effect on his whole life and personality. It was therefore a considerable relief when, in 1923, Barbie moved away from his family to the Friedrich-Wilhelm grammar school in Trier, initially as a boarder. 'I was finally independent,' is how he described his feelings in a revelatory essay written when he left in 1934. He felt liberated from the pressure of being the schoolteacher's son: 'It was a major aspect of my education.' In 1925, however, the whole family moved to Trier. Once again, 'I had to live with my mother and father. I was happy, but I was also disappointed.' He clearly felt the effects of his unhappy home life: 'The terrible hardships which I suffered during [those years] will be my secret forever, and have repercussions on my future . . . Those years made me a wise man, teaching me how bitter life can be, and how terrible destiny.'

In 1933, both his father and brother died. The Barbie family was plunged into depression and tumult at the very moment that Adolf Hitler became Germany's Chancellor. The deaths were 'a terrible blow for my mother and myself,' wrote Barbie. 'I must say that destiny, through the death of my father, has completely destroyed my most cherished hopes.' After several attempts, Barbie finally passed his graduation exams in 1934, but with just average marks. 'This year's events,' he wrote, 'have left me restless. Like every other true German, I am attracted by the powerful national movement, and today I serve alongside all the others who follow the Führer.'

By this time, Hitler had been Chancellor for more than a year. All the alternative political ideologies had been radically suppressed. German schoolchildren had become the victims of relentless indoctrination, resisted only by those whose parents were outright opponents of the Nazis. Even then they usually had to join the Hitler Youth movement. Only those who emigrated were spared. Barbie was by then twenty. Too old for the excuse of political naivety, he positively discriminated in favour of Nazism, and was not only a member of the Hitler Youth movement but also the personal assistant of the local Party leader.

University was barred to him after graduation. With his father's death the family had no money to finance further studies. Unemployed and without the prospect of a secure professional career, he went instead for six months to a Nazi Party voluntary work camp in Schleswig-Holstein. Willingly enthralled by the intense ideological atmosphere, he emerged a fully committed supporter of the Third Reich. He relished the life-style, comradeship and self-importance that attachment to the Party gave. As he admitted forty years later in Bolivia, he became a life-long Nazi dedicated to Hitler and German supremacy, and learnt a violent contempt for those who failed the racial and moral tests which the SS state immortalised.

On 26 September 1935, after submitting to tests for his racial and medical purity, Barbie joined the SS. Member no. 272,284, he was destined for the *Sicherheitsdienst* (SD), that elite corps within the SS whose life was devoted to enforcing Nazi ideology and protecting the Party. Very few emerged from that training course as anything less than resolute Nazis.

It was during those early days of the SS that Barbie says he saw Himmler and Heydrich close up. In 1979, Barbie met Himmler's adjutant General Karl Wolff in Bolivia and for one week reminisced about his life: 'I once played handball with Himmler in the head-quarters courtyard. He seemed very stiff, shy but very polite. One could have a normal conversation with him. He knew how to command respect. Heydrich was the intellectual. Very different.' After he left Berlin, Barbie saw neither of his chiefs again.

His first attachment was in Berlin, as an assistant in department IV-D of the SD main office. Within weeks he was posted to police headquarters in Alexanderplatz to start that training as an investigator and interrogator which was to be so admired and exploited by different governments over the next forty-five years. After a few weeks' attachment to the murder squad, he was transferred to the vice squad, headed, as Barbie affectionately remembered him, by 'Uncle Karl'. It was Barbie's first taste of power, and it left a memorably strong impression.

Berlin at this time was corrupt, corpulent, seedy, debauched and overwhelmingly decadent. As it struggled to survive the approaching inferno, the capital was a wonderland for the self-appointed morality police, and a revelation for the schoolteacher's son. Every night, 'Uncle Karl' took his team out to raid bars, brothels and nightclubs:

One evening, Uncle Karl, who knew every pimp in the city said, 'OK, lads, tonight we're going to raid the Usambara bar.' I've never experienced anything like it in my life again. We sat around the bar in plain clothes. At three in the morning, all the whores from the Friedrichstrasse and Puttkamerstrasse came in with their pimps to settle the night's accounts. I had never seen such rows or heard such language. And then the unbelievable fights which started when the pimps began to hit the whores. It was a bizarre dream show. In the middle of it, Uncle Karl went outside and called up the blue police maria, and everyone was arrested and carted off.

On other nights, Barbie would play the innocent punter looking for a prostitute: 'They would say to me, "Come on, titch. Two marks for a moll." Once inside, I'd pull out my ID card and shout, "Criminal police." ' Just reliving those moments forty years later reduced Barbie to tears of laughter. 'I'd arrest them. They had to serve special punishment when the Olympics were on, and they didn't like it. Nebe, the police chief, ordered them all to peel potatoes for the sportsmen. He called it, "Peeling for the Fatherland." '

When he was not pursuing whores, Barbie was already persecuting Jews, especially those involved in the fur trade, or homosexuals. He remembers with relish an assignment with an SD squad after his transfer to Düsseldorf in 1936. Their destination was an unique homosexual club. As usual, they entered the club in disguise and sat around waiting until the chief stood up and all the men realised they were caught in a raid. Barbie was staggered by what followed. Each homosexual admitted to being a senior officer in the Nazi Party, the Hitler Youth movement, or even the SS. To Barbie's approval, their punishment was swift and severe. All of them were physically beaten by Barbie and the other SD officers, and then jailed. 'If I think of all those homosexuals in Germany today,' said Barbie forty years later, 'I think I'd hand my German passport back, if I had one.'

By the end of 1938, Barbie's career in the security services was assured. When Party membership lists were reopened in 1937, he automatically joined, as member no. 4,583,085. In the same year he passed through the SD school at Bernau and was sent to the exclusive leadership course in Berlin's Charlottenburg. For those chosen few, military service was a mere formality. For three months, from September 1938, he served with the 39th Infantry Regiment, before returning to Charlottenburg for his final training and exams. The first test was boxing, an experience he never forgot. His opponent was a full 30 cms taller. 'He beat me so hard that I was sick everywhere. But I had to quickly pull myself together and do a leapfrog over eight men, and I was still feeling sick.' He was, by his own account, not a physically tough man. On 20 April 1940, he graduated and was promoted to SS Untersturmführer (Second Lieutenant).

Five days later, he was married. The bride was Regine Willms, a stocky twenty-three-year-old daughter of a postal worker from

Osburg. She had left school early, trained as a cook and then worked as a maid in Berlin. In 1937 she joined the Party and began working in Düsseldorf in a Nazi Women's Association children's nursery. When they met, Barbie did not have a permanent home. Unusually for the times, he moved into her apartment before they were married.

Within days of the ceremony, Barbie rejoined his SD detachment and was thrown into von Rundstedt's two-million-strong army invading the Low Countries and France. At this time Barbie was not a member of the Gestapo, which was section IV in the SD, but was assigned to section VI, intelligence. According to Barbie, his unit got as far as the outskirts of Dunkirk, arriving some time after the last British soldiers had scurried for survival across the Channel. With the port overcrowded, the unit was ordered back to the Hague in Holland, to await 'Operation Sealion', the invasion of Britain. Two weeks later, in early May, the channel crossing was postponed. Barbie's unit was put under the direct command of Willy Lages, the SD commander in the Hague, and then shortly afterwards transferred to the *Zentralstelle* in Amsterdam, the 'Central Bureau for Jewish Emigration'. His responsibilities included rounding up German emigrés, freemasons and Jews.

Holland's 140,000 Jews proved to be the most vulnerable Jewish community in Europe. Sixty per cent were concentrated in Amsterdam and after the occupation found it extremely difficult to leave the country. Only 30,000 were to survive the war. Educated and comparatively wealthy, in 1940 they were already well aware of Nazi policy towards the Jews. More than in any other European country, the Dutch Jews actually understood the full implications of the German promises to deal with the Jews. But with considerable subtlety, the *Zentralstelle* moved quickly to dampen those fears and gave assurances which Jewish leaders enthusiastically accepted. It was only a temporary lull; some were not deceived and there was a rash of suicides.

Barbie was at the forefront of these activities, excited by the responsibility but even more excited by the licence to manipulate and deceive. The first personal report written about him in October 1940 reflected his flair: sent from Holland to his commanding officer in Germany, it said that he had 'thrown himself energetically and intensively into SD work'. According to his commanding officer,

Barbie was a 'disciplined, hardworking, friendly and honest officer, a faultless comrade, who was excellent at his work and an honour to the SS'. A month later, his hard work and loyalty was rewarded and he was promoted to Obersturmführer (First Lieutenant).

The Germans imposed the first of a series of discriminatory measures against the Dutch Jews in October. Jewish businesses were subjected to compulsory purchase for trivial compensation, and Jews were summarily dismissed from state employment. Soon after Christmas, anti-semitism escalated from bureaucratic harrassment to physical assault. Acting on the orders of the *Zentralstelle*, organised groups of Dutch Nazis began attacking Jews on the streets in Amsterdam. It followed the by then customary pattern which had been established in other European cities – humiliation followed by beatings. There was outrage, but little more. In February, the *Zentralstelle* ordered Dutch paramilitaries to increase the pressure.

Groups of uniformed Dutch stormtroopers began attacking Jewish homes and businesses. To their utter surprise, instead of cowed submission they met with fierce resistance. Not only did the Jews protect themselves, but non-Jews joined in the fight. The glorious defence was short-lived, but during a running battle, a stormtrooper was wounded and died. On 12 February 1941, the German command used his death as a pretext to seal off Amsterdam's Jewish quarter. Barbie and the SS were mobilised. Early that morning, all but one of the bridges across the canals were raised; the SS had effectively created a Jewish ghetto. 'Three hard weeks followed,' is how Barbie remembers the 'raging' battle, as the Germans and Dutch paramilitaries rampaged along the canals and through the narrow streets. 'The Jews were upstairs in their houses, and we were in the streets.' The intense fighting lasted for just two days and the unrest for two weeks, but the climax for Barbie occurred on 19 February, in the south of the city.

Two Jewish refugees from Germany, Cahn and Kohn, had opened a popular ice-cream parlour called *Koko*. Using improvised weapons and with the help of friends, they had beaten off several attacks in previous days. Their ebullient confidence and evident self-satisfaction was enough to provoke a counter-attack. Barbie and his team arrived at the parlour with strict orders, on Barbie's own admission, only to arrest the Jews, and not to harm them. With the brazen initiative which was to characterise all his exploits throughout the war, Barbie led the charge.

As the first man to burst through the barricaded door, he threw a bicycle into the doorway to prevent anyone barring it behind him. As he turned, one of the defenders squirted ammonia into his face. Although stunned (later he was to need treatment), he rushed forward. Among the twelve Jews inside the bar, he saw Cahn. 'He had a nice bald head. I still had enough strength to pick up an ashtray and smash him on his head. He was badly wounded.' Everyone inside was then arrested.

In the immediate aftermath, on 22 February, SS troops stormed through the Jewish quarter with appalling brutality. Four hundred and twenty-five Jews were arrested, most of whom were subsequently deported to Mathausen concentration camp where, after considerable suffering, they died. The arrests were followed by a strike which was ineptly handled by Barbie's commander, Sturmbannführer Wilkens; he was reprimanded and transferred. This was of little concern to Barbie, who was finding life more pleasant than he had imagined possible. The SS had, after all, won the battle, and they celebrated in royal style with members of the Dutch Nazi Party and senior police officers: 'We drank until eight in the morning. An amazing party, marvellous comradeship. Unrepeatable. And that's what one survives on when one's exiled like this.'

After three days' leave, Barbie returned to duty and claims that he was ordered to finish the job. Cahn and his friends had been condemned to death. 'I was put in charge of the firing squad. One of the condemned asked to hear an American hit record, and then we shot them. I really felt quite ill seeing their brains squirting out all over the place.' For his services, on 20 April, Barbie was awarded the Iron Cross, second class.

Pressure on the Jews increased. On 14 May, a bomb was thrown into a German officers club in the Jewish quarter of Amsterdam. Although the evidence suggests that it was thrown not by Jews but by a resistance group, the Germans decided that the Jews should suffer the reprisals; this time they adopted a more subtle approach. On the morning of 11 June, Barbie arrived at the offices of the Jewish Council, the organisation set up by the Germans to represent Dutch Jews. To the astonishment of the two co-presidents, Abraham Asscher and David Cohen, Barbie politely introduced himself and shook both of them by the hand. Barbie confessed that the Germans had a problem, although he confided that it would be relatively easy to find a solution. Three hundred Jewish apprentices had been forced to leave their training camp, the lieutenant explained; but, after reconsideration, the Germans had decided that the boys should be allowed to return. Rather than collecting the boys by driving around the streets, the Germans wanted to write individually to the boys and advise them of the good news. Barbie therefore needed a list with the boys' addresses. Faced with so polite and reasonable a man, Cohen handed over the list and Barbie, still the soul of courtesy, bade his leave.

That afternoon, Cohen and Asscher were called down to police headquarters. To both it seemed to be a routine summons, except that they were kept waiting endlessly. At 6.00 p.m., Asscher was allowed to phone his home: paralysed with horror, he listened to the news that the Germans had just completed a massive round-up of young Jews. An hour later, the two numbed leaders were taken to SD commander Lages' room. The boys had been arrested, said Lages, as a reprisal for the bomb attack. Cohen and Asscher's pleas for mercy were curtly ignored. To complete their misery, they were taken out of the building past the Jewish boys, who were standing in long rows. Both whispered despondent words of comfort, but soon found themselves alone and miserable on the street. All the boys were deported to Mathausen and were dead before the end of the year, some of them used for early gas experiments in summer 1941.

Just days after that coup, Barbie's daughter, Ute Regine, was born in Trier. His notification of this fact to headquarters in Berlin on 4 July was from Amsterdam, but it is unlikely that he stayed for much longer in the city. Although it does not appear on his official service record, he travelled east via Königsberg and was attached to a special commando group whose mission was to support the German invasion of Russia. During the initial weeks of that ferocious advance, Barbie was employed fighting Russian partisans with a Gestapo unit. It was an introduction to cruder methods of interrogation and to the low value that Germans placed on their enemies' lives. Homes were needlessly destroyed, women and children murdered and men brutally tortured to extract information. If Barbie is a sadist, it was during those months in Russia that he recognised the possibility of satisfying his pleasure.

In spring 1942, he was recalled to Berlin and assigned a delicate mission which needed a French speaker. He was sent as security chief to Gex, a French town on the Swiss border now under German occupation, to kidnap Alexander Foote, an agent working for Moscow with Leopold Trepper. Foote was living in Geneva. Barbie's brief was to arrange his kidnap and bring him back to occupied France. Barbie's base in Gex was a house which actually stood on the Franco-Swiss border. During the preparations for the kidnap, Barbie walked into the house in France, changed his clothes and walked out the other side into Switzerland. Fundamental to the success of the mission was a successful border-crossing by car. Barbie claims that he solved this problem by befriending the chief of the Swiss customs post in Gex. In return for helping him to meet his girlfriend in France, he was promised that he could drive through the border without a search. Headquarters in Berlin gave the green light, Barbie put the rehearsals into practice, but Foote suddenly disappeared. Barbie's next posting, in June, was to Dijon.

France in summer 1942 was still a very pleasant command for German soldiers. The French were relatively benign, there was good food and the occupiers enjoyed a privileged existence; Dijon was quiet, with very few partisan attacks. But at German military command headquarters there was a firm sense that the days of sympathy were drawing to a close. The unoccupied southern part of France, ruled by the collaborationist French government, was hosting too many anti-German groups. Lyons, France's second largest city, had become in name at least the capital of the nation's resistance. Plans were drawn up to occupy Vichy France. It just needed an excuse to implement them and that was conveniently provided by the Anglo-American invasion of French North Africa. On 11 November, the German army crossed the demarcation line. Klaus Barbie, recently transferred from section VI to section IV, arrived in Lyons as head of the Gestapo.

THE BETRAYAL

With hindsight, France in 1940 was in no state either to oppose the invading armies, or to organise an effective underground resistance to German occupation. Over the previous decade, deep political divisions, aggravated by a spate of public scandals, had resulted in the chronic series of weak governments that characterised the last days of the Third Republic. The mood of the country was one of despondency and exhaustion. The government's reluctant declaration of war in September 1939 was, to the majority of the French, an ominous harbinger of chaos – instant bloodshed and devastation seemed inevitable.

Instead, the first eight months of the war were comparatively uneventful, and when the invasion finally came in May 1940, a dispirited, disorganised, even mutinous French army was no match for the outstanding military tactics of the Wehrmacht. There was scant enthusiasm to defend the 'rotten' Third Republic, and with considerable relief, France capitulated on 17 June at the end of a campaign that had lasted only six weeks. Her proud military reputation in ruins, her government divided, her people so paralysed by confusion that some even welcomed the swift victory of the invaders, it seemed impossible to believe that France would ever be able to produce a resistance force capable of troubling Barbie's Gestapo in Lyons.

The German army had reached the outskirts of Lyons on 1 June. Terrified by the ferocious bombardment of Bron airport, about half the city's population of 500,000 immediately fled south. Only a few disparate army units, including a company of Senegalese troops, patriotically stood their ground waiting to defend the town. Contemptuously, the Germans held back until 19 June, two days after the government's formal surrender, and entered the city virtually unopposed. Barely any townspeople were on the streets to see the conquerors march in, watch the Swastika replace the Tricolour, and witness the handful of brave but futile acts of resistance. 'What

29

silence,' commented an awed but melancholy observer. 'One could sense the flow of the Rhône.'

The occupation of Lyons lasted less than three weeks. Suspicious of the French, Hitler was as uncertain then as he remained throughout the war about the role France should play in the Thousand Year Reich. Total occupation seemed an unnecessary liability and since France had, unprompted, delivered a government which seemed more than willing to collaborate, dividing the country was an ideal solution. Paris and the north would be ruled by the German army while below the demarcation line Marshal Pétain and Pierre Laval, based in the spa town of Vichy, would head an ostensibly independent government of fourteen million people. Hitler's solution produced a very uneasy peace but it momentarily silenced most anti-German feelings.

The German army pulled out of Lyons on 7 July. In the cellars of the Prefecture lay twenty-six rotting corpses of black Senegalese soldiers who had been captured outside the city, the first victims in Lyons of German racialism. News of the massacre provoked no demonstrations of anger or resentment. The German withdrawal was simply greeted with relief and the city, like the rest of the country, resumed life as if little had changed. Only those who were determined to oppose both the Germans and the armistice faced an unenviable dilemma. To stay meant acceptance of the defeat, to answer de Gaulle's ambitious call to join him in London would be akin to betrayal, even treason. Most decided to stay. If they were soldiers, their only act of resistance was to hide their weapons in the hope of using them in the impenetrable future.

For those very few Frenchmen who, in summer 1940, instinctively felt that they could neither live nor collaborate with the Germans, Lyons was a natural destination. South of the demarcation line, it was the nearest 'free' city to the capital. Politically conservative and without the pretensions of Paris, it stood at the crossroads of the nation's transport system, divided by the rivers Rhône and Saône with rail and road connections to every city. Its sheer size and its warren-like network of passages and streets made it, in the early years of the war, an ideal refuge for those seeking anonymity. The former capital of Roman-occupied Gaul became the 'natural birthplace' of the French Resistance.

Resistance in the early months meant little more than a discreet and seditious discussion of opposition to the government. Among those who had emigrated to the south were many of the nation's leading journalists, who felt unable to write for Paris's censored press. Some managed to print a handful of primitive pamphlets appealing for support and opposing the collaborationist government. Others scrawled slogans on walls. But the popularity of the First World War hero, Pétain, seemed indestructible. When he visited the city on 18 November, he was greeted by no fewer than 150,000 people. De Gaulle's answer to this was an appeal from London for the streets to be deserted for one hour on New Year's Day. The response appeared to be overwhelming but in fact meant very little.

A lack of political leadership frustrated the immediate growth of the Resistance. The dismay and disillusionment with pre-war politicians persisted into the occupation. None of them became leaders of the underground movement and none of the violent pre-war animosities ever disappeared. France's defeat provoked a bloody civil war between pro-Armistice and Resistance factions which the Germans skilfully and ruthlessly exploited. It took more than a year for some of the antagonists even to consider temporarily setting aside their differences to face the common enemy. Lyons was the setting for the sensitive negotiations and vital compromises which led to the creation of the national Resistance movement. But it was a difficult and hazardous birth, repeatedly thwarted after Barbie's arrival.

During the first year, three distinct, non-communist resistance movements developed, all based in Lyons but each determinedly independent of the others because of the political views and personalities of their leaders. Henri Frenay led the largest group, 'Combat', Emmanuel d'Astier de la Vigerie headed 'Libération', and Jean-Pierre Lévy founded 'Francs-Tireurs'. They were an incompatible trio. Frenay was a diligent, methodical ex-officer, an organiser who was simultaneously careful and brave, yet aggressively ambitious to become leader of the whole secret army. Equally brave, Astier had the opposite temperament: a swashbuckling, hot-headed charmer, he found Frenay lacklustre and unattractive. Levy was at neither extreme and tried to act as conciliator.

The groups had different specialities and strengths among various professions in different areas of the country. In theory they had

31

penetrated the government, the telephone and postal services, the railways and the police. All had tenuous links with small but committed groups of refugees stranded in France: expelled Alsatians, Belgians, Poles, rootless survivors from the Spanish civil war and Jews escaping persecution were determined to fight the Germans, even if the French were reluctant. But the three groups were handicapped by political and personality struggles. During that first year their leaders met to discuss common aims but then withdrew to protect their separate identities, political views, methods and membership. Active support for the Resistance had probably diminished by the end of the year. Deprived of money, weapons, and experience, it was a victim of the harmony created by Vichy and Berlin.

France's cosy fiction ended on 21 June 1941 with the German invasion of Russia. Overnight, the French communists, who had until then been compromised and politically disarmed by the non-aggression agreement in 1939 between Nazi Germany and communist Russia, submerged themselves into the underground and declared war on the occupation army. Resistance groups began negotiating, more pamphlets appeared and sabotage increased. For the first time, unarmed German soldiers were assassinated on the streets, provoking, as intended, vicious reprisals. Dozens of innocent Frenchmen were summarily shot, straining French tolerance of the occupation and undermining the comforting myth that the Germans were, if not welcome, at least decent friends. The honeymoon relationship was shaken but it was not destroyed; most of those executed were imprisoned communists.

Building an underground army posed enormous risks. The tradecraft of a guerrilla war still had to be learnt: isolation cells, dead-letterboxes, cover names, safe houses, chains of command and above all rigorous discretion. Ignorant and inexperienced, all the groups were riddled at best with novices, at worst with informers. Lyons, as a Resistance mecca for all of France, was inevitably heavily policed. Diligently and obediently the Vichy police around Lyons carried out continuous swoops, successfully arresting not only fledgling members of the Resistance, but also agents sent from Britain by the Special Operations Executive (SOE).

The relationship between the Resistance movement and the SOE was a delicate one. There are innumerable historic landmarks establishing the almost unshakeable antagonism between Britain and France and old prejudices born with the Battle of Hastings and the burning of Joan of Arc at the stake were inevitably reconfirmed when the British abandoned the French in June 1940 and fled back across the Channel from Dunkirk. Propagandists in Berlin and Paris found little difficulty convincing many Frenchmen that the British were not their natural allies. Their message seemed to receive irrefutable confirmation when, on 4 July 1940, the British (after issuing an ultimatum that it should either join the Allies or scuttle itself) destroyed the French fleet at Mers-el-Kébir, with the loss of 1267 French sailors. This severely complicated Britain's relationship with the Resistance not only in France, but also in London. The French nation heard only about the carnage and not about the warning and ultimatum.

Throughout the war neither the British nor the American government were prepared to treat de Gaulle as the official representative of a French government in exile. Both allies were unsure to the point of actual distrust about exactly how much support he could command in France and what policies he would pursue once the country was liberated. The same distrust spilled over into SOE and other Resistance operations.

In summer 1941, without consulting de Gaulle's Free French forces, SOE headquarters in Baker Street parachuted the first of a dozen British agents into the area near unoccupied Lyons to contact sympathetic Frenchmen and train them into the nucleus of a fighting force. During the first fifteen months, five networks were established around the city: NEWSAGENT, PIMENTO, HECKLER, GREENHEART and SPRUCE. Most of the agents arrived suffering from a combination of bad training, inappropriate equipment, appalling breaches of the fundamental rules of self-protection, and vicious personality differences with their intended colleagues.

All the agents sent to Lyons had to co-operate either with Phillipe de Vomécourt or Georges Dubourdin. Vomécourt was domineering, intemperate and reckless, but also brave and imaginative. Dubourdin was the opposite. An impossible mix for any newcomer who, parachuting into a dark, hostile country, expected at least friendly support. Only Virginia Hall, a sober thirty-five-year-old American, proved a sure guide and friend. Despite her artificial leg, she built a credible relationship with the local gendarmerie, passing herself off as an American journalist.

Among the early arrivals were Ben Cowburn, a Lancashire oil technician, and radio operators Denis Rake and American-born Edward Wilkinson, neither of whom had sets. Cowburn immediately began organising small but successful acts of sabotage, but the other two wandered desperately around the zone looking for a base, a radio set and the organisation which could channel their courage and training into some recognisable achievement. On 13 August they met a newly-arrived SOE agent, Richard Heslop, who had just landed by boat, and all three headed towards Limoges. Two days later they were arrested by French police. All three denied anything but a passing acquaintance – a futile excuse since both Wilkinson and Rake had brand new banknotes which ran in perfect consecutive order, and identity cards which, although allegedly issued in different towns, were written in the same handwriting. To Heslop's fury, Rake immediately admitted his identity. All three were imprisoned for three months, simultaneously punished by the French yet begrudgingly protected from the Germans.

On 28 June 1942, three other British agents arrived by parachute near Tours: Brian Stonehouse, a fashion artist turned radio operator, and two brothers, Alfred and Henry Newton. They were met but not greeted by Vomécourt. Brusquely Vomécourt ordered Stonehouse to separate from the Newtons and travel to Lyons. After a long delay because of illness and mishaps, he finally began transmitting for several SOE groups operating out of Lyons, but not for the Newtons.

Although separated in age by nine years, Henry and Alfred were known as 'the twins'. Before the war, as the 'Boorn Brothers', they had been acrobats in a circus, travelling around Europe with their parents, wives and children. This happy way of life was brought to an abrupt end when, in 1942, the ship carrying both their families to safety was torpedoed by a German submarine and they were all drowned. Not surprisingly, the Newton brothers were keen to exact revenge. Under the code names 'Auguste' and 'Artus', their SOE mission was to train French groups in sabotage. Their vendetta went sour from the outset.

Their own account, written by Jack Thomas and published in 1956, reflects their considerable bitterness. Called *No Banners*, it is filled with colourful descriptions of their successful exploits against the jackbooted Hun, their bravery and unquestioned patriotism at the risk of a horrible death. There was no reason for Jack Thomas to query the Newtons' account because it had been completely accepted by SOE officers after the war. It is, however, as will be seen, seriously flawed. The purpose of exposing these flaws is not to undermine the undoubted courage of the brothers but to reveal the methods and style of Klaus Barbie.

According to the Newtons in this account, the reception party on the landing field greeted them with insults. Surprised and despondent, they spent their first night uncomfortably in a farm house, where their money was 'stolen' before daybreak. They were then dispatched with little kindness to Lyons to await their contact, Vomécourt, whom they knew under the code name 'Walter'. That meeting was arranged to take place four days after their arrival. The rendezvous was a Lyons restaurant, where to their obvious discomfort four Germans, described by Thomas as 'Gestapo agents', were eating at the next table.

'Suddenly a waiter bawled from the middle of the floor: "Messieurs 'Auguste' et 'Artus', si'l vous plait." With beads of cold sweat breaking out on their faces, Henry and Alfred sat motionless. They did not need to turn their heads to know that the four Germans had stopped eating, that their ears were pricked for just what might come next.' The waiter loudly told the two that he had a message from 'Walter' that he could not make the meeting. Thinking on their feet, the brothers managed to persuade their German neighbours that the whole episode was a sexy joke.

The brothers met 'Walter' a few days later. They were shocked by his contemptuous manner. The French, he told them, needed money and arms, not more Englishmen to fight the Germans. At the end of this harangue, Alfred claims to have cautioned him quietly about his poor security, especially at the restaurant.

'It might interest you to know,' said Alfred, 'that one of the gentlemen in question – the one in the light-cream trench coat, the owner of the Alsatian dog – was Herr Barbe [sic], Sturmbannführer Barbe, the local Gestapo chief.'

'I know him,' 'Walter' said. 'That doesn't stop me going about my business.'

This was June, a full five months before Barbie arrived in Lyons. It is the first of many distortions in the brothers' account.

The brothers and Vomécourt were never able to reconcile their differences after this first argument. The brothers doggedly tried to build a network but say they were frustrated by 'Walter' who, until the last weeks of their operation, kept them away from Stonehouse who was supposed to transmit their messages to London. It is a curious complaint because Stonehouse is quite emphatic: 'I never met the Newton brothers again after we arrived in France, and as far as I remember, it wasn't my job to be their radio officer.'

Despite these problems, the brothers did build up the GREENHEART network, basing it partly in Le Puy, a small town nestling in high, rolling hills a hundred kilometres south of Lyons, and partly in Borne, a small village outside Le Puy, the area for the parachute drops. They arranged a few drops and organised some limited sabotage missions, but they still felt aggrieved at being undervalued and undermined, and were furious that their French associates continuously broke all the most fundamental rules of security. After the war, they expressed exasperation at the desperately isolated struggle they undoubtedly endured in the early days when the Resistance was still surviving its baptism of fire.

The condition of the Resistance in Lyons was critical: it was fragmented, militarily weak, politically divided, and cut off from Britain, its only sure supplier of material. It seemed to be suffocating at birth. The SOE's task was made increasingly easier as the French began to realise that the Germans were draining their country systematically of its food and its industry; but the Resistance still lacked a national leader in France itself.

On the clear, cold night of 1 January 1942, three parachutes floated down over a marsh east of Arles from an Armstrong Whitely twin-engined plane personally commandeered by the British Foreign Secretary, Sir Anthony Eden. One of his secret deliveries into France was Jean Moulin, code-named 'Max'. His task was to convince all the different factions of the Resistance that they should unify under one leader, General de Gaulle.

At the outbreak of the war, Moulin was Prefect of Eure-et-Loir, living in Chartres, a town south-west of Paris. At the time he was France's youngest prefect, noted for his dark, handsome features, his charm, intelligence and administrative skills. Politically, Moulin was a fervent supporter of the Republic: left wing, but not an extremist or a radical; a man of principle. When the commandant of the newly-arrived German troops in Chartres ordered him to sign a declaration that a group of air-raid victims had been brutally massacred by dissident Senegalese soldiers, he refused. Jailed and brutally beaten, he cut his own throat with a piece of broken glass rather than face the temptation of conceding in the trial of strength the following day. It was 18 June, the same day that de Gaulle made his historic appeal to the French to rally to his flag.

Moulin was taken unconscious to the local hospital but, after his recovery, was dismissed by the Vichy government because he was unwilling to collaborate with the Germans. In November 1940 he 'retired' to the south coast in the unoccupied zone and immediately began exploring the possibilities of escape to England to meet de Gaulle.

For a year, while he waited, Moulin toured as much of France as possible, contacting members of the Resistance, most significantly Henri Frenay, the leader of 'Combat'. They met in Marseilles, shortly before Moulin left for Lisbon to catch a plane to Britain. Frenay's briefing on the state of the Resistance focused on its ambitions rather than its achievements, but Moulin already knew enough to impress the Gaullists in London who were in desperate need of inside information.

De Gaulle saw immediately that Moulin was the first Frenchman to arrive from the occupied mainland with the qualities of leadership necessary to transform the fractious resistance movement into a cohesive force which could win the Free French in London the vital recognition of the Allied governments. Over eight weeks, Moulin was intensively briefed on de Gaulle's policies, given basic training for fighting an underground war and provided with a completely new identity. When Frenay met him again in January, it was 'a different Jean Moulin'. Besides a new moustache, he had a firm mission, with power and directives. Agnes Bidault witnessed that first reunion. 'I remember him taking out of his waistcoat pocket a tiny note of paper, hidden in a matchbox. It was the directives for the Armée Secrete which could only be read through a microscope. It was something completely new for us all.'

Moulin's message to Frenay was simple and brutally blunt. Frenay could only hope to wage an effective campaign against the Germans if he was properly equipped with money, guns and, most important of all, radios. The only source was London and to tap that source Frenay had to be prepared to accept de Gaulle as leader.

Within a few days, Frenay had agreed. Moulin immediately gave him 250,000 francs in cash, half of the funds he had brought from London. The two other groups did not come to heel so quickly. Both Lévy and Raymond Aubrac from 'Francs-Tireurs', and Astier from 'Libération' were willing, even keen, to talk to Moulin, but they were not convinced that money and supplies alone could unite the three movements under de Gaulle. Only Moulin's diplomatic skills could convince them that it was possible to work with Frenay and with the communists. According to Frenay, 'From the first day, "Max's" relations with the movements were excellent. At the time there was a lot of friction between us. Impartially, using considerable skill, he brought us all closer together without meddling in everyone's internal affairs.'

Frenay's glowing post-war testimonial hides the bitter acrimony between himself and Astier, and between himself and Moulin, which continued during the months after Moulin's return – damaging arguments which sometimes raged for hours without conclusion. Patiently and helplessly, Moulin watched the antagonists continue their blood-letting while he methodically organised radio receivers, safe houses, dead-letterboxes, links with de Gaulle in London and finance for each group. But by August even he could not conceal the problems created by the failure of the leaders to agree to unite under de Gaulle. There was an unmistakable crisis of morale. Potential recruits were often discouraged from joining the Resistance because of its splintered and argumentative leadership.

De Gaulle's solution, which he communicated to Moulin in October, was to set up a co-ordination committee to which all three movements would affiliate. Ostensibly they would retain their separate identities. Both to ease Moulin's task and to prove where the real power lay, de Gaulle sent his envoy twenty million francs to distribute amongst the Resistance leaders. Within days the three agreed to de Gaulle's proposal. It was the first step towards unity and, more importantly, de Gaulle had imposed his leadership on the movement. With his envoy now firmly in control, not only money, but arms and equipment were parachuted into France. Each shipment increased Moulin's power and influence just at the time when the potential threat to the Resistance capital of France from the Germans became fact.

'Operation Attila', the German army's plan for crossing into Vichy France, was implemented on 11 November 1942, just three days after the Allied landings in French North Africa. General von Rundstedt noted in his diary that the French army was 'loyal' and 'aided our troops', and that the French police were equally helpful. Eighty SS officers arrived in Lyons the same day. Thirty were dispatched to outlying areas. The others, including Barbie, stayed in the city.

Surprisingly, the Gestapo had not decided in advance where to site their headquarters. It was only four weeks later that the fifty-strong SS team moved into sixty rooms on the second and third floors of the Hotel Terminus next to the Perrache railway station. Their living and sleeping quarters were on the second floor. Twenty rooms on the third floor were reserved for interrogation. The prisoners were to be brought daily from Montluc prison. According to the official French police investigation conducted after the war, the rooms at the Terminus were not specially equipped with torture equipment. That would only come in June 1943 when the Gestapo, clearly suffering from an increased work load and insufficient space, moved into the vast Ecole de Santé Militaire on the Avenue Berthelot.

The first SD commander for Lyons and the region was Rolf Müller, but he transferred in early 1943 to Marseilles. His position was temporarily filled by Fritz Hollert who was noticeably disgruntled when he was replaced that summer by Dr Werner Knab, a thirty-four-year-old lawyer born in Munich. Knab changed the whole tone of the Lyons SS team. He arrived directly from Kiev in Russia where he had been a commander of the area's SS and SD forces. During his posting he had been a Gestapo chief and an active member of *Einsatzgrüppe C*, a squad of elite SS men organising and carrying out the mass murder of tens of thousands of Jews, gypsies, communists and whomever else the Nazis considered undesirable. These murderous duties, according to a 1943 report recommending him for promotion to colonel, he carried out with, 'quite extraordinary skill'. A thin, impenetrable, ambitious officer, he spoke both French and English, having spent four and a half months in London and Stratford-upon-Avon. He arrived in Lyons without a scruple for human life and with complete dedication to his cause. In Barbie he found a very willing subordinate and disciple.

Rolf Müller assumed total responsibility for security over the city and region. He allowed none of the usual arguments to arise (as had arisen in Paris during the early days of German occupation of France) between himself and the Wehrmacht about who was in control. When arguments did later develop, they concerned the degree of ruthlessness necessary to suppress the Resistance.

The SD in Lyons was organised into six sections. Section I, under Lieutenant Kassler, was officially responsible for management and trusteeship of seized goods. (According to a French police investigator, Kassler left France at the end of the war with at least twenty-five million gold coins, while other subordinates left with millions-of-dollars-worth of jewels and securities.) Section II was a small legal department, while section III tried to control the French economy, and especially the black market.

Section IV, the Gestapo, was headed by Barbie himself. He divided his own department into six sub-sections specialising in the resistance and communists, sabotage, the Jews, false identity cards, counter-intelligence and the intelligence archives. At the beginning, about twenty-five German officers worked directly under him. Twelve months later, as the Gestapo set up branches in other towns in the region, the number of officers under his direct orders increased. His leadership was efficient, dynamic and totally uncompromising. To the amusement of other Gestapo officers, Barbie was an outright 'workaholic'.

Barbie's domain outside Lyons covered 15,000 miles stretching from the north of the Jura mountains along the Swiss border, and south down the Rhône into the Hautes-Alpes. When Italy withdrew from the war in September 1943, Barbie immediately became responsible for Grenoble and another 3,000 square miles. With frenetic energy he often crossed his 'official' boundaries to operate also in Marseilles and Dijon. Overall, his territory was a mixture of long plains and rugged, wooded, mountainous areas with inaccessible villages and isolated farms. Potentially it was a troublesome area, but for the moment most of the French were still happy to be safe from the ravages of war. The single-minded twenty-nine-year-old lieutenant had as much power as a medieval tyrant. His rule was uncontrolled and unlimited. It was in fact a return to the Dark Ages, only Barbie did not even feel answerable to God.

The SD's section V, the *Kripo*, investigated crime. Not surprisingly, it was the smallest of the sections. Section VI was responsible for espionage, intelligence and infiltration. Elsewhere in the German Reich, it would have reported directly to Schellenberg's Amt VI in Berlin, but there are doubts about this in Lyons. After the war, the Allies, anxious to exploit the expertise of German intelligence, exonerated many Amt VI officers as being less criminal than the rest of the SS. Under Kommandant Talmann and August Moritz, section VI in Lyons not only exploited the enormous amount of information offered by collaborating Frenchmen, but also unhesitatingly encouraged the murder of anyone considered to be an enemy of Germany or of Vichy France.

Gestapo rule over Lyons in the first weeks was hesitant. Despite German penetration of the city over the previous months, the SS lacked sufficient information to make more than a few arrests. Barbie correctly assessed that, despite the sincere offers of help made by René Cussonac, the pro-German Lyons police chief, the city's force was considerably weakened by the inclusion of Resistance sympathisers in its ranks. Over the months he built up a cadre of trustworthy Frenchmen, of whom he said twenty-five years later, 'Without them I could never have done my job so well.'

Of the five SOE networks operating when Barbie arrived, including the Newton brothers' GREENHEART, only PIMENTO, which was organising resistance among railway workers, was to survive his immediate onslaught. As will be seen, his treatment of those British SOE agents whom he captured reveals that he made a sharp distinction between the British and the French. Barbie's earliest successes were against the SOE.

Under the armistice agreement, the German military were not allowed to operate in the unoccupied zone but this ruling had been blatantly ignored by the Germans – especially by the Abwehr and Gestapo. German agents had operated throughout the zone, using false papers provided by the Vichy government and getting help from the Vichy police.

The greatest danger to the SOE had been an elite SD squad based in Charbonnières, west of Lyons, and working under the cover of the armistice commission, which specialised in monitoring illegal radio transmissions. Several months before the Germans crossed into Vichy France, a squad of disguised Abwehr radio-detection vans had efficiently pinpointed the small but careless group of

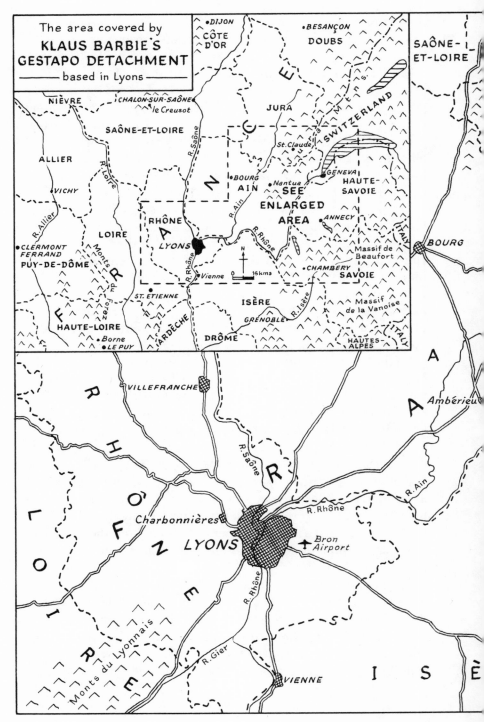

The area covered by
**KLAUS BARBIE'S
GESTAPO DETACHMENT**
—— based in Lyons ——

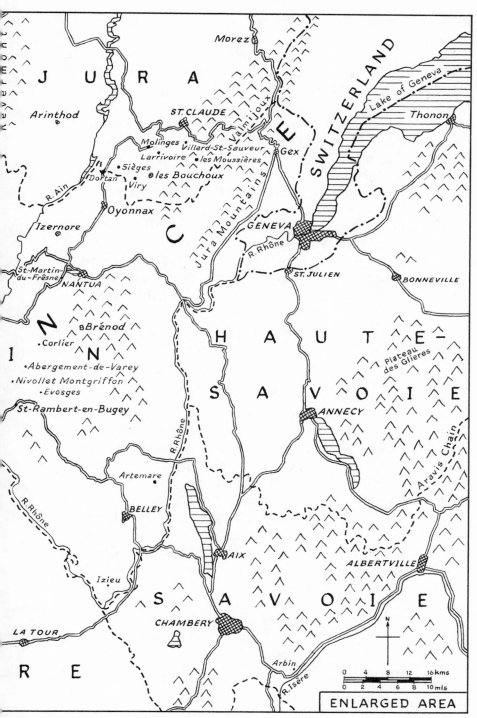

Revermont

J U R A

Morez

Arinthod

ST. CLAUDE

Valmijoux

SWITZERLAND

Lake of Geneva

Thonon

Molinges   Villard-St-Sauveur

Larrivoire   •les Moussières

•Sièges

Dortan   •les Bouchoux

Viry

Gex

Jura Mountains

C E

Izernore

Oyonnax

GENEVA

R. Rhône

St-Martin-
du-Frêsne

NANTUA

ST. JULIEN

BONNEVILLE

I

N

N

•Brénod

•Corlier

•Abergement-de-Varey

•Nivollet Montgriffon

•Evosges

St-Rambert-en-Bugey

H A U T E -

S A V O I E

Plateau
des Glières

R. Rhône

Artemare

ANNECY

Aravis Chain

BELLEY

R. Rhône

AIX

ALBERTVILLE

Izieu

S A V O I E

LA TOUR

CHAMBERY

N

Arbin

R. Isère

0   4   8   12   16kms
0   2   4   6   8   10mls

R E

ENLARGED AREA

British radio officers who had been sent to the Lyons area by Baker Street.

On 24 October 1942, a clear two weeks before the Germans officially crossed into unoccupied France, Brian Stonehouse realised that he had been detected. He was still resolutely tapping a long message to London when the Vichy police burst into his room. The subsequent interrogation was conducted by both German and French officers. 'Everything was so confused that I stupidly confessed that I was a British officer, but I wasn't tortured even after Barbie arrived in the city.'

Soon after, Peter de la Chêne of the NEWSAGENT network was arrested. Interrogated but not tortured by Barbie, he revealed nothing and was sent to a concentration camp. His fellow radio operator, Robert Burdet, for whom Barbie offered a six-million-franc reward, quickly left the city and escaped through Spain. Harried by the Gestapo, Virginia Hall and other members of the group disappeared into the countryside and the network was destroyed.

HECKLER's radio operator, André Courvoisier, was Barbie's next victim. His department's handling of the arrest was an exceptional piece of carelessness, with none of the hallmarks of skilled police investigation.

For three weeks Courvoisier had suspected that he was being followed. Bicycling home on 27 February 1943, he saw the dreaded black Gestapo car. He passed his house and only returned late that night when the car had gone. Taking his radio set and five revolvers he hid them immediately in a locker in his factory. Disregarding basic security rules, he then returned home where he was arrested by the Gestapo at 7.00 the following morning. There had been no time to destroy the papers which listed the members of the whole network and the hiding places of spare radio sets – clearly incriminating evidence, but completely overlooked by Barbie during his search. Hours after Courvoisier's arrest became known, Resistance sympathisers were able to destroy the paperwork and hide the radios in fields outside the town. Courvoisier, meanwhile, was taken to the Hotel Terminus, interrogated and severely beaten, losing many of his teeth. Despite the appalling pain, he stuck to his cover that he was an escaped prisoner of war. In between interrogations, he worked in the kitchens at the Montluc prison, and it was here in early April, as he took food to prisoners in their cells, that he met Henry Newton.

The brothers had been worried since early February that, despite their efforts, their security had been breached by careless French helpers. By March, according to the account written by Jack Thomas, they were convinced that the Germans had obtained their full description from a Frenchman dressed as a cleric, whom they called 'the Bishop'. They had rejected his offer of secret film of the German construction of the 'Atlantic wall', fearing that the deal had been set up by the Germans to confirm that they were British spies.

Awaiting denunciation at any moment, the brothers had spent the last weeks of March hidden in a factory, waiting for finalisation of their escape to Spain and then back to England. As fast as their escape routes were established, the Gestapo efficiently arrested their contacts. Dragnets masterminded by Barbie pulled in the owners of safe houses, radio operators and couriers with money belts intact. At last, by 4 April, it seemed that a safe route had been established.

That evening, the brothers sat down to a farewell meal. With them were their most trusted friends: Alphonse Besson ('Thermogène'), his wife Germaine ('Bohémienne') and Monique Herady ('Fernande'), their courier. Just before 9.00 p.m., as they were finishing, there was a knock at the door. Hearing German voices, the brothers ran up the stairs. From down below, one of the German officers shouted out, ' "Auguste", "Artus" ', their code names. After a brief but vicious fight, they were arrested by Barbie and taken to the Hotel Terminus for interrogation. They had few doubts about what awaited them.

Under the laws of war, Barbie was fully entitled to order the execution of all five: the British because they were spies and the French because, as members of the Resistance, they had broken the armistice agreement signed by the Vichy government. Before leaving England, the Newtons, like all other SOE agents, were told that on arrest they should try their best to stick to their cover stories. Should that prove impossible, either because of the circumstances surrounding their arrest or because of torture, each agent was asked to hold out for at least twenty-four hours so that the remainder of the network had time to disappear. Once in France, it was not always easy to follow the instruction handed out in Britain.

M. R. D. Foot, the SOE's historian, describes the agent's plight as follows: 'If arrested, he did his best to tell his cover story; but seldom with success. Arrest usually meant discovery, discovery usually meant torture, followed by deportation, deportation usually meant death. There were exceptions.'

The Newtons' own account of their treatment in Hotel Terminus is dramatic. In separate interrogations, both denied from the outset that they were British agents. They claimed that they were crashed RAF pilots trying to get back home. Alfred, at the end of the first interrogation by one of Barbie's subordinates, feared that he would not be able to withstand the appalling torture promised for the next day. It was while he was escorted to that second session on the third floor that he passed an open window and, in a flash, threw himself out into the void. Ever vigilant, the Germans had strung wire netting across the courtyard: miraculously, he survived the fall with a broken leg, broken fingers, a fractured shoulder and concussion. Medical facilities in the Montluc were spartan and his cries of pain were heard throughout the prison.

Henry, the dominant brother, was meanwhile interrogated by Barbie. He makes the bizarre claim that Barbie accused him of being the Czech responsible for the assassination of Reinhard Heydrich in Prague in June 1942. The questioning, according to Henry, was continuously punctuated by a series of wild and vicious blows. Once he lashed out at one of Barbie's assistants. His reward was to be beaten half unconscious. Then, on successive days, he was subjected to electric shocks, nearly drowned in an ice-cold bath (one of Barbie's specialised tortures), strapped to a table and hit with a stick, and burnt with a red-hot poker.

Even Alfred, despite his injuries, was not spared. Barbie deliberately hit him on his sensitive wounds. Like his brother, he too refused to break his cover story, even when he was about to be shot against the prison wall.

Back in the cells of Montluc, after the 'days of punishment and interrogations [which] succeeded each other monotonously', Alfred's courage was bolstered when he heard the two women, 'Bohémienne' and 'Fernande', singing messages to him as they passed beneath his cell window – only to be deflated again when he saw his brother Henry brought back to the prison lifeless on a stretcher.

46

All five of those arrested were transferred in May by train to Fresnes prison in Paris. According to Thomas:

> To Alfred's incredulous joy, he found himself in the same com-
> partment as Henry, 'Thermogène', 'Bohémienne' and 'Fer-
> nande'. It was a wonderful reunion, particularly as the guards
> stationed in the corridor made no attempt to stop them talking to
> each other. They spent their journey to Paris checking their cover
> stories and figuring just how much the enemy had been able to
> find out.

After some weeks in Fresnes, the brothers were transferred to Buchenwald concentration camp where, despite appalling conditions, they survived the war. Their return to England was an anti-climax. Sad, lonely, and feeling the terrible futility of their sacrifice, they both suffered chronic sickness before they died.

The Newtons' story, as related by Thomas is, however, an inaccurate one – however colourful. There are three living eyewitnesses to contradict their account.

André Courvoisier, who saw Henry nearly every day for six weeks in Montluc, is quite emphatic that the agent was neither tortured nor even injured. 'There was never a mark on Henry. But I do remember the day when he gave me a ring which he asked me to pass on to "Fernande". He seemed to think that he would not survive the next few days.' Four days later, Henry asked Courvoisier to retrieve his ring, 'because the danger had passed'. Courvoisier remained friends with the Newtons after the war and is still convinced that they were brave men.

Madame Besson, 'Bohémienne', still lives in Lyons on a small pension. Her account completely discredits the Newtons' story. She insists that she neither saw the brothers in prison after their arrest nor sang messages to Alfred from the Montluc prison yard. She has also denied that she was either interrogated or tortured and she is sure that when she saw the brothers on the train, neither of them had any marks suggesting torture. Moreover, during that journey the German guards prevented any conversation. Mrs Besson did not even speak to her husband, whom she never saw again.

The third account contradicting the brothers' is Barbie's own. Reminiscing to General Wolff in 1979 about his successes against the SOE, his recollection was undoubtedly confused, if only because forty years had elapsed. He may well have grouped many events into one story and almost certainly he exaggerated his achievements. But it is an account which contains two remarkable coincidences with earlier parts of the Newtons' story.

At the beginning of 1943, recalled Barbie, he heard that two British agents were landing between Toulouse and Lyons on a sabotage mission. Hidden from view, the Gestapo watched the agents parachute down and then followed them to a small factory. Shortly afterwards, the Germans were spotted and the SOE agents began shooting, only to be forced to surrender when they ran out of ammunition.

Both protested that they were British soldiers, producing military ID tags which had been hidden in their shoes. Barbie insisted that they were dressed as civilians and were therefore spies, who could be shot. Both became very depressed. Barbie remembered that one of them even threw himself out of the window but was saved by a net stretched across the courtyard. The other agent, Barbie remembers, was quite different: 'He was surprisingly easy to break. He confessed immediately and revealed a Resistance camp near Grenoble.' With just the threat of torture, Barbie had extracted the information he wanted.

It is indisputable that at 5.30 p.m. on 5 April, the day following the Newtons' arrest, Barbie and a squad of Gestapo officers arrived in Le Puy and arrested four people: Charles 'Charlot' Causse, Pierre Pestre, and M. and Madame Jean Joulian. All four had worked with the Newtons but, because of personal differences with other Resistance workers in the Newtons' Le Puy network, had formed their own group. All of them were taken the same day to Montluc and interrogated by Barbie. Three days after the arrest, the squad of Gestapo officers returned to Le Puy and dug up the Joulians' garden where they discovered eleven hermetically sealed cylinders containing guns and ammunition; these had been parachuted to the Newtons' network. At the same time, 'Charlot' and Pestre were released. Madame Joulian was released only three months later. Her husband returned from the Mathausen concentration camp at the end of the war.

Only one member of the Newtons' GREENHEART network is still alive, Madame Labourier. She and her husband joined the Resistance in early 1941 and were early members of Virginia Hall's

NEWSAGENT network, transferring to GREENHEART soon after the Newtons' arrival. She first heard about the brothers' arrest from a fellow Resistance member who reached the Newtons' factory hideout at daybreak, twelve hours later. He immediately returned to Le Puy with the news.

Despite the arrests in Lyons and Le Puy, the Labouriers decided not to rush into hiding, but to continue life as normal. Madame Labourier was at her local hairdresser's when she heard about the release of 'Charlot'. Barbie, he reported, had forced both himself and Madame Joulian to confront Henry Newton in Montluc. What 'Charlot' did not reveal was that, without physical torture, Henry had confessed to Barbie, and that 'Charlot' secured his own release in return for helping the Germans. Barbie had skilfully exploited Henry's confession.

After their return to Le Puy, the three who were released had very little contact with the Labouriers, who began working with the Maquis in the hills outside the town. On 11 February 1944, ten months after Newtons' arrest, Barbie arrived at the Labouriers' home. Her husband, warned of the Gestapo's imminent arrival, had fled, but Madame Labourier and her son Marcel were arrested. While the son was taken away for interrogation, she was kept for two days under house arrest and then released. Barbie, she says, warned her that her son would be killed if she left the town. Exploiting a technique he was to use throughout his reign in Lyons, he calculated that she would nonetheless be tempted to alert other members of her group and that his agents could follow her to the Maquis in the hills. This time the trick did not work. Aware that she was being shadowed, she gave the necessary warnings, but without alerting the Germans.

It was at the beginning of March that she saw Barbie again. He was standing near her husband's garage wearing a light-brown raincoat and black trilby hat. Courageously she went up to him ('he had serpent eyes') and asked about her son. 'Your son,' he replied, 'is very stubborn.' Marcel did not survive the war.

On 18 March, Madame Labourier was rearrested. She was just one of many picked up in a massive swoop. Taken with the others to Clermont-Ferrand, she says that was interrogated by Barbie. He was wearing her father's ring, which she had last seen on her son's finger:

I screamed at him, 'What have you done to my son?' He hit me in the face a few times. He asked me about my Resistance group. I didn't say anything, and he didn't torture me. A few days later I was sent to Ravensbrück concentration camp. It was terrible. When I got back at the end of the war, 'Charlot' acted funny. He had not been rearrested. The Newtons later thought that he had betrayed us.

Emotions in Le Puy, as in the rest of France, were very high in the immediate aftermath of the war. Old scores were settled with little ceremony. Known collaborators were lucky to be given even the semblance of a trial. Some committed suicide after a visit from the survivors of a betrayed local Resistance group. Others were just shot in the street. Even more, however, escaped any punishment. Their victims had disappeared into the concentration camps and never survived. Those who did return were often too exhausted, sick and bewildered to seek out their denouncers. After the initial blood-letting and feuds, collaborators and resistants alike just wanted to resume a normal life. Madame Labourier remembers only that 'Charlot' turned away when she saw him again for the first time in the street. 'After sixteen months in concentration camps, I just didn't care any more about what had happened.'

The Newtons were advised by the War Office after the war that they would be unwise to return to Le Puy. They would, they were told, reawaken some old antagonisms.

THE BUTCHER

Manipulating people was not always a delicate skill, artfully practised by Barbie, but often a crude tool used for his own survival. His successes against the Resistance were the consequence of his uninhibited resort to ruthless attrition, and the recognition by his victims that he would suffer no misgivings, not even momentary human self-doubt, before resorting to violence. His first and overwhelming loyalty was to himself. The party, the ideology and the nationalism were just vital props for his own self-esteem. He is one of that rare breed of men without conscience who could as happily have served as a commissar for Stalin as he did as a Gestapo officer for Hitler. His seeming air of authority which, over the next forty years, was to put so many in awe and respect of him, was not the product of special qualities of leadership or intelligence, rather it sprang from his unhesitant and unrestrained dedication to his own success. Limited though he may have been by lack of education, he survived and flourished precisely because the Nazi state encouraged its Gestapo officers to be ruthless to prevent any challenge to its authority. That inhuman audacity became part of his very character. Reminiscing with pride in 1979 about his time in Lyons, he disclosed, 'The reason why the French are so interested in me is because I wounded their Gallic pride. I proved to them that they're stupid.' He could never forget that his father had been severely wounded by the French in the First World War.

Like all other Gestapo chiefs in France, Barbie had to rely on French sympathisers, collaborators and informants to operate effectively: 'At the beginning it was very hard for us. We had very few contacts. Everything was new. I had to build an effective team, carefully hand picking each recruit. We were showered with denunciations of the Resistance by the French and I usually tried to find long-term collaborators from amongst the denunciators.' The rush to help the occupying army was sufficient to convince him of German superiority. His prejudice was confirmed when more than 50,000 Frenchmen fought in German uniforms later in the war. It

51

was a paradoxical hatred. During his interrogation in 1944 of twenty-year-old teacher Roseline Blonde, he put forward in near-flawless French his own theory about his French-sounding name: his family was probably amongst those Protestants expelled from France by Louis XIV. At that moment, Blonde thought that he was a Francophile; he even praised the Palace of Versailles. Then suddenly he was interrupted by a French collaborator who wanted to put some questions. Barbie turned angrily and screamed, 'You are the servant here and I am the master.'

For the Gestapo officers, life in Lyons in the early days of occupation was indeed a pleasure. At lunchtime, Knab had arranged that the whole staff should eat together, with himself presiding at the centre of the high table. Barbie sat on one side, Hollert on the other, the others in descending order of rank. They were impeccably served by French waiters. But quite frequently Barbie, dressed in civilian clothes, walked alone from the Ecole de Santé to a nearby bar, sometimes the *Moulin à Vent*, to eat a meal while chatting with the regular customers. One of these, Jean Laborde, says that the *Moulin*'s patron knew who Barbie was and even listened to him denouncing 'the terrorists' – who, he claimed, did not even have the courage to attempt to kill Barbie when he regularly walked alone from the Ecole to the restaurant.

In the evenings Barbie, like other officers, made a regular tour of the best restaurants, choosing from the *Grillon*, *Les Glaces*, *Balbo* or the *Lapin Blanc*. His regular French girlfriend and companion at such times (according to Hedwig Ondra, one of the SS secretaries in Lyons) was known among the Germans as Odette, but to the Lyonnaise as Antoinette 'Mimiche' Murot. Barbie returned on leave to his wife only once during his whole period of service in France.

Feeling about Barbie amongst the other Gestapo officers was divided between loathing and respect, the latter tinged with fear. No one was allowed to forget that he dispensed summary justice not only to the French, but within the Gestapo itself. With pride Barbie told General Wolff how he dealt with one officer whom the French police chief revealed had raped a local girl. Barbie claims to have said to the officer, '"This evening at six o'clock you're to be in the cellar with the rest of the officers. There'll be a rope and you're going to hang yourself."And he did it. I kicked the chair away. . . .

One becomes tough when one's young. I don't think I could do the same any more today.'

There was, however, little fear of Barbie amongst those fifty-odd Frenchmen who worked closely with him. They were part of Barbie's 120-strong 'personal army', all members of the most aggressive pro-Nazi groups in the town which Barbie gradually drew towards him. One of the most infamous of these, from the French Nazi Party (the PPF), was François André, an ex-communist. Known as the 'Gueule Tordue', his face had been atrociously deformed in a road accident. With a mouth twisted into the shape of a gaping wound, he had no need to convince anyone of his natural brutality. His deputy, Antoine 'Tony' Saunier, was the group's treasurer. In late summer 1943, with Barbie's agreement, André established the Mouvement National Anti-Terrorist (MNAT), announcing that its task was to meet terror with terror and warning, 'Millionaire Jews, bourgeois freemasons, you who subsidise and arm the assassins, you will pay with your life.' Motivated more by a desire for criminal self-enrichment than by political calculations, these men exploited the absolute power that Barbie and the Gestapo gave them to steal at random; murder invariably followed the theft. The money or jewels were handed to Saunier who, after taking a percentage for his own purposes, divided the remainder between the 'staff' and the Germans. They became an imitation Al Capone gang, except that they did not have to disguise their activities or fear retribution from the State. Their underworld *was* the State and they were allowed to enjoy the best that Lyons could provide. Within months, the MNAT had become so identified with the Gestapo that in early 1944 it was given offices in the Ecole de Santé.

Besides the mobsters were the political fanatics, men and women eager to denounce and remove their real or imagined enemies. According to August Moritz, the head of section VI responsible for collaboration, queues formed every day at the special kiosks for denunciations. 'We had so many that we couldn't even check most of them.' Invariably the information was given to André's group to investigate, with unfortunate results for the victim.

But even Barbie confesses to mistakes. One of his best French agents, Robert 'Pierre' Moog, he admitted, turned out to be a double agent:

We had a special way of checking a collaborator's loyalty. We dressed them in German uniforms when we went on an anti-partisan raid and made them shoot at Frenchmen. 'Pierre' managed to do that – although while doing good work for us, he did good work for the other side as well. After the Gestapo headquarters was bombed in May 1944, we discovered that 'Pierre' had disappeared with two suitcases filled with documents.

Not all the double agents escaped. Barbie remembers with grim satisfaction how a Frenchwoman, acting as a collaborator, led his men into a trap which killed four of his agents. 'When I established that she was a member of the Resistance, I had her executed and her body thrown into the Rhône.'

Besides André's MNAT, the Gestapo also drew support from the specially formed French Gestapo, the *milice*. Pétain's original plan had been to rally the *anciens combattants*, the veterans of the First World War, to his support by sentimentally recalling memories of their final and glorious victory in 1918. Recruitment to the Légion Française at the beginning was not a problem. Many wanted to participate in rebuilding the spirit of France. But within a year, the Légion's undisguised collaborationist image decimated the ranks. Pétain, increasingly anxious to demonstrate his own government's ability to police the country and defeat the resistance, turned to Joseph Darnand, who in 1941 had created the Service d'Ordre Légionnaire (SOL). Darnand possessed impressive credentials as a French nationalist. Severely wounded during the First World War, he had been decorated several times for outstanding bravery, even for the defence of France in 1940. But in common with many others, he had rapidly reconsidered his position and believed that France should fight with the Germans against the communists. Among SOL's twenty-point programme were the slogans, 'against Bolshevism, for nationalism; against Jewish leprosy, for French purity; against pagan freemasonry, for Christian civilisation.' Known as the 'Black Terror', his paramilitary force – dressed in khaki uniforms, black ties and Basque berets – fought on the streets as the most aggressive defenders of French fascism. On 5 January 1943, Pétain announced that the SOL were in 'the forefront of the maintenance of order in France, co-operating with the French police. To make their work easier, I believe they should be given autonomy.' Darnand was appointed head of the newly formed *milice*. Wel-

comed, Barbie immediately entrusted Joseph Lecussan, the regional *milice* chief, with enforcing the policies which turned most
Frenchmen against Vichy.

In summer 1942, after some negotiation, the Germans had
convinced Vichy Prime Minister Laval that Frenchmen should be
encouraged to volunteer to work in German factories. Appealing to
national solidarity, Laval tried to disguise the reality by explaining
that the Germans had agreed to release one POW for every three
volunteers. But faced with insufficient volunteers, the Vichy government announced on 17 February 1943 the Service du Travail
Obligatoire, compulsory labour in Germany. In practice, every
Frenchman was automatically liable. After receiving their call-up
papers, they were to report to STO offices for transport to Germany. When men failed to report, the *milice* or Gestapo hunted
them down or took reprisals against the local population.

One of the first dragnets in Lyons for the draft-dodgers was on 1
March 1943. Six hundred men had failed to report for an STO train.
At 5.30 that Monday morning, Wehrmacht soldiers, directed by the
Gestapo, sealed off Villeurbanne, one of the town's largest work-
ing-class suburbs. An hour later the Gestapo, with the soldiers,
conducted a house-to-house search. Whenever the front door was
not immediately opened, bursts of Schmeisser sub-machine-gun fire
smashed the lock. Every man aged between seventeen and fifty-five
was arrested and hustled to local cafés which had been temporarily
requisitioned. Those without exemption from the STO were herded
to the Place de la Mairie, and stood waiting, covered by anti-tank
cannons and machine-guns. At the end of the morning, 300 men
were taken to the local railway station where their families gave
them food and clothing and said a brief farewell. Their destination
was Mathausen concentration camp.

It was the prelude to a massive three-day Gestapo dragnet
through the city, starting on 7 March. Frenziedly trying to fill their
quotas, German soldiers and *milice*, directed by the Gestapo, drove
through the town's streets corralling any group of men unfortunate
enough to be on the pavements, especially as they left the
cinemas and factories. Fathers of ten children were as vulnerable
as eighteen-year-olds. Subdued by bursts of sporadic shooting, all of
them were herded into waiting railway carriages for the journey
across the Rhine.

As the dragnets increased, thousands of young Frenchmen went into hiding. As the safest places were the countryside, forests and mountains, Vichy and the Germans were suddenly confronted by small bands of desolate, hungry and bitterly hostile Frenchmen roaming the country. They were natural recruits for the still disorganised and divided Resistance, one of whose members in a casual moment, discussing their possible use, had described them as the *maquis* (from the Corsican, 'scrubland'), hence the name.

The other victims of the Gestapo manhunt in Lyons were the Jews: the country's second largest Jewish community lived in the city. Virulent anti-semitism has a long and tragic history in France and long before the country's defeat French conservatives were blaming their country's predicament equally on the communists and the Jews. Nevertheless, in the years before the war thousands of German, Austrian and Czech Jews had sought and been given temporary refuge in France. Some sought extra insurance and became French citizens. It proved to be of little avail after France's defeat. On 20 July, Laval's government announced a commission to review recent naturalisations. Within a short time, six thousand Jews became stateless. A month later, Vichy announced the abolition of laws against anti-semitic propaganda. Once they had got into their stride, by the end of September, thirty-one camps for stateless Jews had been set up in Vichy where hundreds of Jews were to die of hunger and exposure during the winter. All these policies were taken at the initiative of the Vichy government.

Senior officers at Gestapo headquarters and the German Embassy in Paris were somewhat surprised by this rapid burst of Vichy anti-semitism. Hoping to develop collaboration, they had been reluctant to initiate any persecutions. But among the more junior officers, Theodore Dannecker, an obsessive anti-semite, portrayed Vichy's measures to Berlin as the reason why complete implementation of Nazi policies against the Jews, including their deportation, would not damage collaboration. Dannecker's persistence was rewarded.

At the Gestapo's request, on 14 May 1941, French police rounded up 3,700 Jews in Paris. Three months later, on 20 August 1941, just three weeks after Goering had spoken to Heydrich for the first time about the 'Final Solution', a four-day round-up by French police began in the capital. To Dannecker's disappointment, only 4,320

Jews (all men) were finally delivered to the Drancy internment camp; he was even less satisfied in December, when a subsequent raid produced only 743 Jews. Prudently, some Jews had moved south to the unoccupied zone, and especially to Lyons. In the town and surrounding area, the Jewish population had swollen from 3,000 to approximately 70,000. As more Jews fled, Dannecker insisted that stronger anti-Jewish measures were needed. Support for him in Paris was mixed but in April 1942 he found very willing allies in Laval and René Bousquet, the secretary-general of the police. Over the following weeks, a series of discussions between Bousquet and the Gestapo produced an agreement for further round-ups and accelerated deportation of Jews from Drancy to Auschwitz. French agreement was fundamental to the German plan because only the French police had sufficient manpower and orga-nisation to comb the country for the Jews. Officially, only stateless Jews were to be deported, but Bousquet not only privately agreed that French Jews could be included but also inquired whether the Germans could also deport Jews interned in Vichy camps. Anxious to fulfil the target he had personally given Adolf Eichmann of delivering 100,000 deportees (soon reduced to 40,000), Dannecker willingly agreed to that proposal and also to Laval's request that children also be deported, 'to avoid the separation of families'. The result of those agreements was a series of raids by the French police in the occupied zone, starting on 16 July, in which 13,115 people were arrested.

Keen to show their total sympathy with those raids, Laval and Bousquet ordered a series of similar round-ups in Vichy. Lyons was their first and natural target. On 26 August, in the 'grey Lyons round-up', 1,000 were arrested and interned in the Vénissieux work camp. Disappointed by the small number of arrests, Laval ordered repeated raids during the following weeks, directed exclusively at foreign Jews. The number of arrests was again small, but the protests provoked by the police rampage were massive. Stunned by their ferocity, the Vichy government was forced to call a pause.

By the time Barbie arrived in Lyons on 11 November, 41,951 Jews had been deported from France to Auschwitz, less than half the number which Dannecker had promised Eichmann. The orders from Paris were to complete the task. Under Barbie, Jewish affairs were the responsibility of sub-section IVC, under Hans Welti and

57

Erich Bartelmus. Within weeks of arriving, in early January 1943, Bartelmus led a series of raids, rounding up 150 Jews in the town.

The most important raid that year, however, was on 9 February in the Rue St Catherine – the headquarters of the Fédération de Sociétés Juives, the national co-ordinating headquarters of all France's Jewish organisations. Barbie arrived very early in the morning, arrested those who were already inside and waited to arrest anyone who arrived during the day. From the outside, the unsuspecting visitor had no idea that the Gestapo were behind the door. Most of those who came wanted advice on escaping from the Germans, and false papers or financial aid. Amongst those who arrived was Michel Kroskof, a Polish artist who was looking for recruits to his Resistance group. Like the others, Kroskof was seized and interrogated immediately by Barbie; but, unlike the others, he resolutely stuck to his story that he was only trying to sell his paintings and was not Jewish. Barbie tried to trick him by telling a subordinate in German that the prisoner would have to be executed. Kroskof, who carried false papers describing himself as a Frenchman, pretended not to understand and was released. More than one hundred others were not so lucky. Eighty-six of them were deported to Auschwitz, to their deaths. The telex from Gestapo headquarters in Lyons to Paris announcing their arrest and deportation was sent on 14 February and signed by Barbie – conclusive proof that he was directly involved in persecuting the Jews.

No one knows how many Jews the Lyons Gestapo had arrested and deported by the end of the war. The local magistrate claimed that a total of 7,591 people were deported from Lyons; Bartelmus went on many raids, but the deported Jews were not segregated and his records were destroyed. However, many more Jews than were arrested escaped across the borders into Switzerland and Italy, or hid in the countryside, some joining the Resistance.

Barbie, unbelievably, claims that he only became anti-semitic after the war – but, as thirteen-year-old Simone Legrange discovered, whatever the motivation, the brutality was the same. Denounced by a neighbour, Legrange and her family were taken to Montluc prison and put in a cell together. The first German they saw after their arrival on 6 June 1943 was, according to Legrange:

. . . a smiling man. At first I found him very, very charming. He was dressed in light grey, carrying a cat which was a darker shade of grey. He came towards us very nicely, stroking the cat. First he looked at my father, then my mother, and then came to me and said I was very pretty. Still stroking the cat, he put it gently on the table and asked my mother where her other children had gone. We really didn't know. They'd gone into hiding in the country two days before and we didn't have their address. Slowly, he came up to me and took hold of my long hair, rolling it gently along his hand. When he reached my skull, he yanked it as hard as he could and repeated his questions over and over again. He slapped me and knocked me onto the floor and picked me up with the end of his foot . . . [Simone was then separated from her parents.] He knocked me about all day. My face was completely torn to pieces. My lip was split. I was covered in blood, and I hadn't eaten. He took me to my mother's cell. He had the door opened and called to my mother, 'Well, there you are, you can be proud of yourself.' The beatings continued for five days.

Having failed to break their spirit, Barbie ordered the family's deportation. In Auschwitz, Monsieur Legrange was shot in front of his daughter, and his wife was sent to the gas chamber after being caught stealing some discarded cabbage leaves.

Barbie naturally disputes that he ever interrogated the Legrange family. As proof he insists that he hates cats. He also denies that he *knew* the final fate of the Jews he deported from Lyons: the proving of that knowledge is crucial to his present prosecution. Dr Kurt Schendel, who worked in 1943 and 1944 in the Paris liaison office of the Gestapo's Bureau for Jewish Affairs, was one of those responsible for negotiating with Heinz Roetke, the head of the Gestapo's Bureau for Jewish Affairs, and Alois Brunner, a special assistant to Adolf Eichmann with the brief to organise the acceleration of the Final Solution. Schendel had many discussions with both SS men about the deportations (except that they were called 'evacuations' or 'family reunification') and in 1972 he swore an affidavit to the Klarsfelds that it was common knowledge in Paris that Barbie was not only leading the arrests of the Jews, but also organising summary executions at Montluc of those arrested. According to Schendel, one of the committee members of the UGIF (Union Générale des Israélites de France) in Lyons, Raymond Geissmann, had tried at the end of 1943 to persuade Barbie several times not to shoot the arrested Jews, but Barbie had replied, 'Shot or deported, there's no difference'. This suggests that Barbie knew from the SS officers working in the Jewish Bureau in Paris, and definitely from Knab, what the real fate of the deported Jews was likely to be.

The main prison used by the Gestapo in Lyons was the fortress of Montluc. Constructed in the beginning of the nineteenth century, it is sited near the Perrache railway station, just a mile from the centre of town. Within weeks of its requisition by the Gestapo it became, even by Gestapo standards, appallingly overcrowded. With unrestrained vengeance, the PPF and the *milice* had embarked on a massive wave of arrests and were depositing their prey with the Germans. The first solution was to build wooden barracks in the courtyard for the Jews. But when that proved to be only a temporary relief, the Gestapo organised regular 'clean-outs'. Any inmate who had been imprisoned more than a few weeks, was automatically sent to a concentration camp in Germany.

Jean Nocher was one of the first to be arrested and imprisoned in Montluc. His day began at 7.30 a.m. with physical and verbal abuse hurled at him and the other prisoners by the armed German guards. His only relief from solitude was to catch a glimpse of the other prisoners, although some of them looked terribly bruised and swollen after a night's interrogation. Joining the long procession of prisoners, he was allowed just three minutes at the wash basins. Back in his cell, plagued by vermin, Nocher received little water and hardly any food. Others did not go back to their cells but were taken away, often without their clothes, for interrogation:

> Their return in the evening was something awful to see, their bodies just a mass of open wounds, burns and blood. Once, in the next cell to mine, was a poor devil moaning quietly. The Gestapo had made him lie down naked, with his back against the sharp edge of a shovel embedded in the ground. Then they whipped his stomach with a lash. His backbone was fractured and his legs paralysed.

The Gestapo institutionalised torture when it requisitioned the massive Ecole de Santé Militaire on the Avenue Berthelot in June 1943. Under Knab's direction, three enormous cellars in the west wing were converted into cells where prisoners were kept for some days before being transferred to Montluc. After the initial interrogations in Room Six on the ground floor, the prisoners were taken to specially-equipped rooms on the fourth floor. Each room had one or two baths, a table with leather straps, a gas oven, pokers which were heated inside the oven, and crude electrical prongs. The baths were filled alternately with freezing and boiling water. According to André Frossard, he was undressed and his wrists were tied to his heels. Then a stick was pushed underneath his trussed arms. Barbie and the other interrogators pushed their victims under the water, resting the stick across the bath: '. . . it was like an axle around which they turned me, dragging me by the hair'. When the victim nearly drowned, the interrogators attempted to revive him with kicks and blows.

One of Barbie's early victims in the Ecole was Maurice Boudet, a member of the Resistance, who was arrested on 9 July 1943. 'He was a monster. He always had a cosh in his hand. He beat without hesitation and encouraged others to do the same. When I was unconscious, he pushed me into the freezing bath, then the cosh again, and acid injected into my bladder. He really enjoyed other people's sufferings, and even hung people up in front of us with music playing in the background.'

Using these appalling methods, Barbie did achieve considerable success against the Resistance. It was not only the torture which produced the results, but also his impassioned determination to defeat his opponent. Once on the trail of a Resistance leader, with the scent in his nostrils, there was little that could restrain him. Unable to control that ambition, and impatient when faced with determined opposition or defiance, he resorted to torture. Professional interrogators and intelligence experts insist that torture is counterproductive because the victim will often confess to anything just to stop the pain. While that remains an unanswerable argument, it is a sad truth that every intelligence agency in the world has used and continues to use torture. Barbie's case, however, is special. Some of his victims insist that he was a sadist and actually enjoyed using torture. Others make no mention of it. The majority of his victims did not survive to report on his demeanour. All that is certain is that in his terms he scored his 'successes' using both guile and torture.

For more than a year Barbie hunted for one Albert 'Didier' Chambonnet, the regional Resistance chief responsible for the Alsace, Haute-Savoie, the Ain and the Jura. There were three stages in the discovery: firstly the discovery of the Frenchman's

Resistance code name; then his real name; and then the man himself. On 30 March 1944 Lisa Lesevere was arrested and a Gestapo search produced photographs which were to be used for false papers of recent recruits to the Maquis. By coincidence, Lesevere was carrying a letter addressed to a certain 'Didier', a low-ranking officer responsible for dead-letterboxes. But she did know the Resistance chief.

Shortly after her arrival, Barbie asked her to give him the real name of 'Didier'. Lesevere pretended not to understand. Dogged and impatient to extract his due, Barbie began hitting the young woman and then summoned four assistants, including 'Gueule Tordue'. Lesevere was hung from the ceiling by her wrists and beaten. The following day she was undressed, beaten and pushed into the bath. She fainted, was revived by a doctor, to find Barbie and his agents laughing and offering her a drink as if nothing had happened. For nineteen days, the torture sessions continued. When her torture temporarily ceased, she was forced to watch others suffer, including her own fifteen-year-old son, whom Barbie had discovered. His parting words to his mother were, 'Don't forget that I am very soft'.

As the brutalities intensified, so did her resistance against divulging anything. But then, after a mock execution, Barbie revealed that another girl from her own network had betrayed her. Lesevere was tied, stomach-down, onto an upturned chair, and 'Gueule Tordue' began hitting her with a spiked ball hung from a cosh. Her vertebral column was broken and she fainted. Her first image when she awoke, lying on the floor, were the legs of a young girl and the sound of her playing Chopin's *L'Héroïque* on the piano. Barbie leaned over her, stroking her hands: 'What you have done is magnificent, my dear. Nobody has held out as long as you. It's nearly over now. I'm very upset. But let's finish. Go on, a little effort. Who is "Didier"?' Lesevere said nothing. Hitting her on the face, Barbie shouted, 'I don't want to see this stupid young woman any more. Get rid of her!'

Just six days earlier, Mario Blandon, 'Didier's' chosen hit-man and bodyguard, had also been arrested. Blandon had joined the Resistance in 1942, distributing pamphlets for 'Combat'; after shirking the STO he was condemned to death in his absence. As the *chef d'action immédiate* of a Groupe Franc, an urban Resistance group, his prime task was to assassinate collaborators and traitors. 'I killed many more Frenchmen than Germans,' says Blandon with some pride, 'and I never gave them any warning.' Each murder was followed, he says, by a very good meal.

It was likewise without warning that Blandon himself was trapped, betrayed by a collaborator whose identity he has, despite considerable effort, never discovered. With three others, Blandon was en route to carry out another murder when he drove into a roadblock – waiting, he believes, especially for them. Three days later he was driven alone by the Gestapo to the Ecole de Santé. 'Don't worry,' said Barbie, 'your friends are dead and you are going to join them.' Blandon admits that he was terrified, especially when Barbie pushed an album of photos in front of him to identify fellow members of the Resistance. 'Fortunately, Barbie didn't recognise me, even when I was looking at my own photo.'

The torture began on the second day. It continued daily for eighteen days. Stripping him almost naked, Barbie beat Blandon repeatedly, burnt him with cigarettes and pushed him under the bath water:

> The worst he did to me was pushing three-inch needles through my rib cage into my lungs. I often collapsed and he threw me into the corridor to recover. I feigned unconsciousness and saw him inflict even worse tortures on others. Women were undressed and beaten, one even holding her three-year-old child; and one woman was forced to submit to Barbie's huge sheepdog. At the end of each day, we were all dragged, bleeding heavily, to the cells below, and the killings continued. One night there was a lot of noise and Barbie came down the stairs pushing someone ahead of him. He kept three steps behind him . . . [here Blandon paused] . . . you see, I was watching this with the eye of a professional killer and I knew exactly what was going to happen. Barbie shot the man in the back of the head. The head split apart while the man somersaulted to the bottom of the stairs like a rabbit. To get that effect, you need to be exactly three steps behind. Barbie just laughed, the same laugh that I recognised twelve years ago in his first television interview.

Blandon was also tortured on occasion by Barbie's assistants while Barbie looked on, eating a sandwich and drinking a beer. Once he gave Blandon a cigarette saying, 'this could be your last'; a few minutes later the beatings started again. The climax was the sudden confrontation with 'Didier' himself. Blandon then realised that the whole group had been betrayed. He swears that neither he, nor his chief, were in any condition to give even a grimace of recognition. The following day Blandon was sent to Paris to join the long journey of the infamous 'train of death' to Dachau, during which 932 people died. 'Barbie's tortures were bad, but Germany was even worse.'

Few who survived to describe the experience suffered more than Father Bonaventure Boudet, a member of a French mission who was arrested on 9 July 1943 and interrogated by the Gestapo at the Ecole. At the end of the war, Boudet could not even remember how many interrogation sessions he had endured; some had lasted twenty-four hours; the last session had continued for three days. Besides violent beatings, he was savaged by police dogs, hung to a hook by his wrists and given electric shocks, then hung by his legs until blood trickled out of his nose, ears and mouth. While he was hanging upside down, his head was immersed inside a bucket filled with soapy water. His final agony was acid, injected into his body, which caused insufferable agony in his urethra and kidneys.

Boudet also watched as others were tortured. Fingers and toes crudely cut off with kitchen knives, women's breasts severed and nipples torn off, limbs being burnt and severed from the body. One victim was actually scalped and his eyes torn out.

Hedwig Ondra, born in 1923 in Austria, also witnessed the results of these tortures. Young and desperate to see something of the world, she had applied in 1941 for a job as a secretary in Paris. It promised glamour and foreign travel. To her surprise she discovered that her new employers were the Gestapo in the Avenue Foch. In November 1942, impressed by her fast typing, the personnel department appointed her as Knab's secretary. The work, she says, was too varied. Frequently, while typing Knab's regular situation reports to Berlin or Paris, she was summoned to the fourth floor to type a 'confession'. The Frenchman in question, who had invariably been tortured before she arrived, would dictate an agreed statement which was translated to her by a German priest: 'They were experiences I would rather forget.' In early 1944, she pleaded that she was on the verge of a nervous breakdown and was transferred. In 1963, she went voluntarily to the state prosecutor in Munich to testify that Barbie was 'a very brutal man'.

Curiously, it was not Barbie's brutality which was to win him his greatest coup.

THE COUP

On 7 June 1943, René Hardy, code-named 'Didot', boarded a train bound for Paris at the Perrache station in Lyons. His journey ended when he was arrested by the Germans, eighty miles further on at Chalon-sur-Saône. What followed that arrest plunged the Resistance movement into a severe crisis which remains shrouded in mystery to this day. Every aspect of the saga is disputed by at least one of the participants and, usually, not only for personal but also for political reasons. The only certainty is what finally happened two weeks after Hardy was arrested: Moulin was captured, arrested and tortured by Barbie and died soon after. Had he lived, post-war French history might have been very different. For forty years France has demanded an answer to the question: did René Hardy betray Jean Moulin?

Henri Aubry, a founder member of Combat, had written to Hardy summoning him to meet his chief, General Delestraint, appointed by de Gaulle as head of the Armée Secrete. The rendezvous was to be the metro station at La Muette. The purpose was to promote Hardy to head of the Armée Secrete's Third Bureau. From extraordinary carelessness, Aubry's message to Hardy, which mentioned Delestraint's code name 'Vidal', was not written in code. Even worse, it was left in the 'Dumoulin' letterbox which was already known to the Germans. Hardy, however, knew the box was no longer safe, and never collected the message – but by pure coincidence he was due to leave for Paris at the same time anyway for an entirely different meeting. Soon after Aubry's message was left at the box, it was picked up and brought to the Gestapo headquarters. The Germans knew that 'Vidal' was an important Resistance leader. It was clearly an unique opportunity.

Barbie ordered two French informants, Jean 'Lunel' Multon and Robert 'Pierre' Moog, to travel immediately to Paris to help the capital's Gestapo with 'Vidal's' arrest. Both had just arrived from Marseilles where, because of their betrayals, the Resistance had suffered a crippling wave of arrests. Ignorant of the web that was fast being spun around him, Hardy travelled under his own name and arrived at Perrache. To his horror, he saw and recognised Multon, whom he knew to be a traitor. Nevertheless, confident of his cover, he boarded the train. Barbie's agents sat in the very next compartment.

It was at 1.00 a.m. when, acting on Moog's initiative, the French police boarded the train at Chalon-sur-Saône and arrested Hardy. He was taken off the train while the two denunciators continued towards Paris. There are two very different versions of what then followed.

According to the most definitive account, written after long investigations by Henri Noguères, a noted historian of the French Resistance, Hardy was taken to the local police station and held for three days. For the first two days the questioning was quite cursory. It was only on 10 June, the third day, that Barbie arrived, and after a short time took Hardy back to Lyons in his car. Once inside the Ecole de Santé, Noguères believes, Hardy lost his nerve – perhaps because Barbie threatened to kill Hardy's beautiful fiancée. Whatever the reason, Hardy left the dreaded Gestapo interrogation headquarters just eight hours after his arrival, and he emerged completely unharmed. It was only several days later that he contacted other members of his group. Contrary to the most fundamental Resistance rule, he deliberately failed to mention that he had been arrested and that he had spent eight hours in Barbie's office. His explanation for his absence was that, having seen Multon, he had jumped off the train; only after he was sure that he had not been followed had he returned. In the meantime, Multon and Moog had successfully organised Delestraint's arrest and, as a bonus, two other Resistance agents had fallen into their net.

It was only after the war, in March 1947, that the story told by Hardy of his arrest and interrogation by Barbie was exposed as untruthful. His explanation for the cover-up was that, at the time, he was afraid that he would have been blamed for Delestraint's arrest. His account of the hours with the 'Butcher of Lyons' was less credible.

Hardy claimed that he had told Barbie that he was a businessman and a sympathiser of Nazi Germany. Having won Barbie's confidence, he then offered to collaborate in any way he could, although he insisted it would inevitably be limited. Barbie, he claims, accepted that offer with the threat that, should Hardy double cross him, his fiancée and her family would suffer. He insisted that Barbie never realised the importance of his prisoner.

Over the years Barbie has given several accounts, all of which differ significantly on the sequence of events following his arrest of Hardy at Chalon-sur-Saône. But all his accounts are identical on the two crucial issues: firstly, that by the end of their 'discussion', Barbie knew that Hardy was 'Didot'; secondly that the Frenchman had agreed to collaborate and betray the whole Resistance network.

Barbie's version in 1979 was that Multon had told him several days before 7 June not only that 'Didot' was travelling to Paris to meet Delestraint, but even the exact train and seat number. With Multon on the train, Barbie himself went to Chalon-sur-Saône and watched with satisfaction as Hardy was arrested:

> As he passed me he seemed very confident. Once he was in the prison cell, I walked in and took his glasses, held them up to the light and said, 'plain glass'. He realised immediately that he had been betrayed and asked me who I was. 'That,' I said, 'you'll soon find out. But let me tell you what I know. These identification papers were made in England and your real name is René Hardy, in charge of railway sabotage.' He was terribly shaken. When he'd recovered he said, 'I give up. What's going to happen to me?' [By then the two were in Barbie's car heading for Lyons.] 'I'll give you five guesses. We'll arrive at 8.00 a.m. in Lyons and at 9.00 a.m. you'll be standing against the wall.' He went quite pale. 'Well, can't we talk about it?' I realised that he wasn't made of hard stuff. 'But I'll only talk,' he said, 'as long as you don't take me to Montluc.'

Barbie claims that Hardy spent about a day at the Ecole de Santé, giving him a detailed description of the 'Plan Vert', the railway sabotage plan. In the meantime he was waiting for a telex from Berlin which would contain Himmler's personal approval for Hardy to be used as a Gestapo agent. Soon after it arrived Hardy was released, 'although of course I had two men follow him'.

Barbie's first official account, given thirty-one years earlier in 1948 – in a sensational disclosure to Comissaire Louis Bibes, a French government official investigating Hardy's alleged betrayal of Moulin – was somewhat different. In this version Hardy's breakdown only occurred when they arrived in Lyons, after Barbie had found a letter from his fiancée in his pocket. 'Moreover,' Barbie told Louis Bibes, the investigator, 'he wanted to give the impression of being an important leader. So I said to him, "The best way to become a leader is to help us get rid of the others." Twenty-four hours later he agreed.'

A year earlier, in 1947, Barbie had written his first, unofficial, account of his arrest of and subsequent relationship with Hardy for Robert Taylor, the American CIC agent who recruited him to work for American Intelligence. In that account, Barbie claimed that he was actually on the train with Multon and that he left it two hours before it arrived at Chalon to alert the police to arrest Hardy. He claimed that, after his comments about the glasses, Hardy 'suddenly stretched out his hand and assured me that he had the fullest faith in his future fate . . . In that moment, I decided to trust Hardy.' During the following two days, Barbie claims, the two spoke for hours about life, their work and the war. Hardy was, according to this account, well cared for and comfortable – and sufficiently relaxed by alcohol to reveal a few secrets. Barbie did not press him then: '. . . to his great astonishment I released Hardy from confinement. In return he gave me his word of honour that he would seize the right moment and would help me under any circumstances . . . He came to me every evening after his release, gave me reports and slept in my office.'

At this point Barbie's 1979 account turns into pure fantasy. On the one hand, he claimed that Hardy had in 1943 given him details of events which had not yet occurred; on the other, although he had told Bibes in 1948 that he had lost contact with Hardy after August 1943, he now claimed that Hardy had given him details of the Normandy invasion plan.

Noguères, not surprisingly, distrusts Barbie's account. In a conflict of evidence between a Gestapo torturer on the one hand and an alleged French traitor on the other, the choice is virtually impossible. Nonetheless, the events which followed Hardy's release tend to support Barbie's version.

The news about Delestraint's arrest sent a shudder throughout the movement. To Moulin in particular, it seemed an awful premonition. Realising that the Resistance was heavily penetrated by the Gestapo, he was morosely fatalistic about his own future. 'I am sought now by both Vichy and the Gestapo, who, partly owing to the behaviour of some members of the Resistance, know everything about my identity and activities.'

Events now moved rather quickly. Moulin's first priority was to appoint a temporary successor for the hapless Delestraint. He also wanted to reorganise completely the military groupings throughout France. He expected considerable opposition, especially from Frenay on some matters and from Aubry on others. Nothing less than a meeting of the top Resistance leaders could settle the various disputes. On Saturday 19 June, it was decided that the military leaders of the Resistance should meet two days later. Everyone expected a long and hard session. During the preceding forty-eight hours, they held a series of preliminary discussions in the streets, bistros and parks of Lyons.

None of the meetings was more important than the encounters around Sunday lunchtime near the Pont Morand by the Rhône. Between 11.30 and 3.00 p.m. Aubry met Gaston Defferre, then a senior Resistance official. Nearby, sitting on a park bench was René Hardy and another man. The stranger's face was always partially or wholly hidden by a newspaper. None of the Resistance leaders alive today has any doubt that the stranger next to Hardy was Klaus Barbie. Calling Hardy over to him, Aubry told his *chef de section* that an important meeting had been fixed for the next day and that he wanted Hardy to be there. Because of security, the exact location had not been decided. Hardy was just told to be at the Caluire funicular at 1.30 p.m., where a guide would meet and escort them to the safe house. The two then went their separate ways.

Just before midday on the following day, a pretty blonde woman, Mme Delétraz, arrived at a Resistance safe house in Lyons. A former member of the destroyed 'Gilbert' network, Delétraz had been arrested some months previously by the Gestapo. She had volunteered to help the Germans, but in fact was a double agent. Visibly distressed, she explained that she had just come from the Gestapo headquarters. Two hours earlier she had heard someone called 'Didot' tell the Germans that the leaders of the Secret Army would be meeting later that day, and that de Gaulle's delegate would also be there; he could not tell Barbie where the meeting was to be held. According to Delétraz, Barbie ordered her to follow 'Didot' to the house and then return to the Gestapo, who would be waiting in vans near the top of the funicular. She claims that she left the Ecole de Santé as fast as possible but her warning was never passed on to the Resistance leader.

Barbie agrees with most of Delétraz's account but insists that in the event he found the location by following yellow chalk marks left by Hardy. French investigators dismiss the chalk story but accept Barbie's claim that he gave Hardy a 6.35mm-calibre pistol. Barbie also claims that his assistant, Heinrich 'Harry' Stengritt, paid 'whole suitcases of money' for information, but this has not yet been established.

Security for the meeting was unusually lax. The location was a doctor's surgery in a big villa in Caluire, a suburb of Lyons, overlooking the town. It was a good cover because a stream of visitors would not normally attract attention. Dr Dugoujon, the owner, was a sympathiser but not an active member of the Resistance. According to the plan, Dugoujon would continue seeing patients while the committee met in an upstairs room. In theory, only a small handful of people would know the exact location. The other participants were to meet at selected places in Lyons and be guided to the house. But in fact more people than usual knew about the meeting and even its location. Moreover, contrary to the procedure on previous occasions, no lookouts or armed sentries were posted around the house.

Moulin arrived late at 2.45 p.m. with Raymond Aubrac and two other Resistance leaders. Aubry, Hardy and three others had already arrived. Because Moulin was late, the receptionist assumed that they were ordinary patients, and led them into the downstairs waiting room. Just a few minutes later, Aubry heard the creak of the gate leading in to the small courtyard. Casually, he looked out of the window; he saw a large group of leather-jacketed men, armed with British-made Sten guns, dash over the grass and burst into the house. Turning to the others he gasped, 'We've had it. How weird. It's the Gestapo.'

Barbie was the first to burst in. He claims that he fired a burst of machine-gun fire into the ceiling and ordered everyone to put up their hands. The French deny that there was any shooting, just a 'small man, shouting in excellent French, "Hands up. German police".'

Barbie went first to Aubry, hit him around the head, pulled his arms behind his back and handcuffed him. Then to Aubry's sur-

prise, Barbie called him 'Thomas', a code name he had only
recently begun to use: ' "Thomas", it doesn't look as if things are
going well. You looked a lot happier yesterday at the Pont Morand.
I was reading my paper. But it was such a beautiful day that I
thought that I would let you enjoy it because I was going to see you
again today.'

According to Barbie in 1947, 'The interrogations were only for
show. I suddenly realised that the Resistance leaders were missing. I
was afraid that they had been warned shortly before the raid. Then
I thought of the waiting room.' In fact, downstairs in the waiting
room, Aubrac and Moulin hoped that they would be mistaken for
genuine patients. When Barbie first came into the room, he hardly
noticed Moulin sitting under a picture of horses. But any hopes of
escape were soon dispelled. Within a few minutes everyone, including the innocent, had been punched, roughly frisked and lined up
facing the wall. Moulin just had time to pass to Aubrac some
documents which had been hidden in the lining of his jacket before
both were handcuffed. As they chewed and swallowed the paper,
Moulin whispered to Dugoujon, 'My name is Jean Martel'.

After the initial shock, a tense and awful silence settled on the
house. Hardy's presence was a surprise. Aubry had invited him
without telling anyone, because he wanted some support for his own
arguments against the others. It was also Aubry who claimed that he
immediately noticed Hardy standing slightly apart from the others,
without handcuffs. His hands were instead bound with a loose
chain.

According to Barbie, but disputed by some of the French, the
prisoners were immediately brought to him individually for questioning in the dining room. Once again there are two very different
versions of how Barbie ran that first interrogation, and more
important, what he actually achieved. He claims that Hardy had
given him a complete list of the participants and that he immediately
confronted each of them with their real identity. Moulin, he asserts,
was identified by Hardy, who was hiding in a cupboard in the dining
room. According to a prearranged agreement, Hardy knocked on
the side when he heard Moulin's voice.

Barbie's claim that he had identified everyone, including Moulin
before leaving the house, is refuted by the French who insist that
Moulin's cover was only blown two days later. Dugoujon is quite

sure that there has never been a cupboard large enough to conceal a man in his dining room. But he and the others remember Barbie hitting them with a wooden chair-leg. Laughingly Barbie denies hitting anyone. 'They say that I used a piece of Henry II furniture. I don't know how old the furniture was. In any case I didn't hit them. I just destroyed them psychologically.'

It was during the interrogations that there was a series of shouts and then a burst of shooting. Hardy had escaped. According to Hardy, he had hit his guard as he was getting into a waiting car. As the German lost his balance, Hardy dashed for some shrubs and rolled down a hill. To a French eyewitness outside, the complete lack of alarm shown by the heavily armed SS men was quite striking. The Germans mounted only a cursory search and inside the house Barbie seemed quite unconcerned. It was enough to convince many in the Resistance that Hardy had betrayed the meeting, a view which is supported by Barbie:

> As planned, Hardy gave Stengritt a shove, dropped the chains and ran. We shot at him, but of course didn't intend to hit him. But then everything went wrong. The next day there was a message that the French police had arrested the man who had got away. The chief of police was very proud of his force and I had to congratulate him. When he brought Hardy to our headquarters I had to give him and some other policemen the normal reward – 20,000 francs. The money didn't matter because we had a whole room-full – dropped by the British. When Hardy came he was wounded. He had shot himself in the arm to make everything look genuine. It was very annoying. After some thought I realised that the only solution was to let him 'escape' again. So instead of sending him to Montluc, I sent him to a German Red Cross hospital. Then, a few days later, I arranged with the doctor that one night the guards should be taken off duty for fifteen minutes. I told Hardy the plan and he escaped through the window.

Hardy, of course, disputes the whole account, saying that he was brave, clever and lucky. 'Escape,' said Hardy, 'always seems fantastic to those who haven't done one.' Knowing that he could only have escaped by breaking a padlock on the window, jumping two floors, and then despite a wounded arm, heaving himself over a wall, all of those who were left back at the house in Caluire, and who survived the war, have been quite willing to accept Barbie's version. To escape from Barbie no fewer than three times needed more than luck and skill alone.

Soon after Hardy's escape, the others were driven to the Ecole de Santé. The interrogations, threats and beatings began soon after their arrival. The first session ended at 11.00 p.m. that night. All of them, including Aubry, Aubrac, Moulin, were loaded into a lorry and taken to Montluc.

Early the next day Barbie raided Aubry's home. His haul included four million francs, a mass of seriously incriminating documents and the arrest of some other Resistance workers. He then returned to the Ecole de Santé to continue the interrogations. Three of those arrested, but not Moulin, were taken to Barbie's room. Each of them was brutally beaten and ordered to reveal the identity of 'Max'. Aubry, his shoulder dislocated by Barbie's blows, faced three mock executions during those first twenty-four hours.

It was during the second day, 23 June, that Barbie won his prize. Someone still unknown, possibly tortured beyond endurance, revealed Moulin's identity and he was immediately brought from Montluc for his first interrogation. When Dr Dugoujon saw him return that night, he could scarcely walk. There was a bandage around his head. On the following day, he was taken back to Barbie's office for further questioning. Looking through the peephole of his cell door, Aubrac saw him return. Unable to walk, he was supported by two German soldiers. He was barely recognisable. An hour later, a prison officer fetched Christian Pineau, another prisoner who later became a minister in de Gaulle's government. Pineau had been allowed to keep his razor and had become the unofficial prison barber. According to Pineau, he followed the officer through the silent prison to a courtyard where a man was lying motionless, stretched out on a bench. A guard stood nearby with the gun slung across his shoulder. 'Shave him!' Pineau was told by the officer. To his amazement, Pineau realised that it was Moulin:

> He had lost consciousness, his eyes were hollowed as if they were buried in his head. He had an ugly bluish wound on his temple. A low moan escaped from his swollen lips. There was no doubt that he had been tortured by the Gestapo. Seeing me hesitate, the officer said again, 'Shave him!' I asked for some soap and water. The officer brought some and then went away. Slowly I tried to shave him, trying not to touch the swollen parts of his face. I couldn't understand why they wanted to put on this macabre performance for a dying man. When I'd finished I just sat next to

73

him. Suddenly, Moulin asked for some water. I gave him a drink, then he spoke in a croaking voice a few words in English which I didn't understand. Soon after he lost consciousness. I just sat with him, a sort of 'death-watch' until I was taken back to my cell.

Pineau was not the only one to see the results of Barbie's interrogation that day. Until 1943 Gottlieb Fuchs was the Lyons Gestapo's official interpreter. On his own admission, he was Barbie's favourite. Fuchs claims that on Friday 25 June, in the afternoon, he was sitting alone in the reception at the Ecole de Santé when he heard an enormous noise on the first floor, just by Barbie's office. 'I saw Barbie in his shirtsleeves dragging a lifeless body down the steps. Its hands and feet were tied up. He stopped for a moment on the ground floor to get his breath back. Then he started dragging the body again down more steps towards the cells in the basement. The man had been badly beaten around the face and his clothes were torn.' Fuchs later discovered that Barbie's victim was Moulin.

Over the years Fuchs has contradicted minor points of his own account of that incident. But he has been consistent about what he heard Barbie say when he emerged from the basement: 'If he doesn't die, I'll finish him off in Paris tomorrow.' Fuchs says that he then went down to the cells and found Moulin severely tortured and in a semi-coma – the same condition in which Pineau was to see him four hours later.

Barbie's post-war account of Moulin's interrogation is, in all its versions, very different. For one thing, Gestapo headquarters in Paris, having heard about the arrests, ordered that everyone should be brought north immediately. Clearly the generals in the Avenue Foch wanted to question the leaders of the French Resistance themselves and not leave it to a mere lieutenant. Barbie had an obvious interest in concealing that, against these orders, he had already worked on Moulin himself.

But everyone, including Barbie, agrees that throughout his interrogation Moulin did not reveal anything and did not betray one member of the Resistance. It was probably on the afternoon of the first day that Barbie pushed a piece of paper in front of the already beaten Moulin and shouted at him, 'I want names'. Moulin, still insisting that he was Jean Martel, a decorator and gallery owner from Nice, picked up the pencil and drew a sketch of his tormentor. Barbie says that he then took the piece of paper and wrote *Jean*

Moulins (*sic*) on it and pushed it over to the injured man. According to Barbie, Moulin just crossed out the *s*. 'It was because he had finally admitted his real identity that, when he was taken back to his cells, he spent the next three hours banging his head against the wall, trying to commit suicide. I later punished the guards for not preventing it.'

Barbie's claim never to have 'touched' Moulin is plainly ridiculous. After the war he claimed that Moulin was handed over to the French police just a few days after his arrest, 'perfectly healthy and uninjured'. In his later versions, contradicting himself, he describes how he personally accompanied Moulin to the Gestapo head-quarters in Paris. Barbie's only regret in 1979 was that his wife had not kept the sketch which he had sent to her: 'It would be worth $50,000 today. But one doesn't think about those sort of things.'

Moulin travelled to Paris towards the end of June. Barbie went with him. He was taken directly to a large villa in Neuilly, the home of a fugitive millionaire, which had been requisitioned by General Bömelberg, the head of the Gestapo. Only the most important members of the French Resistance were imprisoned there, those who according to the Germans were to be given 'honourable treatment'. In neighbouring rooms were Delestraint and Aubry. Neither saw Moulin at the villa. Aubry's last view of Moulin was in Bömelberg's office in the Avenue Foch. Unconscious, Moulin lay stretched out on a chaise longue. According to Aubry, Barbie was in a neighbouring room, 'clicking his heels in an exaggerated way in front of Bömelberg who stood there chain smoking.' Aubry says he also heard Bömelberg say to Barbie in French, 'I hope he will pull through. I wish you good luck.' It's an unlikely touch but supports all the available evidence that Bömelberg and the Gestapo leader-ship were at pains to conceal their gross mishandling of Moulin, and their utter failure to extract either information or a propaganda coup from their star prisoner.

On 29 June in Berlin, six days after Moulin had been identified, Ernst Kaltenbrunner, head of the whole SS in Berlin, sent a secret report to Joachim von Ribbentrop, the Foreign Minister. Headed, 'The Secret Army in France', it contained a description of the events at Caluire and an account of Hardy's arrest. 'During the course of his interrogation,' wrote Kaltenbrunner, 'the head of railway sabot-age, Hardy, alias "Didot", made a full statement and, amongst other things, confessed to having worked out a plan of about 150 pages on sabotage operations to be carried out on the railways under the Anglo-American invasion plan.' (Hardy naturally denies the whole account, insisting that he could never have remembered the massive 'Plan Vert'.)

About Moulin, Kaltenbrunner wrote: ' "Max" himself did not come to the meeting. He had probably been arrested in a French police raid.' The Gestapo in Paris had deceived Kaltenbrunner to conceal their bungling. Now, attempts by German doctors to resuscitate him having failed, Bömelberg's only problem was how to dispose of the dying Moulin.

Secretly, on 7 July, an unconscious body on a stretcher was placed on a military train bound for Frankfurt, Germany. Moulin was dead on arrival. Some evidence suggests that he died en route at Metz. By 9 July the body had been brought back to Paris and cremated at Père Lachaise. De Gaulle's ambassador to France, more knowledgeable than anyone else about the organisation, plans and resources of the Resistance, had died without the Germans gaining any benefit from what in other circumstances would have been presented as a major triumph.

Barbie had, in the meantime, returned to Lyons. Just one of those arrested in Caluire still remained in his care, Raymond Aubrac. Aubrac was soon to discover that Moulin's death had not affected Barbie's attitude towards torture. On the contrary, he was even more determined to get the information which was denied him by Moulin's death.

Aubrac had already suffered under interrogation. Three days after his arrest, on 24 June, soldiers had taken him from his cell at Montluc and driven him to the Ecole de Santé. 'We were thrown like dogs into the cellars. I was afraid, very afraid. I knew the reputation of the "Butcher of Lyons".' After a short time, his wrists handcuffed behind him, he was taken to Barbie's office on the first floor. 'The door banged behind me. He was by the window. Not a very big man, a little tubby. I was twenty-nine, he was thirty. I never really saw his eyes because he always stood against the light. For a moment the atmosphere seemed so relaxed. It was summer and he was in his shirtsleeves.' Aubrac's illusions were quickly dispelled. Barbie was holding a truncheon. 'He looked mockingly at me, enjoying his power, even looking forward to torturing me.'

Over the next days there was never a moment when Barbie even bothered to try subtlety and guile to seduce Aubrac into co-operating. He had decided that the temptation to end the violence would be the only incentive to Aubrac to betray his cause. He thereupon launched into an orgy of extraordinary viciousness, which many others must have endured who did not survive to recount their ordeal: 'He screamed at me, "Where are the arms? Where is the money?" I didn't answer. He screamed, "Filthy pig" and began hitting me violently on my head. I soon fainted which was a consolation because I couldn't then feel any pain. But when I came round, he immediately began hitting and kicking me again.'

During at least two interrogation sessions Aubrac remembers quite clearly regaining consciousness to see Barbie sitting behind his desk with a very beautifully-dressed young woman on his lap:

She never said anything and they even kissed full mouth in front of me. It was his way of showing virility. Her presence spurred him on. Looking back I sometimes even think that he wasn't that interested in getting any information. Fundamentally he was a sadist who enjoyed causing pain and proving his power. He had an extraordinary fund of violence. Coshes, clubs and whips lay on his desk, and he used them a lot. Contrary to what some others say, he wasn't even a good policeman, because he never got any information out of me. Not even my identity or that I was Jewish.

Courageously, and despite his injuries, Aubrac refused to give up his cover – 'Claude Ermelin' from Tunisia. His wife, Lucie, had contacted him the day following his arrest. Enclosed in a bundle of clean clothes addressed to 'Claude Ermelin' was a half-completed crossword puzzle. Among the dirty clothes which she collected a few days later was a completed crossword puzzle – within it a message, by now sadly outdated: 'Maxwell'.

Desperately, the shocked and disorganised remnants of the Resistance council secretariat searched for ideas to mount a rescue operation although they still did not know exactly where Moulin and the others were held. It was a forlorn attempt. The move to Paris destroyed whatever chance there was.

Independently, Lucie Aubrac soon heard that her husband had not been moved to Paris, and was still at Montluc. Theirs being an uniquely romantic and indestructible relationship, it was quite natural for Lucie to consider immediately her own plans for freeing her husband. Only a few months earlier she had rescued him from a hospital where he was also under arrest.

On 23 June a well-dressed, attractive woman whose papers carried the name 'Guislaine de Barbantane' arrived at the Ecole de Santé. She told the receptionist that she wanted to see the German officer in charge of the Caluire affair. She was shown into the captain's office on the first floor. Entering with apparent resolution and self-confidence she saw a man of her age, dressed in a light suit and pink shirt; a beautiful girl rested in the background. It was somewhat bizarre. It was not what she had expected. She had carefully thought out her approach.

'Good morning, M. Barbie. I am a friend of one of the patients you arrested at Dr Dugoujon's in Caluire. You cannot keep him because he has very serious tuberculosis. He has to take special medicines.'

'What's his name?'

'Ermelin.'

'How long have you known him?'

'About a month.'

'Where does he come from?'

'Tunisia.'

Barbie burst out laughing, threw Aubrac's file onto the desk, and pulled out a photo of their son: 'And who is he?'

'That's my godson. He was with us on holiday. He's an orphan. I look after him.'

'Your friend's name is really Valette. He doesn't need medicine but a cigarette and a glass of rum. Understand?'

Lucie burst into tears (genuine tears because she believed that Aubrac was to be shot). 'I'm crying because I'm ashamed. I'm expecting his child. How am I going to confess my sin to my parents? For someone like me it's a disgrace to have a lover.'

Barbie seemed quite moved. 'Ah, Mademoiselle. Men, men, you should never trust them.'

On 29 June Lucie tried to see Barbie again. It must have been during a break in her husband's interrogation sessions. His mood had changed. Quite brusquely, pushing her into the corridor, he shouted, 'I've already told you, it's all over for your friend. I don't want to see you any more.'

Undeterred, she tried indirect approaches. Gestapo officers working in other departments were gently 'seduced' with gifts and charm to get their help in persuading Barbie that she should have one last meeting with Raymond. At last, on 20 October, she was told that Barbie had finally agreed. She was expected at Gestapo headquarters the next day. But by then seeing Raymond was no longer so important.

Over the previous weeks she had been keeping a close watch through binoculars on the daily movements of the lorries carrying the prisoners between the prison and Gestapo headquarters. She had also recruited eleven members of the Armée Secret to help her hijack the lorry carrying Raymond. The attempt was timed for 21 October, the very day she was due at the Ecole de Santé.

That morning, the group took up their positions. The lorry failed to emerge – there had been a breakdown. The group dispersed, and quickly changing into different clothes Lucie rushed to the headquarters. Raymond, convinced that his wife had been arrested, pretended that he did not know her.

'What,' shouted Lucie, 'you don't recognise me? You are a real bastard. You knew me only too well. I'm expecting a child of yours. And this child must have a name. I don't care if they shoot you or deport you, but you've got to marry me.'

Raymond realised that an escape plan had been set in motion. 'Wearily', he agreed and they were given permission to meet once more to formalise the marriage. Lucie left the Ecole de Santé knowing that Raymond would undoubtedly be travelling that night in a lorry back to Montluc. She alerted her group and they took up their prearranged positions, several of them armed with specially acquired silencers.

As expected, the lorry emerged from the Ecole de Santé into the night. Two armed soldiers sat in the front with the driver, three more in the rear with orders to shoot any prisoner who tried to escape. The fourteen prisoners were chained in pairs; Raymond had deliberately chosen a partner who looked daring and strong. A darkened van, its side windows removed, slipped out unobtrusively in front of the lorry. Inside sat Lucie. Another van and a car followed behind. After just four minutes the first van began to overtake the lorry and as it drew level with the driver's window three silenced machine pistols spattered the front cab. The lorry came to a sudden but safe halt by the kerb in the Boulevard des Hirondelles. All three Germans had been killed outright. The soldiers in the back jumped out in surprise, only to be sprayed similarly with gunfire. Two were killed, one escaped. Within weeks the Aubracs had been flown back to Britain, Lucie having discovered, in the meantime, that she was in fact genuinely pregnant. Brave and successful as Aubrac's rescue was, it still remained an isolated victory against Barbie that year. To some it seemed that Lyons had been transformed from the 'Resistance capital' to the 'Gestapo capital'.

Moulin's arrest had been a real catastrophe for the Resistance. For those who had worked closely with those arrested, the ensuing months were very difficult, not least because of the certainty that there would be further betrayals. The Resistance was quite used to picking up pieces and patching up damaging blows, but the destruction which followed Caluire was considerable. Organisationally, everything had to be moved within twenty-four hours. That meant immediate exposure for dozens of people as well as further confusion and inevitable arrests.

Politically, Moulin's arrest had immeasurable consequences. Moulin was not just a leader of a group of disparate guerrillas; he was developing a political movement. Had he survived, he would undoubtedly have possessed considerable political influence after the German defeat. With his disappearance, the communists seized opportunities which otherwise they would have been denied. For France, these were crippling consequences in the immediate postwar years.

For the victor, naturally, came the rewards. First a personal congratulatory letter from Himmler to the 'Einsatzkommando', including Barbie, 'for their high efficiency in the pursuit of crime and their indefatigable devotion to the battle against Resistance organisations in France.' In November he was awarded the Iron Cross, First Class, with sword.

Berlin's only criticism of his conduct that year was his failure to produce more children to increase the Aryan stock. In his reply he explained that the birth of his daughter Ute had been very difficult and his wife needed a year's rest. During this time Dortmund had been bombed, forcing his wife to move to her mother-in-law's in Trier. The overcrowding in his mother's house and the fact that he had returned home only once in two years, had prevented them satisfying SS requirements.

THE DEVASTATION

The liberation of Oyonnax on 11 November 1943 was a mere thirty-minute event, but it was a symbolic, even historic gesture.

This small town, sixty miles from Lyons, lies in the south of the Ain province whose inhabitants and terrain proved over the next nine months to be ideal for Maquis life and operations. The town's 'liberation' was in fact just a parade, organised in the utmost secrecy by Major Romans-Petit, the leader of the Maquis in the Ain, and probably one of the best Maquis leaders in France. A First World War hero, he had come from Paris in December 1942 determined to fight the occupation. During that first year about one thousand men had joined him in the hills. Virtually unarmed, with very little food and inadequate shelter, their only strategic asset in the summer of 1943 was the rugged countryside in which they lived and the potential support of the inhabitants. The Maquis, he felt, needed a show of force, a demonstration that they were more than law-breaking hillbillies. With the town sealed off and communications cut, his men were drawn up in the town square, ready to perform an act they had been rehearsing for some weeks in the hills.

Dressed in his captain's uniform, with white gloves and wearing all his decorations, Petit shouted at the top of his voice, 'Maquis de l'Ain, follow my command.' According to Petit, the small but rapidly growing crowd of curious sightseers looked on with, '. . . complete amazement, followed by delirious happiness. Men, women and children shouted, "Long live the Maquis, long live France!"' At the war memorial, Petit laid a wreath with the message, 'From tomorrow's victors, to those of 1914–18.' Emotional scenes followed a rousing performance of *La Marseillaise*, and with everyone in tears, Petit returned with his motley army to the hills to start the campaign against the occupation.

In September 1943, Richard Heslop, now code-named 'Xavier', had been sent by Colonel Maurice Buckmaster, the head of SOE's French section, on a reconnaissance mission to the area. In his briefing, Buckmaster told Heslop, 'We need to know everything there is to know. This is an important area, and when we invade Europe your groups will have a major job to disrupt communications and delay German troop movements.' Heslop's mission was to assess the Maquis throughout the whole of south-east France. Depending on his recommendations, the Allies would decide whether or not to devote special attention to the area. 'If you recommend that we go ahead,' said Buckmaster, 'then you will be in charge of all the Resistance in the provinces.' Over fourteen days, Heslop covered the four provinces over which Barbie ruled. As if on a Cook's tour, he was efficiently picked up and deposited in a seemingly endless review of Maquis camps, men on parade and caches of hidden arms. 'What saddened me most,' he wrote, 'was the low morale of the men who had been hiding for months in the Maquis camps. They were depressed.'

The first area Heslop saw was the beautiful mountains of the Haute-Savoie. Fine for holidays, he concluded, but too dangerous for guerrilla warfare where Maquis groups could easily be trapped. The next stop, the Ain, attracted him most. The countryside was an ideal mixture of rolling hills, valleys, plenty of woods and hiding places, but also lush pastures suitable for parachute drops and landings. The Ain 'was real guerrilla country'. Most important of all, Heslop was convinced that he and Petit could work together.

Within forty-eight hours of delivering a favourable report to London, Heslop was flying back towards Lyons with an American radio operator, Paul Johnson, an ex-OSS agent. Their network, code-named MARKSMAN, was set to revenge Barbie's destruction of the other SOE operations in late 1942. Filled with enthusiasm, Heslop immediately began the routine but vital hunt for landing zones, places to store supplies, the selection of safe houses, particularly for Johnson to use for his transmissions, and, with Petit, the appointing of group leaders. But he also needed a quick boost for morale. The remedy was an RAF drop. As the parachutes floated earthwards in a series of drops during October, the young Maquis began to shrug off their feeling of desperate isolation and enthusiastically started training sessions for their campaign against the Germans.

The news of increased guerrilla activity in the Ain did not take long to reach Gestapo headquarters in Lyons. Reports from collaborators in Oyonnax had mentioned that the Maquis were carrying newly-supplied British guns. Daily, vital rail traffic was being disrupted as Maquis groups blew up lines in remote country areas. Even the special trains which had been built to clear the lines of explosive charges had been hit. With monotonous regularity, the Maquis were looting supply trains and carrying off consignments of food, which they now used to sustain their increasing numbers. Maquis groups had scored major hits, destroying the power station at Le Creusot and a major ball-bearing factory at Annecy. Wehrmacht patrols driving through country districts were being attacked and, on occasion, even completely wiped out.

Knab had to face the unpleasant fact that the Ain was fast becoming bandit country, damaging not only the Wehrmacht's morale and prestige, but also endangering German security. He wanted to retaliate immediately. General Pflaum, commander of the 157th Reserve Division, agreed. With continuous rumours of Allied plans to land in the south of France, his operational priority was to guard the vital supply line to Germany and the Reich's border with Switzerland. Pflaum's immediate problem was that most of the troops in the area were reservists and garrison troops unsuited for fast operations. To Knab's irritation, Pflaum had first, as a matter of routine, to consult his corps headquarters; the Gestapo had little patience.

On 6 December, in the small town of Nantua, just ten miles south of Oyonnax, an unpopular married couple who dealt on the black market and were known collaborators, were seized by the local Resistance, stripped naked, daubed with Swastikas and made to walk through the streets. Knab was determined on immediate reprisals. Eight days later, a special train carrying 500 German soldiers drew up without warning at the station and within an hour had sealed off the town. Throughout the day, they aggressively searched every house, arresting 120 men who were deported to concentration camps. Posters, signed by Knab, announced that the arrests were a punishment and a warning to anyone else who tried to besmirch the reputation of the German forces. At the end of the operation, it seemed to the Gestapo to be a good opportunity to teach another town the same lesson. A group of officers, with some milice, drove up to Oyonnax and arrested the deputy mayor, the former mayor and an industrialist. Their bodies were left on the roadside outside the town. The town had paid the price for its temporary liberation.

Christmas in 1943 was not celebrated by Gestapo officers in Lyons with quite the same merriment as it had been the previous year. Germany's military position had deteriorated. The Wehr-macht, defeated in North Africa, was facing its grimmest test in Russia and Italy. Hedwig Ondra remembers that there was a stiff, formal staff party with Christmas decorations, but that afterwards she and a group of friends cooked for themselves some Austrian and German specialities and sat together talking about home. Barbie and the senior officers enjoyed the temporary seasonal truce with a feisty raucous celebration during which enormous amounts of food and wine were consumed. Nothing, however, could disguise the serious deterioration in German security.

Heslop and Petit had spent Christmas touring Maquis camps, eating excellent food which had been stolen from German convoys, satisfying themselves that morale amongst the considerably swollen ranks of the Maquis had improved. Thanks to Heslop, the Maquis were now well-armed, fed, and clothed, while their dependents were being supported with money sent from London. But these improved conditions did not conceal the very real dangers they faced. The Gestapo had captured 'Brun', one of the saboteurs at Le Creusot; he had been slowly tortured, and his naked body was left on the town hall steps as a warning. It was one of the more painful consequences of their gruelling war – that success provoked more atrocities.

On 9 January, two German soldiers were shot dead at the station in Lyons. According to Barbie, he was accosted by an army lieutenant demanding immediate reprisals to contain the fury of his troops. 'I told him not to worry. I had a good idea. I arranged for some cells doors [at the Ecole de Santé] to be left open the following night when there was certain to be an air-raid alarm and sirens. Sure enough they went off, and the idiots in the cells thought they could escape. They came up the stairs, right into the machine-gun post I'd set up. We killed twenty-one of them.' (A post-war investigation reported that twenty-two were killed.) Barbie's justification was perversely self-serving:

We were in the right, because they shouldn't have shot our soldiers in the back. It was against all the laws. We never thought that we would have to put up with such atrocities. But it had all started in Russia. That's how I got into all this. But there, it was the women whom we really feared. If you fell into their hands . . . if you saw what they'd done to one's comrades, then you really became hard. There was nothing else but to do the same.

But as intelligence agents both Knab and Barbie realised that, regardless of individual 'successes', the Gestapo's resources were too limited to fight what had become a small army. Anticipating that the threat to German forces would grow, Barbie sought new allies or at best reinforcements. The choice was very limited. The local *milice* were given more responsibilities and even more power. *Milice* courts had been established throughout France in January, but in Lyons the 'trials' rarely lasted more than a few minutes; the conclusion was always the same. It was unusual for victims of the *milice* to be given a trial at all. On the same day as Barbie staged the prison escape, Joseph Lecussan, the regional *milice* chief, personally arrested eighty-year-old Victor Basch, the national president of the League of Human Rights, and his wife. He shot them the following day, sticking on Basch's corpse a placard: 'Terror against terror – the Jew always pays.' The murders would have been of no concern for the Gestapo, but they alienated the *milice* even further from the French and diminished their value for the Germans.

Barbie's alternative ally was the Wehrmacht. After weeks of discussions, Pflaum agreed to launch the first 'search and destroy' mission against the Maquis in France. The plan was to encircle the large area south of Nantua, between St Martin-du-Frêne, Artemare and Ambérieu, and launch a pincer attack starting in the hills around Brénod, sweeping down to the plains on the southernmost part of the Ain, nearest Lyons. No one would be allowed to leave their parish or village; there would be a curfew between 8.00 p.m. and 6.00 a.m.; no one was to be allowed to use a car or bicycle; all trains would be stopped and telephone lines cut. With the area sealed off and all movement frozen, thousands of German troops were to be deployed to comb through the villages and countryside hunting for the Maquis. The Gestapo's mission was to exploit the disruption caused by the Wehrmacht and ferret out the whereabouts of the Maquis, using their traditional methods. The prize was the capture of the Maquis' command staff.

On 5 February, as the German forces were manoeuvring into

position, Heslop, Johnson and 'Colonel Chabot' (Henri Girousse), the temporary commander of the Ain, with other members of the Maquis command group, were slowly trudging their way through exceptionally deep snow in very hilly terrain towards Brénod. Heslop was expecting more RAF drops. Soon after settling into a remote farmhouse at Le Mollard, overlooking Brénod, a messenger brought the news that German soldiers had just occupied the town. Heslop and 'Chabot' decided to wait rather than rush off. Walking through deep snow was not only very difficult, but also left a very noticeable trail for the Germans to follow. For the moment, there seemed to be very little need for concern. It was only during the day, as the sound of gunfire from German troops attacking a Maquis camp on a nearby wooded hill intensified, that news about the scale of the German operation trickled through. At nightfall, Johnson heard from London that there would be a drop that night. Heslop felt that he had little alternative but to organise the reception party while Johnson remained in the farmhouse. The next day, the German attack on Camp Michel intensified. Several hundred German soldiers had gradually worked their way through snow drifts and were wearing the Maquis defenders down. Marius and Julien Roche, two brothers working with the command staff, watched from a hill as fourteen German trucks and artillery arrived in Brénod. As they watched, a Messerschmitt flew overhead firing its guns. Back in the farmhouse, Johnson had already seen a column of German soldiers marching up from the town towards the farmhouse. Within minutes, the house was empty and twenty-four people were trudging south-west towards another remote farmhouse, La Ferme de la Montagne at l'Abergement de Varey, known locally as 'le petit Abergement'. For three days they trudged through the deep snow, with little food and under constant fear of being caught by a German patrol. Unknown to them, they were walking straight into the very area that Barbie had selected for his personal attention. He had translated the 'search and destroy' mission into a scorched-earth operation.

Barbie already knew that 'Chabot' was in the area. On the first day of the operation, he had sent 'Gueule Tordue' to interrogate 'Chabot's' family; but the family was already in hiding and 'Chabot's' father-in-law convincingly pleaded ignorance. Nevertheless, for Barbie, the hunt was on. His first victims on 6 February were in the pretty village of St Rambert-en-Bugey, at the south-westernmost tip of the operational area. Fifteen people were arrested and one Jew killed outright for resisting arrest.

He then set off for Evosges, another small but undistinguished village about ten kilometres away. Travelling behind him were five army trucks carrying about 100 Wehrmacht soldiers, and also several black Citroën cars carrying five collaborators including Lucien Guesdon and Robert 'Pierre' Moog. Inside his own car was Erich Bartelmus, one of the most sadistic torturers in the Lyons Gestapo. Driving along the twisting, narrow, snow-covered roads, it would have taken Barbie about an hour before he turned the final bend and saw the grey stone house of Jean Carrel, a roadmender, at the entrance of the village. Until Barbie's arrival, the 150 villagers of Evosges had hardly been aware of the war. Throughout the sixteen months of occupation, they had continued their farming isolated from politics, only troubled by shortages and the price of their produce. Except for those few who had seen the rare German convoy speed down the main *route national* between Bourg and Belley, the majority of the villagers had not even seen a German soldier.

There are two accounts of what occurred as Barbie's car stopped outside Carrel's house: the one Guesdon gave in July 1945, and that of Georges Brun, a villager whose family have lived in Evosges since 1650. The accounts are identical. Before Barbie's arrival, the village had already been surrounded by troops to prevent any escapes. Leading the way, Barbie burst into Carrel's house and found him in bed. Outside, there was some shouting. Someone had opened the barn door and found it stacked with bags of flour, bearing an official swastika sign. These had been stolen by the Maquis. Dragging Carrel undressed down the stairs and out of the house, Barbie personally shot the twenty-eight-year-old man without any questions asked. Georges Brun, then aged fifteen, heard the shot as he and some other villagers were being herded along the main street towards Carrel's house by German soldiers. All of them were ordered to stand in front of the body. Everything had happened so quickly that Brun, like the others, was totally bewildered.

Brun's twenty-one-year-old brother Julien was one of the few who tried to escape with his lifelong friend, Jean Jiet. Both of them had been avoiding the STO and knew the consequences of arrest.

At first they hid in a barn, but the owner, fearing reprisals if they were caught, screamed at them to leave. Running off into the fields they lay in the snow until they decided to make a bolt, but were immediately spotted. They were captured, beaten, and dragged back to the village.

Leaving the terrified group at Carrel's house, Barbie walked thirty yards to the soldiers guarding Julien Brun. Without any preliminaries, he asked Julien to lead him to the nearby Maquis camp. According to Guesdon, Julien 'categorically refused'. According to Georges, Julien just did not know the way. The result, testified Guesdon in 1945, was that 'Barbie shot him immediately'.

Georges Brun heard the shots but remained mystified. An hour later, he was released and walked slowly back to his house. 'When I saw him there, I became mad. You can imagine how I felt. I was only fifteen and there was my brother's body. My friends had to lock me up because I was determined on vengeance with the gun I had hidden.'

After searching the village, Barbie left at about five in the afternoon. The two bodies were brought in and most of the young men said goodbye to their families and went into the hills. Georges Brun stayed to console his father. 'We just didn't think that they would come back.'

Early the following morning, soldiers again surrounded the village. Barbie felt cheated. The operation was three days old and he had not discovered any positive leads to the Maquis. Boiling with frustration, he resorted to senseless violence. Within minutes of arriving, he had arrested the mayor, Jean-Marie Jaquemet and ordered him to stand on the street with his family. A peremptory command, and Jaquemet's house was set ablaze. While the Germans were momentarily distracted by the flames, Jaquemet told his wife and two daughters to escape. Seconds later, he was shot in the stomach. Seeing the soldiers pull back the bolts to shoot him again, the wounded mayor covered his face with his hands. The bullets blew his fingers off and he fell to the ground. His family, running across the fields, heard the final *coup de grâce* fired into his head. For Barbie, it was just the beginning.

Evosges was ransacked and pillaged. Eight more houses and the village's six cars were burnt. Among the new arrests were Georges Brun's cousin, André Madiglier, and Astride Brun, both of whom had given food to the Maquis. They were taken to Barbie, who was still standing by Jaquemet's body and burning house. He gave the order and they were shot. Barbie then drove out of Evosges, no doubt forgetting at once both its name and its tragedy. Georges Brun still suffers today. 'They would not allow us to bury the bodies for eight days. We had not expected them to be so cruel. We had not imagined they could do anything like this.' The tragedy is compounded for Georges because he has no sons and with his death the Brun family, who have farmed in Evosges for over three hundred years, will disappear, except from the village graveyard.

Barbie's next stop was Nivollet-Montgriffon, three miles northwest of Evosges. By then he had successfully extracted some accurate information, perhaps from the three young *maquisards* whose bullet-riddled bodies were found in the hills outside Evosges when the snow melted. After a house-to-house search the town's deputy mayor, Marius Chavant, a member of the Maquis, was arrested at midnight in his house. He was shot fifty yards from his home for refusing to reveal where his son and the other young men from the village had escaped to. Four other bodies, including the village cheesemaker's, were also found when the snow melted.

It was 8 February, the middle of the German operation. The disruption throughout the region was enormous but the military results were meagre. Hundreds had been arrested, many of whom would be deported and disappear for ever. Dozens of houses had been burnt and many innocent civilians had been killed in the most brutal circumstances. The cost to the Maquis however, although they were on the run, was so far slight. Heslop, also on the run, was moving west from Corlier towards L'Abergement de Varey, when he heard that the RAF was dropping supplies indiscriminately over the area. Most of it was falling straight into German hands. There was now chaos as well as grief. In an attempt to save at least some of the arms, Heslop began a cross-country march which ended summarily when he fell through a snow drift and cracked his shin.

'Chabot', Johnson and the twenty-two others had marched for three days to reach L'Abergement de Varey. As they slid down the final hillside towards the remote farmhouse, they were too exhausted to notice the signs of a sudden evacuation, only twenty-four hours earlier, by another Maquis group who had been denounced. It was past midday and informers had already alerted Barbie.

While 'Chabot' cautiously walked around outside the house, the others took off their clothes to dry, and lay exhausted on the floor. Marius Roche and his twin brother Julien, were amongst them:

> We were exhausted when we arrived. It was the first and only time that we didn't set up a guard at once. Even when a peasant woman breathlessly burst in shouting, 'You've got to leave, the Boches are on the way,' we didn't take it seriously. It was two hours later that there was the unmistakable noise of Germans and *milice* driving up the long, tree-lined road, followed by an immediate burst of shooting. I looked at my twin brother, and said 'Adieu'. We were twenty-two and inseparable.

Just grabbing their clothes and without a chance to dress, everyone ran out of the house. Miraculously, a sudden snow flurry covered the farmhouse, cutting all visibility. Ducking behind the cover of hedges surrounding the house, they hid and waited, unable to move because heavy machine-gun fire was raking the whole area. Only the farmer's wife, in another house, managed to run. But after twenty yards she was stopped by a German dressed in civilian clothes, who spoke good French: it was Barbie. After a short interrogation he released her, but as she walked away from the gunfire, a German grenade fell nearby, injuring her slightly. The German soldiers had by now pinpointed the *maquisards* behind the hedges and began lobbing grenades and mortars in their direction. Some of the group, unable to withstand the terrible cold, crept back into the house. The shooting intensified and a *maquisard* fell wounded near Johnson. As the German fire closed in on their targets, both 'Chabot' and Johnson realised that the only hope for survival was to withdraw, leaving those in the house shooting wildly at the Germans. By the time they had reached the woods at the top of the hill, several more retreating *maquisards* had been wounded; there was no alternative but to leave them in the snow.

It was some days later that the eight survivors and Heslop returned to the farmhouse. Those who were wounded in the rush for the woods had been brutally treated, their faces completely crushed by hobnail boots. The imprint of the hobnails was still visible. Inside the destroyed building were the charred, limbless and unrecognisable bodies of the remainder, including Julien Roche. The owner of the farm had also been killed.

The operation ended four days later. In its wake, the Germans had left a trail of destruction, death and grief. The Maquis had been disrupted but militarily they were undefeated. Within days Heslop had contacted London and a massive re-supply operation began with as many as nine planes simultaneously dropping canisters over the Ain. With new arms came a flood of recruits, spurred on to join the struggle because of the recent atrocities.

Any frustrations Barbie felt because of failures in the countryside were relieved by 7 March, when the Gestapo in Lyons arrested 'Chatoux', an important member of the region's Resistance movement. Interrogated in the Ecole de Santé, quite probably by Barbie, 'Chatoux' immediately betrayed his whole underground network. Over the next weeks, 101 Resistance workers, including the regional chief, Albert Chambonnet, were picked up at Barbie's direction. The movement lost key supporters in the police, medical profession and post office, and many of those responsible for false documents and the distribution of newspapers; a devastating blow to the region's fight against the Germans and a major coup for the Gestapo.

Gestapo successes against the Resistance were matched by those of the Wehrmacht. During the winter, the RAF had dropped supplies to the Maquis of the Haute-Savoie onto the Plateau des Glières, a high remote mountain table near Annecy. Down in the valleys, the Germans carefully noted where the parachutes were landing and in mid-February began to move thousands of soldiers towards the area. Now well-armed and believing he possessed the tactical advantage, Tom Morel, the Maquis leader, decided that the plateau would make an ideal location for a stand against the Germans. Maquis leaders throughout the region were invited to head for the plateau and join the trial of strength. Heslop refused. The idea was contrary to every rule of guerrilla warfare, which was to exploit mobility in hit-and-run tactics rather than stand and fight. His remained a minority view.

As more RAF supplies landed, German spotter planes pinpointed the *maquisards'* positions and finally began their attack on 25 March. With 8,000 soldiers and two air squadrons on alert, the German assault began with a massive bombardment. Then the Luftwaffe and the troops, among them the crack Airborne Division, launched a massive attack. There was no escape from the plateau and only a handful of the 450 *maquisards* survived the battle.

Greatly encouraged by their success, the German High Command decided to press their advantage against the Maquis and on 31 March ordered 8,000 troops to be moved north back into the Ain and into the Jura to take part in 'Operation Frühling' (Operation Spring). Unlike the wild scrub and irregular wooded hills of the Ain, the Jura with its steep mountains, deep valleys and rivers was less suitable for guerrilla warfare, but the Maquis had always been stronger here than in the Ain and had for some time been cutting the vital rail link between Lyons and Germany.

During the first week of April, General Pflaum again discussed with Knab the exact locations where, according to Gestapo intelligence, the Maquis were concentrated. Knab wanted the attack to start in Nantua, then drive towards the northern part of the Ain, with special attention to the area around Oyonnax, Arinthod and St Claude in the Jura. Pflaum agreed. During the night of 6/7 April, German troops moved into position to seal off all access to the operational area. At 8.00 a.m. on 7 April Pflaum gave the orders for a three-pronged attack to start, concentrating around Gex, Oyonnax and St Claude. At his disposal were five regiments of mountain troops, a regiment of panzers, light artillery and infantry, and a regiment of Cossacks. Ominously, Knab had persuaded Pflaum that no French forces, even the *milice*, should participate in the operation. According to Pflaum's post-operation report, Knab had alleged that 'they were too timid in carrying out executions and in burning houses'.

On the first day, the German forces made no contact at all with the Maquis in Gex or Oyonnax, but in the north they were pinned down by heavy and accurate fire from well-fortified positions around St Claude. This picturesque town with a population of 10,000 sits astride the meeting-point of two valleys. Surrounded as it is by high mountains, access to the town is only possible along narrow, winding roads hugging the wooded mountain-sides. Surprised by the Maquis' strength, and hindered by the terrain, the German troops had to wait until nightfall before they could escape. Their casualties on the first day were five dead and thirteen wounded. After quickly consulting Knab about Gestapo intelligence reports, Pflaum ordered reinforcements to encircle the town. The first *maquisards* were captured on 9 April; they were handed over for interrogation to the SS detachment led by Barbie.

Barbie had not left Lyons at the beginning of the operation. Mid-morning on 6 April, a squad of a dozen German soldiers led by Gestapo officers and *milice* drove from Lyons to the tiny and extremely isolated village of Izieu. Local *milice* had allegedly heard from Henri Bourdon, a farmer, that for the past year the village's largest house had been used as a school and refuge for Jewish children, aged from three to fourteen. One of them, Theo Reiss, actually worked in Bourdon's fields. Until then none of the villagers had been concerned for the children's safety; the village was so remote from the war that there was no sense of secrecy about their presence. None of them even knew at the time of the two German lorries which had pulled up in front of the house, or of the panic that followed inside. The school's director, Miron Zlatin, was told by the Germans that the children were to be evacuated for their own safety. Immediately suspicious, he tried to dissuade the Gestapo officers from moving the children; having failed, he told the children to pack their belongings and climb into the lorries.

Julien Favet, a farmhand, was working in the nearby fields at the time. Usually one of the children brought his lunch and, when no one came, he returned to the village. As he walked into the drive, he saw the children filing out of the house. 'The Germans were loading the children into the lorries brutally, as if they were sacks of potatoes. Most of them were frightened and crying. When they saw me, they all began shouting, "Julien! Julien!"' As he moved towards the children, a rifle butt was stuck in his ribs. In the midst of the confusion and noise, there was a loud shout. Theo Reiss had tried to jump out of the lorry and escape. 'They grabbed him,' remembers Favet, 'and started beating him with the butts of their rifles, and kicking him in the shins.' Held back by a soldier, Favet was helpless. 'Then a German came up to me. I'm sure it was Barbie. For a moment he looked at me, spoke to another German, then said, "Get out." I left, walking backwards.'

There is no reliable confirmation that Barbie did go to Izieu, but his involvement in the arrests and subsequent deportation is beyond doubt. At 8.10 that evening, a telex signed personally by Barbie was sent to Gestapo headquarters in Paris: *The Jewish children's home in Izieu (Ain) was closed down this morning. A total of 41 children aged 3 to 13* [sic] *were arrested. Additionally, all the Jewish personnel – comprising ten people, including five women – were also arrested.*

Money or other valuables were not discovered. Transport to Drancy follows 7.4.44. Signed Barbie. Reiss, another child and Zlatin were deported on 15 May to Reval, Estonia, and shot. The others were dispatched to Paris. Just six days after leaving Lyons, on 13 April, the children and adults were reloaded onto another train destined for Auschwitz, where with just one exception (Lea Feldblaum, a young assistant), they were all gassed.

Barbie has persistently denied involvement in the Izieu arrests and deportations. Wanting to distance himself from any responsibility for the war crime of genocide, he insists that his role was purely administrative. 'I signed the telex only because Eichmann's people were not around at the time,' was his explanation when questioned during the Seventies. He chose to ignore that the Gestapo's Jewish sub-section was under his direct command and that he had heard a year previously, from other SS men who had returned from eastern Europe, the final fate of all the Jews whose deportation he had authorised.

With that administrative chore completed, Barbie drove straight to St Claude. The 157th Reserve Division had requisitioned the Hôtel de France as headquarters for the operation, and the Gestapo were allotted offices on the fourth floor. On the first day there was no Maquis to interrogate and Barbie, with his small entourage and one hundred Wehrmacht soldiers, drove eight kilometres south to the small village of Larrivoire. As in all villages, the Gestapo's first suspects were the mayor, the priest and the schoolteacher. Drawing up outside the village school, Barbie marched in and demanded to see the local schoolteacher. It was Good Friday and the teacher, Roseline Blonde, was at home. As a detachment of soldiers went in search of Blonde, other soldiers had already set fire to farmhouses at the edge of the village and begun systematically ransacking the remaining houses, stealing, and drinking whatever they found. Each house was pillaged, then set ablaze. Soon the whole village was burning. Only the village sacristan's house was spared. He was a known collaborator. After the mayor had been found and shot, Barbie demanded that the petrified villagers bring the teacher to him. But Blonde had already run into the hills.

Barbie already knew, probably from the village sacristan, that Blonde was a Maquis sympathiser who had allowed local *maquisards* to use the school for meetings, storage and to check on informers. But by the time villagers had found her in the woods, Barbie had already left with the parting threat that, should they fail to deliver Blonde for interrogation, the whole village would be deported.

Blonde was in a panic. She could see not only her own village burning but also, on the skyline, a fierce red glow from the nearby villages of Sièges and Viry. Their inhabitants were to suffer appalling atrocities. Blonde felt she had little choice. As she reluctantly returned to her village, she was assaulted with undisguised venom by her friends and neighbours. Without exception, they blamed her for their catastrophic misfortunes and insisted that two villagers escort her to St Claude to make sure that she did not change her mind. She left, too alienated from the village ever to return.

Barbie meanwhile had hastened back to St Claude. The Wehrmacht had finally captured some members of the Maquis. At the Hôtel de France, Munich-born Corporal Alfons Glas, a twenty-five-year-old member of the 99th Mountain Infantry Regiment, saw the uniformed Gestapo officer several times over the next two days:

> He was very noticeable by his behaviour: presumptious, even arrogant. We were irritated that he didn't feel any necessity to salute our officers. His belt was always crooked, leaning towards the side where his gun was hanging. He had a 9mm American pistol and always carried an American sub-machine-gun. He walked around town completely unprotected, the sort of man who really didn't know the meaning of fear that he might be shot by someone from the Resistance.

On the afternoon of 8 April, Glas was sitting at a table in the middle of the hotel's dining room on the first floor. Six or seven prisoners arrived in the hotel dressed in normal clothing and were ordered to stand with their arms leaning against the wall. The rumour soon reached Glas that one of the prisoners was Joseph Kemmler, an Alsatian Maquis leader:

> When Barbie came in the room, the prisoners were visibly frightened. After questioning the others briefly, he turned to Kemmler, questioning him in French, and Kemmler just answering, 'never'. Barbie hit Kemmler in the face with his gloved hand. He repeated his questions and then hit him again. After having been hit like this three or four times, Kemmler began to bleed from his nose and mouth. Barbie then walked towards the piano which was a few steps away and, with his gloved and blood-

smeared fingers, began to play the first bars of the song, *Speak to Me of Love*. Then he went back to Kemmler and asked more questions. Again he only got the answer, 'never'. He hit him again.

By then it was night and Kemmler was separated from the others and taken upstairs. The following day the interrogations began again, again in the dining room, although this time behind a glass partition. Glas watched as before: 'Barbie stood in the rear. Kemmler was standing, alternately being hit by two Frenchmen with a rope, half-an-inch thick, which had a metal snap-hook fixed to the end. They kept hitting him between the shoulder and the thigh, never the head. Barbie asked him questions, followed by more blows.' Glas watched the interrogation for about ninety minutes until Kemmler was unable to stand. The two Frenchmen carried him to a chair with arm rests, to prevent him falling down. Barbie then left the room. Glas, with several others, watched Kemmler sit quite still and then with a shudder lean forward. 'About five minutes later, a urine puddle formed underneath his chair. That was how I knew he was dead.' Kemmler's half-burnt body was found several days later in les Moussières, brought there by Barbie himself when he raided the village and shot four men suspected of helping the Maquis.

While Kemmler slowly died, Barbie went outside into the Place du Pré, where the town's population had been ordered by loud-speaker announcements to gather. René Chorier was typical of many who hesitantly walked towards the square. Twenty-three years old, he had dodged labour conscription and had joined the Maquis. It was only by chance that he was in the town to see his father when the German troops arrived. 'They had machine-gun posts on all the roads, and even in the mountains overlooking the town. There was no chance of escape and, knowing that they were about to search every house, it was better to risk going to the square.' Surrounded by more machine-gun posts, about 2,000 men were waiting forlornly to be checked. Amid considerable tension, Chorier watched as Barbie, rushing backwards and forwards, screaming orders at Wehrmacht soldiers, tried to organise a check of all identity cards. 'It was taking too long, so Barbie just gave instructions and began picking people out at random. At about mid-day my mother arrived. She wanted to give me some food. As

Klaus Barbie with his wife and children (*Klarsfeld*)

SS officers based in Lyons: Erich Bartelmus, Werner Knab and August Moritz

Left: Barbie with the SS team (*Klarsfeld*)

Resistance leaders captured by Barbie in
1943: Jean Moulin (*Sygma*) and Raymond
and Lucie Aubrac (*France Soir*)

Moulin's alleged betrayer, René Hardy (*Sygma*). SOE agent Henry Newton with Resistance radio operator André Courvoisier (*Kentish Gazette*)

Izieu: the Halaunbrenner family, the Jewish schoolchildren deported to Auschwitz, and the plaque which commemorates the tragedy (*Klarsfeld*)

LE 6 AVRIL 1944, JOUR DU JEUDI-SAINT 43 ENFANTS DE
LA MAISON D'IZIEU ETAIENT ARRETES PAR LES ALLEMANDS, AVEC
LEURS MAITRES, PUIS DEPORTES LE 15 AVRIL 1944.
QUARANTE ET UN ENFANTS ET CINQ DE LEURS MAITRES FURENT
EXTERMINES DANS LES CHAMBRES A GAZ D'AUSCHWITZ.
LE DIRECTEUR DE LA COLONIE ET DEUX GARÇONS FURENT
FUSILLES DANS LA FORTERESSE DE REVEL.

REIFMANN-LEVAN CLAUDE 11Ans	BEN TITOU RAOUL 13Ans	BEN ASSAYAC ESTHER 13Ans
TEITELBAUM MAX 13	BULKA MARCEL 14	HALAUBRENNER CLAUDE 5
TEITELBAUM ARMAND 11	BULKA ALBERT 5	HALAUBRENNER NINA 9
AMENT JEAN 11	HALPERIN GEORGES 8	LUZGARD JACQUELINE 19
ZUCKERBERG EMILE 6	MERMELSTEIN MARCEL 8	MERMELSTEIN PAULETTE 12
SPRINGER ZYGMUND 8	GERENSTEIN MAURICE 14	SZULZKLAPPER Suzanne 12
ADELSHEIMER SAMUEL 7	GOLDBERG HENRI 14	SPIEGEL MARTHE 11
GAMIEL EDMOND 11	GOLDBERG JOSEPH 12	SPIEGEL SENTA 9
SADOVSKI GILLES 9	BALSAM MAX 13	GERENSTEIN LILIANE 11
LEINER MAX 9	BALSAM JEAN 11	
KARGEMAN ISIDORE 11	WELTNER CHARLES 10	
WERTHEIMER OTTO 13	HIRSCH ARNOLD 16	REIFMANN MOISE 64
BEN ASSAYAC ELIE 11	REISS THEO 17	REIFMANN NOVA 60
BEN ASSAYAC JACOB 10	FRIEDLER LUCIENNE 5	REIFMANN SUZANNE 38
BEN GUIGUI JACQUES 13	KROCHMAL RENATHE 9	HEIGER LUCIE 50
BEN GUIGUI JEAN CLAUDE 6	KROCHMAL LIANE 7	FRIEDLER MARIE 36
BEN GUIGUI RICHARD 8	ARONOWICZ MINA 12	ZLATIN MIRON 40

The SOE and the Maquis de l'Ain: Richard
'Xavier' Heslop, Paul Johnson, Julien and Marius
Roche, and Albert 'Didier' Chambonnet

The Klarsfeld family (*Klarsfeld*)

she began to walk towards me, Barbie went rushing up to her, shouting furiously, and gave her a kick in the buttocks.'

By 4.00 p.m. the SS had finally selected about 300 men. Chorier was among them. 'One of the men began making a fuss about being arrested for no reason. They just shot him.' On the side of the rail truck which carried the 300 to Buchenwald, the Germans scrawled 'Terrorists from the Jura'. The whole town had been punished for the deaths of five Wehrmacht soldiers. As the prisoners were being loaded onto the train, soldiers under Barbie's direction went to *La Fraternelle*, the local co-operative store, and plundered it for that night's dinner.

The next morning, at 10.00 a.m., Roseline Blonde arrived at the hotel. It seemed to her as if she were volunteering for immediate execution. Instead, she became involved in an extraordinary display of a split personality. Sitting eating mushrooms and cream, Barbie interspersed his threats to have her immediately shot with a long monologue about the frivolity of women, the latest book he had read, and about football. Why, he asked the teacher, could French intellectuals not understand German charms and qualities. 'You are an intellectual, you are a schoolteacher. You should be co-operating with the Germans.' Blonde's interrogation was broken up by a farce. A soldier, cleaning his gun, mistakenly fired a shot. The glass partition shattered and there was panic. While Barbie beat the soldier, someone arrived with apparently urgent news. 'They all rushed off like madmen. As Barbie was rushing out, a soldier pointed to me questioningly, and Barbie just said, "Take her away."' Blonde was sent to Ravensbrück.

Over the next four days, Barbie rushed frantically and haphazardly through an area south of St Claude, from Villard-St-Sauveur to les Moussières, Les Bouchoux, Molinges, Viry and then north to Morez. In each village there are accounts of betrayals, arrests, intimidation, incineration, plunder, beatings, torture and finally execution. Read together, the eyewitness accounts amount to a description of uncontrolled, frenzied savagery rather than a calculated investigation to crush the Maquis.

On 13 April, in one typical encounter, Barbie arrested Baptiste Baroni in Molinges. To intimidate the Frenchman, he pushed Baroni outside and showed him the body of Gaston Patel whom he had just executed. Where, Barbie wanted to know, was the local

Maquis chief Dubail, alias 'Vallin'. Baroni pleaded ignorance. Acting the part which so delighted Barbie, he ordered a heavily bruised *maquisard* to be pulled out of a nearby Gestapo lorry and asked Baroni whether he recognised the man. Again Baroni pleaded ignorance. Casually Barbie told the *maquisard* that he was therefore free to leave. After walking a few steps, German soldiers shot him down. Now Barbie dragged Baroni to a farmhouse from which Dubail emerged. 'Here's your chief,' shouted an exultant Barbie, ordering the house's incineration. A few hours later, Dubail was shot. Baroni was sent to a concentration camp, but he survived the war.

With hindsight, it is not hard to judge that these operations were militarily abortive and politically counter-productive. Individual deaths could not destroy the Maquis. Throughout the two-week operation, the Germans went into villages and towns and, albeit temporarily, succeeded in intimidating those inhabitants who were helping the Maquis; but they rarely felt sufficiently secure to venture into the fields and forests to hunt their enemy. By the end of April 1944, they had good reasons for fear.

In his report to headquarters, General Pflaum suggested that the lack of contact with the Maquis proved the success of the mission and that the area was finally 'clean' – a self-serving exaggeration and distortion. More significantly, he revealed a major confrontation between himself and Knab. Senior SD officers, wrote Pflaum, had tried to give orders to the Wehrmacht, and at least two regiments had complained. Apparently they had refused to participate in SD atrocities. The SD had mercilessly burnt down Sièges, wrote Pflaum, because 'the operation had not until then been sufficiently spectacular for them'. His only recourse after furious arguments with Knab was an appeal to his corps command for a directive about the SD's authority over the Wehrmacht. He was reassured that the Wehrmacht was not answerable to the SD, even during a joint operation. His complaint that Gestapo intelligence was not always reliable, was also noted. Pflaum's contemporary report was, however, ignored by a French court at his trial after the war. He was condemned for allowing soldiers under his command (according to his own report) to kill 148 people, many 'while trying to escape', to arrest 923 people and to burn down 204 houses. German casualties overall were six dead and fourteen wounded.

The arguments between the Wehrmacht and the SS were the backlash of their joint frustration at not being able to cause anything more than fear and considerable dislocation among Maquis groups. Railway lines were still being regularly blown up, convoys attacked and Germans killed. However, there was still no suggestion that German military control around Lyons was at risk. German occupation laws were still accepted by the vast majority of Frenchmen. Life in Lyons continued as normal: Knab even issued an order that any Lyons nightclubs which had closed were to reopen. Defiantly, the Gestapo were letting the townspeople know that they did not fear the imminent Allied invasion.

On 26 May the atmosphere in the city changed dramatically. In a prelude to the Normandy landings, seven hundred B17 and B24 bombers attached to the 15th US Air Force carried out a daylight raid over Lyons and other cities in southern France. Starting at 10.43 a.m., 1,500 incendiary bombs and explosives were dropped onto the city. Officially the targets were military sites, power stations and railway lines but, as so often, the bombers unintentionally destroyed much more. Houses, factories and offices collapsed under the onslaught. In Lyons, at least 717 people were killed and 1,129 were injured. Pro-German sympathies and resentment against the Allies rose proportionately. Within four days all the rail lines had been repaired, but the anger remained. Alban Vistel, the regional Resistance leader, cabled the Free French government in Algiers: *Effect on morale even more disastrous than material effect. Population painfully indignant . . . Ready for all sacrifices but useless ones.* [Resistance] *are capable of cutting rail lines more effectively . . .*

The town's only consolation was that among the unintended targets was the Gestapo headquarters at the Ecole de Santé. The buildings were destroyed and an unknown but substantial number of prisoners were killed. A few Gestapo officers also perished. Those who survived could no longer feel immune from the Allies. Gestapo methods did not change. Only the venue. Interrogations were now carried out at the Place Bellecour.

The day after the bombing, a Maquis ambush organised by Heslop attacked a *milice* convoy. Twelve *milice* were killed and thirty-eight wounded. It was the second major attack that week. Earlier, over seventy *maquisards* had ambushed a German convoy at the Bois d'Illiat, killing, according to the Maquis, fifty-two Germans and wounding about one hundred and thirty. Barbie admits that attacks on Germans were answered by reprisals, but there are no records of massacres during the last days of May. The Gestapo were now fully occupied trying to counter an epidemic of attacks on the railways. Obeying the call from London, the Resistance were not only cutting the lines, especially those linking Lyons with Germany, but also destroying bridges and tunnels. Under Heslop's orders, a Maquis sabotage squad destroyed a complete engine depot and fifty-two locomotives at Ambérieu. Another SOE group, PIMENTO, the only early one to survive Barbie's first year in Lyons, wrought havoc on the railway lines linking Lyons with the south and east of the country. The preparation and waiting were finally over. The Nazis were to be challenged and fought to the bitter end.

A rash of major battles now broke out between hundreds of Maquis and the Wehrmacht. As in so many other parts of France, the news from Normandy hypnotised many with hope of early victory, inciting groups of *maquisards* around Lyons to declare their own liberation prematurely. Roads leading into villages were blocked by felled trees; proclamations were read announcing provisional governments; collaborators were executed; everywhere *maquisards* came out of the forests in a show of force.

On 8 June, in Dortan, a mile from the burnt-out shell of Sièges, a Maquis group proclaimed the Fourth Republic. For four weeks the villagers enjoyed their liberation and forgot about the occupation. The Germans, they felt, would be more concerned about fighting in Normandy. Their exhilaration ended when they heard the menacing sound of grinding truck engines and the news that 'thousands of Germans' were poised to attack. Most fled into the hills and woods. Effortlessly, German soldiers and contingents of Russian soldiers from the collaboration army led by General Andrei Vlassov recaptured Dortan, torturing, raping and murdering those who remained. All 178 houses in the town were burned down. As the refugees in nearby hamlets watched their homes burning, they were suddenly attacked by mortar fire, and by machine-gun strafes and bombs from the air. Across the fields, German troops were advancing in a vast chain. There was no escape. For four days the area was pillaged and the inhabitants terrified until the Germans withdrew without even bothering to conceal their activities. All that remained was the local château which was used by both the Wehrmacht and the Gestapo during the weeks as a convenient site for rape and torture.

Dortan's experiences were a carbon copy of similar incidents throughout the Ain: Maquis groups seizing control of towns, villages and hamlets, barricading roads, and waiting for the German attack. With predictably methodical ruthlessness, the German arrival meant the destruction of the liberated village. At least 200 civilians in the Ain were shot dead during the three weeks after the Normandy landings. Panic gripped the Wehrmacht, *milice* and the Gestapo. Without provocation or reason, Germans passing in convoys took fatal pot shots at farmers in their fields, shoppers in the streets or old people in their gardens.

There is little eyewitness evidence of Barbie's own activities during the June and July carnage. He was 'seen' in a few villages and there are accusations that he committed several murders. Ludwig Henson, the Gestapo chief at Chambéry who was answerable to Barbie, claimed at his trial in Lyons in February 1948 that ten executions in Arbin on 21 June 1944 were carried out on Barbie's explicit instructions. 'It was Barbie himself and his men who went to fetch the prisoners and took them to the place where they were executed.' Another Gestapo officer, Ernst Floreck, in a statement to the Lyons court, claimed that Barbie was present and responsible for at least thirteen mass executions between April and July, killing at least 212 people. Floreck, who was himself a self-confessed torturer, described Barbie as 'the biggest bastard of them all'.

There is no reason to believe that Barbie altered his methods of work in Lyons. At Montluc, which was his direct responsibility, the 'cleaning out' suddenly became a daily occurrence. But with railway lines to Germany routinely cut, deportation to concentration camps became rarer. Instead, groups of prisoners were regularly told to come out of their cells, 'without your belongings'. Loaded onto lorries, they were driven by the Gestapo from Lyons either to isolated fields in the country or to small villages throughout the Ain. With their handcuffs removed, they filed slowly towards hedgerows or copses and were ordered to stand forlornly in a line or lie on their stomachs. According to the very few Frenchmen who miraculously survived their wounds, little was said besides a muted farewell. The sub-machine-guns (often of British or American make and seized from the Resistance), were fired and the executioners returned to Lyons. Pressure of work, indifference about the possibilities of detection and the sheer habit of killing meant that the bodies were invariably left where they fell.

Some victims were allowed to write farewell letters to their family, but those written towards the end of the German occupation were never passed on; they were destroyed by the *milice* or Gestapo. Henri Mazuir's letter to his wife, written before his execution in December 1943, survived:

> My darling little girl, Give my love to your mother and to Roger. My last thought will be for you and for my parents. A few tears fall on my letter. They are the last. They are the last gift I can make to thank you for our 39 months of marriage. My poor darling, you are very young and the pain will be cruel. I ask you to think of me in your prayers. God has not abandoned me yet, and in a few moments I will be able to hear mass and take communion. I love you and embrace you with all my strength. Be happy and make a new life . . . Long Live France.

By the beginning of July, the Lyons Gestapo's ability to maintain the security of the region had dropped considerably. Although Gestapo bureaux throughout the area were still receiving reliable reports from collaborators and passing them on to the Wehrmacht, the swift battle against Maquis camps throughout the Ain plain had become essentially a military operation. Determined to restore German control over the vital Rhône-Saône corridor, at least nine thousand German soldiers were mobilised to fight the Maquis for the third major operation that year. The principal targets were the 'free zones' of the Ain and Vercors.

In the Ain, Nantua and Oyonnax were under total Maquis control; German control of other towns depended on the strength of the Wehrmacht contingent present at the time. The Wehrmacht objective was simply to kill as many Maquis as possible, and force the remainder to disperse. On 10 July the Wehrmacht, operating in fast-moving columns from several directions, reoccupied the Ain. Among those forced to move were Johnson and Petit whose head-quarters were in the very pleasant Château Wattern at Izernore, just north of Nantua. Their tranquillity was shattered by the sound of a bombardment. German panzer tanks were heading in their direction but had confused their intelligence and were aiming at a château on the other side of the valley. 'Petit ordered us to retreat towards the Jura,' remembers Johnson. 'There were three hundred creeps with us, including the *sous-préfet* of St Claude and his mistress, who was still wearing high-heeled shoes.' As they withdrew, the RAF indiscriminately dropped tons of arms most of which were seized, to Heslop's fury, by the Wehrmacht.

Two days later, seventy-two RAF planes dropped arms and ammunition over Vassieux, in the Vercors. Within a week the German army had been diverted to surround the plateau area which had been proclaimed a 'Free Republic' forty-three days earlier. Their attack began on 21 July. Within two days the French were crushed, claiming losses of 500 *maquisards* and 200 civilians killed, and 500 houses destroyed.

Significantly, the city of Lyons itself stood isolated from the seeping chaos and bloodshed in the countryside. The Groupe Franc, unlike the Maquis, lacked a hinterland into which it could disappear and the townspeople were unwilling to take risks. Under Barbie's direction, the Gestapo had effectively limited potential armed opposition in the birthplace of the Resistance. There were isolated attacks but they were definitely counterproductive. On the night of 26 July, a bomb was thrown into the *Moulin à Vent*, the popular restaurant on the Place Bellecour, frequented by Gestapo officers including Barbie. No one was seriously injured. At noon the following day, Erich Bartelmus arrived outside the damaged building with five prisoners from Montluc, including the Maquis leader, Albert 'Didier' Chambonnet. All five were shot and their bodies left where they lay as a deliberate warning to others contemplating any attack on the Gestapo. The executions stunned the Lyonnais, who were perhaps unaware that similar shootings were a daily occurrence in the countryside. Loyally, Bartelmus, who now lives in Trippstadt, West Germany, has consistently refused to reveal whether the order to attack was given to him by Hollert or Barbie, but by then reprisals had become so routine that it is possible he simply cannot remember. Fearful of the inevitable condemnation, no Resistance group has ever admitted responsibility for the attack.

'Operation Dragoon', the long-awaited American landing on the southern coast of France, was successfully completed on 15 August. With the Allied armies in the north on the verge of a final breakthrough towards Paris, the German occupation of the south was doomed. Only the 198th and 333rd German Infantry Divisions, and the XIth SS Panzer Division, stood between the American Seventh Army and Lyons. On paper the German army looked impressive, but it was seriously weakened by insufficient supplies and untrained soldiers, and its numbers depleted by movements to defend the north. Berlin gave the command for them to commence an orderly, fighting retreat. At Gestapo headquarters, Knab and Barbie gave the orders for a final 'cleansing' operation.

Heslop and Petit, realising that the speed of the American advance depended on a clear run through the Belfort Gap, mobilised the Maquis to harrass any German defensive position. Throughout the countryside, Maquis groups launched into the final battle with savage gusto. It is a mark of the Maquis's success in the Ain and Savoie, that the speed of the American advance and the rapid retreat of the Germans was far beyond the expectations of Allied planning staff at SHAEF headquarters.

Two days after the Allied landings, the 'clearing' operation at Montluc was accelerated. On 17 August, 109 prisoners, mostly Jews, were taken to Bron airport on the outskirts of Lyons, shot and buried in the bomb craters which pockmarked the field. Three days later, 110 men and women were driven from Montluc to the disused fort of St Genis-Laval. According to a sworn statement by Max Payot, a member of the *milice* who worked in Gestapo headquarters, 'Fritz Hollert, my boss, walked up to me and rubbing his hands gleefully said, "Today we've got some good work to do." At 7.00 a.m., thirty-five of us were in Place Bellecour. At first I thought it was going to be a major police operation, but I realised my mistake [and] understood it was going to be more executions.' When the convoy reached the Fort, the prisoners' hands were tied up, led in small groups to the first floor, and systematically shot. Payot sent the prisoners up the stairs. After some time, 'the prisoners had to walk over a heap of their former comrades. Blood was pouring through the ceiling and I could distinctly hear the victims fall as they were shot. At the end the bodies lay one and a half metres high, and the Germans sometimes had to step onto the bodies of their victims to finish off those who were still moaning.' The bodies, covered in petrol, were then burnt and the building dynamited.

While the fire was raging, we saw a victim who had somehow survived. She came to a window on the south side and begged her executioners for pity. They answered her prayers by a rapid burst of gunfire. Riddled with bullets and affected by the intense heat, her face contorted into a fixed mask, like a vision of horror. The temperature was increasing and her face melted like wax until one could see her bones. At that moment she gave a nervous shudder and began to turn her decomposing head – what was left of it – from left to right, as if to condemn her executioners. In a final shudder, she pulled herself completely straight, and fell backwards.

At Gestapo headquarters in Place Bellecour, prisoners were shot in their cells or at the top of the stairs leading down to the basement. The fate of the 800 prisoners still remaining at Montluc was seemingly sealed.

By 20 August, the German forces were falling back in the face of the advancing American army, fighting a stiff but organised retreat. In Lyons, the German military command under General Wiese was ordered to hold the city until the retreating XIth SS Panzer Division had passed through. It was a difficult mission which he fulfilled with ruthless efficiency, cool nerve and fanatical dedication. Confronted by an insurrectionary strike in Villeurbanne, he ordered Wehrmacht units to crush the uprising; they demolished blocks of apartments where suspected resistants were hiding, and indiscriminately shot anyone on the streets, frantically clinging to their fragile control. The city was gripped simultaneously by terror and hope. For the first time, the Gestapo were compelled to make compromises. In a signed letter to Knab, Yves Farge, a Resistance leader, threatened that Germans taken hostage by the Maquis would be executed as a reprisal should any remaining prisoners in Montluc be killed. Uncharacteristically, the Gestapo hesitated. While forty Jews were taken immediately, probably on Barbie's orders, to be executed, the other prisoners remained for the moment untouched.

On 24 August, Cardinal Gerlier, horrified by the St Genis-Laval massacre, went to Gestapo headquarters, to plead with the Germans to stop the killings. That evening, Knab was again personally threatened by a Resistance messenger that there would be reprisals if any of the 800 prisoners were shot. According to Wilhelm Wellnitz, the Gestapo's telex officer who left Lyons with Knab, the Gestapo chief was forced into concessions because many German

105

soldiers were being shot in the back. The Wehrmacht refused to continue to support the Gestapo's operations. At 9.50 that evening, the prisoners inside Montluc suddenly realised that the Germans had abandoned the prison. Outside in the streets, Resistance fighters who had come to help the inmates heard loud, rousing singing as the embattled and tearful survivors sang *La Marseillaise*.

It is believed that Klaus Barbie left Lyons for the first time on 22 August, and travelled north towards Dijon. Grenoble had been liberated that day and it seemed that German control of Lyons was on the verge of evaporating. The city was drifting towards anarchy. Over the next twelve days, the Wehrmacht, in spite of barricades and sniping, steadily patrolled the town, allowing retreating units to pass through unhindered. Vistel, realising the weakness of the Resistance, spent the last days of the occupation struggling to prevent rather than encourage an attack on the Germans. The Gestapo withdrew from the city undefeated, having methodically destroyed all their records. The absence of any documentary evidence successfully hampered French prosecution of former Gestapo officers.

According to a former American intelligence officer, Barbie confided to him after the war that he had returned to the city during that last week 'to clean up the mess'. Over twenty of his closest collaborators, Frenchmen who could reveal the truth about his crimes over the previous twenty-one months, were murdered. His girlfriend was also allegedly killed. Although he now claims that his right foot was injured during a Maquis attack while he was travelling to Dijon, he told the same American that his foot was injured during the final massacre. He left the city a wounded man. Lyons was finally liberated by the American army on 3 September.

On 14 September, Barbie was recommended for promotion to captain. In his report SS Sturmbannführer Wanninger wrote:

Barbie is known at headquarters as an SS leader who knows what he wants, and is enthusiastic. He has a definite talent for intelligence work and for the pursuit of crime. His most notable achievement was the destruction of many enemy organisations. Reichsführer SS Himmler has expressed his gratitude to Barbie in a personal letter commending his pursuit of crime and his consistent work in defeating Resistance organisations. Barbie is dependable in both his ideological approach and character. Since his training and during his employment in the SD, Barbie has led a regular career as a director of the 'senior service' and, providing that there is no objection, it is recommended that he be promoted as from 9 November 1944 from SS Obersturmführer to SS Hauptsturmführer.

THE FUGITIVE

Wounded and shaken by that last, grim week in Lyons, Barbie was taken first to the St Peter military hospital in the Black Forest and then transferred to Halberstadt. Unlike most other SS officers he was quite realistic about Germany's plight. Despite the shrilly optimistic news broadcasts pouring out of the Ministry of Propaganda in Berlin, his recent experiences convinced him that the war was lost. Yet, as for so many other passionate Nazis, it was impossible for him to imagine any alternative to defending the Reich. So, despite his injuries, he volunteered to fight on.

Posted to Halle in north Germany, Barbie found himself with a ragbag of recruits drawn from every service – sailors, engineers and reservists. After brief training, they were to be thrown into the fight at Baranow-Bruckenkopf in yet another bid to repulse the Allied advance. For Barbie, the elitist, it was a shock. These were not the sort of Germans with whom he was accustomed to fight. 'I took one look at them and thought to myself, "I'm prepared to die, but not with this lot."'

The Allies had finally broken through the Ardennes and were closing towards the banks of the Rhine. Ever anxious to protect his own interests, Barbie obtained a special pass and disappeared into the chaos which was engulfing the country. It was a depressing and bewildering sight for a passionate Nazi. The trains were disrupted, the roads clogged with frustrated military traffic, the towns and cities were already badly scarred by the bombs and the food supply was at a critical level. But there was still some reassurance. The remorseless machinery of the police state was still functioning, albeit not as smoothly, and people remained as obedient as ever. Anxious and isolated, Barbie's only thought was to make for Himmler's headquarters in Berlin. It was like going home for comfort. Near Brandenburg, however, he was stopped and ordered to join another hastily formed unit which would soon be recklessly moved up to the retreating front. Flashing his pass, he once again avoided the final commitment and arrived safely in the burning capital.

The city was dominated by a mood of helplessness, panic and unreality. Barbie went straight to 8 Prinz-Albrechtstrasse, the Gestapo headquarters. All that remained was the basement. Only the cells were occupied – filled with the last enemies of the Reich, most of whom would be executed before the final capitulation. Among them he saw Friedrich Fromm, one of the '20 July' conspirators, impatiently pacing up and down. He was executed soon after Barbie saw him.

Barbie proceeded to Hitler's bunker in the Wilhelmstrasse. There was little reassurance to be found there either. In the yards outside, senior Nazi officials completely divorced from any reality, were lecturing fourteen-year-old members of the Hitler Youth about their duty to the Fatherland, as if there was neither a war nor a defeat imminent. The extraordinarily theatrical scenes above ground accurately mirrored the fantasies of those below. There was a simple choice to be made: either join the charade, or leave. Characteristically unwilling to be sucked into anything that might jeopardise his own safety, Barbie's immediate thought was of self-preservation, but without unnecessary disobedience. 'I had to hold my mouth and just be very quiet. Very quiet. But what could I do? The only alternative was to be posted to my unit based in Hanover. I went to Werner Braune, who was head of personnel – unfortunately he was among the last to be executed at Landsberg in 1951.'

Braune delivered a long speech about why Barbie should stay and defend the Reich in Berlin. Here was another who spoke as if Germany was on the verge of victory. More than ever convinced that he had to leave, Barbie compromised and left for Düsseldorf.

At the beginning of April, in anticipation of the Allied victory, there had been a revolt among the tens of thousands of slave workers who had been forcibly brought from all the German-occupied countries to work in murderous conditions in the Rühr mines and factories. Barbie was a natural recruit to any unit commanded to quell an uprising. Like untamed animals, squads of SS officers moved mercilessly through the disease-ridden and in-fested camps shooting anyone who dared show anything other than total submission.

From Düsseldorf the unit moved to Krupp's capital city, Essen. On the other side of the Rhine, the British and American armies were poised to speed into the heartland of Germany. Slave workers were refusing to go down the coal mines. 'I had a great idea. We could throw them all down into the pits and drown them.' Whether serious or not, there was no time to implement the plan. The threat from the miners was insignificant compared to that from the Allied armies who had crossed the river and arrived in Essen. For the second time Barbie was in the front line, only now there was no retreat. The Allies crossed the Rhine bridge at Remagen on 7 March. Realising that he was a wanted man, Barbie withdrew from the fight. Like a trapped tiger, he travelled frantically through what remained of the unoccupied Rhineland, seeking the security of SS leadership but also for orders which made sense. He was an unwilling and unhappy witness to the collapse of an empire which he wanted to serve loyally even beyond its last gasp.

> My war ended in Wuppertal. We turned a garage into a stronghold. Nearby were two trucks loaded with civilian clothes for the Werwolfs [the abortive German resistance movement]. But no one had made any plans to continue the fight underground, probably because no one thought that we would lose the war. So I buried my gun. The four youngsters I was with and myself changed our clothes, got some false papers from the police headquarters, and headed off through the forests and pastures towards the Sauerland. It was very hard. From one day to the next, I'd become a beggar.

For a short time, they rode on stolen bicycles, facetiously smiling at passing American soldiers. It was, however, a short-lived honeymoon. As the unconditional surrender silenced Germany's military juggernaut, the security net was already tightening. To prevent a resistance movement, the Allied armies were searching and randomly interning most German men of military age. Abandoning the road, Barbie travelled by night and hid in forests during the day. His luck ran out near Hohenlimburg when he fell into an American roadblock.

Locked up in a school Barbie was questioned by a former concentration-camp inmate, acting as a jailor. For three years Barbie's professional skill had been directed at destroying the carefully constructed cover stories of his victims: now it was essen-

110

tial to his own survival that he cover up his past. His first interrogator presented no challenge. With little difficulty he convinced him that he was just an ordinary soldier who was trying to get to Kassel. No further checks were made. According to one American's memory, he was sentenced to fourteen days' imprisonment and then released, but Barbie says that after only a short time he convinced another of his jailors that they were all ordinary, innocent soldiers, and that he should let them escape. Allegedly he agreed. Nearby was a church: 'He told us, "Go in one door and go out the other." We did that and then separated. That's when I began my secret life in the underground.'

Barbie's name at that time appeared on two Allied lists of wanted war criminals – one published in London by the United Nations War Crimes Commission, the other published in Paris by CROWCASS, the Central Registry of Wanted War Criminals and Security Suspects. Both stated that he was a Gestapo officer wanted for murder and torture in Lyons. The failure to identify and arrest such men was not unusual in those immediate post-war months. Despite many public declarations during the previous years by Prime Minister Churchill and President Roosevelt that one of the major purposes of the war was to hunt down and prosecute war criminals like Barbie, virtually nothing had been done to create the machinery to implement those solemn promises.

Even before war was declared on 3 September 1939, the British government, and the Foreign Office in particular, had been most reluctant to become at all involved in showing concern at German brutalities. As long as British nationals were not involved, the civil servants in Whitehall believed, there was no British interest at stake. If anything, the actual declaration of war hardened that attitude. Now there was a war to be fought, and the priority was to defend Britain and defeat Germany; there could be little concern about atrocities against non-Britons.

The first demand for the British government to commit itself publicly to punishing the Germans responsible for atrocities was delivered by the Polish government-in-exile. The Nazi attack on Poland is the historical pretext for Britain's declaration of war and German atrocities against the Poles had, from the outset, been widespread. To the surprise of the Poles, the British were reluctant to take any stand and when pushed would only agree to a short unpublicised protest. Frank Roberts, the Foreign Office official who was to become so closely identified with his Ministry's 'detached attitude', told the Polish representatives that the British government utterly refused to commit themselves to any sort of policy to punish the Germans responsible. It was a position he and his colleagues defended inflexibly for the next two years. Reassuringly for them, their grim determination not to get involved in the war-crimes business had the full blessing of their minister, Sir Anthony Eden.

Eden openly sympathised with his officials' impassive reaction to the reports from Europe, especially reports involving the Jews. Eden supported the Arabs in his Middle-Eastern diplomacy and was, according to his private secretary, Oliver Harvey, 'hopelessly prejudiced' against the Jews. He read with sympathy a comment written by another of his officials, Roger Makins, in 1940, that any commitment to 'hunt down and try thousands of Germans after the war' would be 'virtually impossible to carry out'. The government, he suggested should 'studiously refrain from saying what we propose to do with them in the unlikely event of our catching any after the war.' Eden endorsed that view. Foreign Office policy was clear and agreed: Britain was not to be committed to hunting down and punishing war criminals after Germany's defeat. It was most important, the Office felt, to avoid in any way possible the drawing up of lists of wanted men with the intention of presenting them to the Germans at the end of the war; this had happened in 1918 and had resulted in a humiliating charade because the Allies had been unable to force the Germans to deliver.

To Eden's considerable irritation, Churchill and the cabinet disagreed. Reliable reports had arrived in London of the cold-blooded massacre of hundreds of innocent Frenchmen by German soldiers and Ministers wanted to respond in any way they could. At a Cabinet meeting on 5 October 1942, the Foreign Office was instructed to produce a public statement which would promise retribution for war crimes. Makins immediately began searching for ways to avoid fulfilling what the politicians demanded. He began toying with words to produce a vague and deceptive phrase which would be unenforceable in the future. At the same time he suggested that the BBC be warned not to repeat a broadcast to Europe

112

which mentioned that lists were being drawn up of 'persons guilty of infamous conduct'.

His machinations were sabotaged on 25 October. Genuinely affected by increasing reports of German massacres in France, President Roosevelt spontaneously issued a public protest and promised 'fearful retribution for those responsible'. In one stroke the White House had committed itself to prosecuting German war criminals. Securing that statement was the result of the sort of intense lobbying and pressure which is the natural part of American government – but it had taken nearly ten years to produce the desired result.

Attacks by the Nazis against their German opponents had intensified immediately after Hitler's government was sworn into office on 30 January 1933. Jews, communists, socialists and trade unionists were randomly beaten and murdered. The American newspaper reports were coldly played down by the new Secretary of State, Cordell Hull, and for the next ten years he and his department consistently discounted reports of German atrocities as either exaggerated or unreliable, only giving way when the pressure finally became irresistible. Departmental policy was similar to London's: in public, to remain uninvolved in the domestic affairs of another country; in private, the Secretary could raise the issue in a gentle fashion with the German ambassador. Commitments had to be kept to an absolute minimum and for some time President Roosevelt did little to outface his officials.

The outbreak of war increased the pressure on the Administration to help not only those persecuted in Germany but victims in many other countries which came under German control. Roosevelt made several speeches critical of German aggression, but his reaction on 25 October 1942 to the shooting of innocent French hostages was his first public protest against German atrocities. His commitment to bringing the Gestapo officers responsible to justice was a wry irony considering Barbie's later employment by the Americans.

Churchill had only had a few hours' notice of the President's speech. Clearly it would be embarrassing if he remained silent while the leader of an ostensibly neutral country made a public commitment. In a hastily written speech, Churchill also condemned the 'Nazi butcheries in France' and ended by saying that, 'Retribution for these crimes must henceforth take its place among the major purposes of the war.'

These statements in Washington and London should have been the last nail in the coffin of bureaucratic indifference to the fate of war criminals. The contrary seems to have been the case. Officials and their political masters in both the Foreign Office and the State Department now sought to minimise the damage caused by their leaders' 'reckless' promises. Their first problem was to deal with demands from the governments-in-exile based in London, who were dissatisfied with a draft protest prepared by the Foreign Office. According to the French representative, Maurice Dejean, they wanted something 'more arresting' and committed. Dejean submitted a new draft whose final paragraphs horrified the British and American officials. A 'principal war aim', it said, was 'the punishment, through the channel of organised justice, of those guilty of or responsible for these crimes, whether they have ordered them, perpetrated them or participated in them'. It ended by promising that the guilty would be brought to justice.

Unwilling to commit themselves, the British and American governments attended the solemn declaration ceremony in London's St James's Palace on 13 January 1942 – just as observers. In his welcoming speech, Eden even told Britain's allies that his government did not support their policy. Its implementation, he told the assembled politicians, was the responsibility of their own governments, not of the British government. Each country was to be responsible for prosecuting the crimes committed against its own nationals. The Americans silently concurred and hoped that this might be the end of the subject for some time. It was a vitally important disclaimer which the two foreign ministries clung to until the end of the war.

Again the politicians ruffled the diplomatic waters. At their July meeting in Washington, Churchill and Roosevelt agreed that the Allies should set up a United Nations Commission on Atrocities which would investigate and collect the evidence of German war crimes. According to Churchill, by naming publicly those responsible for atrocities, the Commission would 'let them know that they are being watched by the civilised world, which will mete out swift and just punishment on the judgement day'. The leaders were anxious to respond to public pressure. Here finally was an unambiguous promise to hunt down war criminals. Their officials were less than enthusiastic.

At the State Department, the immediate reaction was to ignore the proposals. Eden's reaction was nearly as cool: 'There may be little harm in the idea. What do we do next?' Its only virtue seemed to be that it would at least head off their allies' demands for action and Britain could resist pressure to endorse the St James's Palace Declaration. But once again the policy-makers' obstructions were sabotaged by their leaders. On 21 August, President Roosevelt again publicly warned those responsible for 'barbarous crimes . . . [which] may even lead to the extermination of certain populations . . . that the time will come when they shall have to stand in the courts of law in the very countries which they are now oppressing and answer for their acts'. The President's declaration depressed State Department officials. With the latest news from Europe, this was precisely the result they had feared.

On 1 August 1942, Gerhard Riegner, the representative in Switzerland of the World Jewish Congress, heard from a German source that the German government had decided to exterminate all the Jews of Europe. Numerous reports of mass executions had already emerged from eastern Europe, but this was something different – the Germans wanted to establish production-line facilities for murder, using prussic acid. Convinced that the report was true, Riegner cabled the news to Rabbi Stephen Wise, head of the American Jewish Congress. The cable was sent through American diplomatic channels so that the first recipients were State Department officials in Washington. Their reaction was cynical disbelief and an immediate decision not to pass the telegram on to Wise. 'Jewish affairs' throughout the war were handled by Robert Reams, who made no secret that he did not trust the Jews and their 'atrocity stories' and for a time successfully prevented their publication in Washington. On this occasion his department's suppression was short-lived. Riegner had also sent the telegram to a British Labour member of parliament, Sydney Silverman. Silverman alerted Wise on 28 August and the State Department was forced to release Riegner's message, but only after securing Wise's reluctant agreement that there should be no publicity until further checks had been made. In the meantime Jewish representatives lobbied every relevant politician in Washington to save the European Jews, but their efforts were fruitless. After the waves of bureaucratic irritation had passed away, Riegner's message became, for a short while, just another story to be treated with scepticism and caution.

In London, the Foreign Office could not be so boldly resistant as their colleagues three thousand miles away. Pressurised by the Prime Minister, the Cabinet and the Allied governments, it had little alternative but to set up the UN Commission. Washington, however, showed little interest. Despite urgent telegrams from its London ambassador, John Winant, the State Department finally confessed that it had mislaid his original letter containing the proposals. During the undignified last-minute rush to meet Eden's formal announcement, on 7 October, that a United Nations War Crimes Commission (UNWCC) would be established in London, the two governments could not even agree on the scope of its work. Both, however, were agreed that it would not include the actual investigation of war crimes.

The consequences of those limitations were quickly recognised by Lord Simon, a pre-war supporter of Chamberlain's appeasement policy. Speaking as the newly appointed co-ordinator of the British government's war-crimes policy, Simon told the House of Lords that declarations alone were worthless. Investigative machinery was needed to track down the wanted men, with policemen and detectives recruited to set up an FBI or Scotland Yard style of organisation. But Simon was a discredited politician and his warning was ignored.

The officials who ignored Simon's warning were the same who were unwilling to accept the accounts of German atrocities. By autumn 1942, all the death camps were already operational. Nearly one million Jews had been slaughtered. Tens of thousands of Europeans had been forced into labour camps. Klaus Barbie, having left Holland, was about to begin operations in France. All the evidence of Hitler's genocide policies was available from scores of eyewitnesses in western and eastern Europe, and from radio intercepts and intelligence reports. Yet in the Foreign Office, Roberts wanted the subject left in a 'dim light' and another official, Geoffrey Robertson, commented on the Riegner telegram, 'I am still somewhat sceptical about this story.' His ministry advised the BBC that it was 'soft-pedalling the whole thing as much as possible'.

The administration in Washington had become dramatically

split. At the State Department, many continued to treat the whole murder programme as a 'wild story'. Others, appointed directly by the White House, were convinced by the reports. The divisions were sufficient to provoke considerable arguments when, in December 1942, Eden bowed to overwhelming pressure and sent a Foreign Office draft of a proposed new declaration. The reports of the 'Holocaust' were finally accepted unconditionally. Information from Europe, it stated, '. . . leaves no room for doubt that the German authorities . . . are now carrying into effect Hitler's oft-repeated intention to exterminate the Jewish people . . .'

Robert Reams was aghast. They were, he believed, simply pandering to Jewish scare stories which should be suppressed. To accept the reports would mean that the governments would have to do something to satisfy demands for post-war justice. But he could not prevent publication. Early in October 1943, reports arrived in London of the massacre of a hundred Italian officers by German forces on the Greek island of Kos. Churchill was particularly affected. The Foreign Ministers of America, Britain and Russia were due to meet in Moscow and Churchill proposed that the three governments sign an agreement that after the war those responsible for war crimes, 'will be sent back to the countries in which their abominable deeds were done in order that they may be judged and punished according to the laws of those liberated countries . . . most assuredly the three Allied powers will pursue them to the uttermost ends of the earth and deliver them to the accusers in order that justice may be done.' Despite objections from Eden, Churchill's draft was signed by the three Foreign Ministers. The Moscow Declaration became the cornerstone of post-war war-crimes policies and should have ensured that Klaus Barbie, for one, was returned to France after the war.

Declarations alone could no longer stop German atrocities, but there was still time to build the machinery to find the perpetrators – had it not been that the same officials who had been unwilling to accept the atrocity reports were responsible for establishing the War Crimes Commission. The announcement of the Commission's establishment in October 1942 had been followed by dilatory negotiations between the governments. Its first meeting, twelve months after the announcement on 19 October 1943, was a portentous preview of the future. The Russian government had officially

117

refused to join and the American representative, Herbert Pell, had still not been allowed by the State Department to leave the United States. When the Commission's chairman, Sir Cecil Hurst, asked Dennis Allen at the Foreign Office for the list of war crimes already accumulated by his department, Allen bluntly rebuffed him. Hurst, he wrote, seemed to have 'some rather odd ideas'. The Foreign Office, it appeared, did not trust the Commission. Allen omitted to tell Hurst that the British government had not yet initiated a scheme even to collate the flimsy evidence of war crimes it had collected.

When Pell finally arrived, the antagonisms which were already developing between the Commission and the British government increased. The State Department was even less interested in helping than the British government and was equally unwilling to hand over any cases for the Commission to investigate. Pell had only been appointed after many others had rejected the Department's invitation. His name was suggested by the President in return for his political support of the White House in previous years; foreign service officers were appalled that such an excitable extrovert should be their ambassador. The harder Pell tried to create the machinery for hunting down war criminals in London, the more reluctant the State Department officials became. With relief, the Department handed over responsibility for war-crimes investigation to the War Department whose Secretary, Henry Stimson, in accepting the new charge, added that because of a 'shortage of personnel' he would be unable to help the Commission. Frustrated at every turn, Pell and Hurst became involved for the next twelve months in a persistent series of arguments with their respective governments about their powers and responsibilities, and the need to create investigative agencies.

Relations were worsening when, on 26 August 1944, General de Gaulle entered newly-liberated Paris and marched down the Champs Elysées. The same newspaper reports in London and Washington which suggested that the end of the war was in sight, also carried reports about brutalities in France during the German occupation. Public interest in plans to bring the Germans responsible to justice was immediately aroused. As the organisation especially established for that task, the Commission was inundated with demands for information. Hurst was embarrassed but was determined to hold his first press conference, despite enormous pressure from the British and American governments to remain silent. An unusually large number of journalists crowded into the Commission's offices.

Asked how many names were on the Commission's list, Hurst replied, 'The list of war criminals is not a very long one. It is meagre.' In the uproar which followed, Hurst stoutly refused to divulge the number. It was in fact just 184 names, fourteen of whom were held responsible for toppling a statue off a pedestal – an unlikely war crime. The following day, the Commission's failure made headline news on both sides of the Atlantic. A few weeks later Pell was recalled, complaining in public that Department officials 'do not want to punish Nazi criminals as thoroughly as they advocate'; Hurst retired on 'grounds of ill-health', while Foreign Office officials concluded, much to their disappointment, that the attractions of closing the Commission down were outweighed by the anger that would be generated in the United States if they did. As the Allies swept through France and were poised to invade Germany, nothing had been done to implement the pledges made by Churchill and Roosevelt. Klaus Barbie and tens of thousands of other war criminals had at that time still very little to fear.

Reviewing the position in his Pentagon office in September 1944, John McCloy, the Assistant Secretary of War, blamed the British for the crisis. Energetic, highly competent, and politically astute, McCloy realised that the British had produced only a pile of official papers, no results and considerable political embarrassment. It was by now obvious, he felt, that only the American and British armies in Europe would have the resources to investigate the crimes. Hundreds of thousands of Germans had already been captured; the US First Army had crossed into Germany and was pressing towards Aachen; but in the absence of an unequivocal directive from their own commanders, the military machine had refused to take on any responsibility for war crimes. SHAEF headquarters, directing the invasion of Europe, had already insisted that it would only investigate war crimes which had been committed against troops under its command since 6 June; the Combined Chiefs of Staff were still considering directives to their armies and would do so until long after the end of the war; the army commanders, faced with the immediate battle, had not even considered the issue. At the War

119

Office in London, senior officials led by the permanent secretary, Sir Frederick Bovenschen, were deliberately creating as many obstacles as possible to prevent the British army taking on any war-crimes responsibilities. He was successful until the end of the war when the British army in Germany found itself with just twelve men ('three scratch teams') to comb through the whole of the British zone.

Taking the initiative to prevent just that happening in the American Zone, McCloy phoned Brigadier-General Weir, the US Army's Deputy Judge Advocate-General, and asked whether he had any ideas about building a war-crimes agency. Delighted by the call, Weir arrived within minutes in McCloy's office with a proposal he had been drafting for some weeks. It involved cutting across no fewer than twenty-five different departments, and giving their powers to the JAG. Despite opposition from the General Staff, McCloy announced two days later that the JAG would be the sole war-crimes agency. Weir was ordered to start immediately. He submitted a plan to expand his staff from four to one hundred and twenty-five but was only allocated twenty-nine, a totally inadequate number for Weir's requirements. His plan, on FBI advice, involved creating a huge police operation equipped with a gigantic punch-card system, special maps and intelligence archives. It was exactly the right idea, but incredibly he envisaged that the whole operation could be based in Washington. A year later, a sadder and wiser man, he confessed that his idea would have only been realisable with a staff of 2,500. But by then most of his staff had been diverted to work for the prosecution of the major war criminals at Nuremberg. Not one of his staff had been available in January 1945 to investigate the most outrageous German war crime against American troops, the slaughter by the 1st SS Panzer group of 102 prisoners of war at Malmédy in the Ardennes forest. The lawyers in Washington were thrilled by the prospect of putting Hitler and his aides on trial on unprecedented charges, such as crimes against humanity and waging aggressive war. The smaller crimes, they felt, could be left to the army in Europe.

In the SHAEF Handbook, issued to all officers, the arrest of war criminals was listed as the fifth most important objective in the occupation of Germany. General Eisenhower had received an order from the Department of the Army at the end of 1944 to set up a war-crimes office; his directive, issued on 24 February, explicitly ordered the newly-established teams to investigate only 'alleged war crimes against members of the armed forces of the United States'. That directive excluded all crimes in concentration camps and the crimes committed against the French and the nationals of other occupied countries. Knowing that very few crimes had been committed against American personnel, the army commands automatically put Eisenhower's directive as a very low priority.

Colonel Clio E. Straight was appointed to head the US Army's JAG war-crimes section in Europe. Born in Iowa, he readily admits that he knew nothing when he was appointed to the post, either about Europe or about the crimes committed by the Germans. Moreover, he was unable to leave his temporary headquarters in Paris until July 1945; he was repeatedly told that there was no transport available to Germany. By that time, seventeen teams were operating independently in the US Zone but because of untrained personnel, lack of transport and money and, above all, a low-priority rating, their work was unimpressive. When Straight finally arrived in Wiesbaden and set up his office, he was overwhelmed by the chaos. Other army units refused to give him even perfunctory co-operation, he could not get facilities that he desperately needed, and the investigating teams were working far away in splendid isolation. There was, he wrote some years later, 'almost a complete lack of appreciation of the impending problem . . . it was still not appreciated that war crimes had been committed on an extremely vast scale . . . It does not appear that steps were taken by the Commands to implement even the directives to arrest war criminals. Responsibility for apprehension and detention was just assigned indiscriminately.'

The investigators, Straight discovered, were frustrated because arrests could only be carried out by CIC (Counter Intelligence Corps) agents, and the CIC did not feel it was their job. 'Sending the [war crimes] directive to soldiers in fighting units, who had a war to fight and then an uneasy peace to maintain, just couldn't produce any results,' he ruefully remembers. Trying to save something of the operation, Straight ordered the investigators to ignore all cases not involving American personnel or concentration-camp victims. 'It was not possible to try all those crimes, there was no useful purpose,' he recalls. Quite simply, Straight's decision meant that

Barbie's crimes were not subject to American investigation. But Straight cannot be blamed. He was the mere victim of the failure of officials in London and Washington to implement the politicians' pledges.

In theory, it should have been relatively easy both to arrest and to identify Barbie. To prevent any resistance movement developing, and for general security reasons, SHAEF directives specified the arrest of anyone who had served in the army or the police or had been an officer in the Nazi Party. Despite the unprecedented chaos into which Germany was plunged, millions of Germans had been arrested and were interned throughout the country – among them, for a time, Barbie himself. Although the War Crimes Commission had finally published a list of wanted war criminals, the most effective list should have been the one published in Paris by CROWCASS, the Central Registry of War Criminals and Security Suspects.

According to the proposals put to Eisenhower in November 1944, CROWCASS would regularly publish three lists: one of the wanted men, another of those detained for specific crimes, and a third listing all German war criminals detained and the camps where they could be found. The method of finding the wanted criminal was theoretically quite attractive. The internment camp would return to Paris a completed form with the name, photograph and fingerprints of each imprisoned German. The information would be punched onto a card and fed into a Hollerith IBM card-index machine, which would then compare the information available on similar cards with the names of the wanted men. It would then be relatively easy to go to the camp and arrest the wanted man. Barbie's name appeared in one of the earliest lists, yet CROWCASS never placed him in any danger. Every aspect of the system failed.

By July 1945, eight million Germans were interned. Punching their names onto cards was overly ambitious. Not even the German High Command ever had the advantage of a complete list. The majority of internment camps either did not receive the lists, or did not fill them in, or failed to return them to Paris. Those that did arrive were invariably either outdated because the internees had been moved to another camp, or worthless because the criminals were registered under false names. In the Paris headquarters there was chaos. The Hollerith machines which had been shipped from

America invariably failed to work, the premises were too small, and the staff were at loggerheads with each other. When Patrick Dean at the Foreign Office saw CROWCASS's first list, he wrote, 'misleading and unreliable'. Barbie was arrested at least twice before being employed by the Americans, yet remained unidentified.

Barbie was first listed on a war-crimes list in the first UNWCC published list in December 1944. Listed no. 48 in the German section, he was named as 'Barbier, alias Kreitz', a Gestapo official in both Lyons and Dijon. Three years later, the CROWCASS list listed him as 'Barbie, Barbier, Barby, von Barbier, or Klein, or Kreitz or Mayer,' wanted for murder. His file number was 57.

After his escape from the school, Barbie was finally reunited with his family, who were still living with his mother-in-law in Trier. Despite the relative comforts, he quickly felt both exposed and frustrated. It needed little imagination to realise that Allied soldiers hunting for former Gestapo officers would start their search at his family home.

After fond farewells, and with the help of friends, he found lodgings in Marburg, a small university town forty miles north of Frankfurt. Robert Schmidt, the owner of 35 Barfusserstrasse, was a committed Nazi who had joined both the Party and the Brownshirts in 1930. He unquestioningly accepted Barbie's pretext that he was hoping to enroll as a student in the local university. His house became the fugitive's principal home until August 1946. A fellow lodger was Hans Becker, an alias which Barbie quickly assumed so that, in the event of a raid, he would have an effective cover story. By either skilful design or pure coincidence, Barbie also lived occasionally at the home of a Fridolin Becker in Kassel. It was from that house, on 18 April 1946, posing as a CID officer called Becker, that he and two others entered a local home pretending that they were looking for a wanted man, believed to be hiding in one of the rooms. Once inside, they stole 100,000 marks-worth of jewellery. In 1950, his two accomplices were arrested and convicted of the theft. The police were unable to arrest Barbie, who by then was working for the Americans; but quite mysteriously, soon after the trial, the jewellery was delivered at police headquarters. The German prosecutors remain convinced to this day that the anonymous delivery was made by an American CIC officer.

Barbie's life in Marburg was comparatively comfortable. Irrepressible and indefatigable, Barbie – the manipulator, the deceiver, the unrepentant Nazi police officer, but above all the unscrupulous survivor – instinctively began the transition from gamekeeper to poacher. At first he resorted to the very same activities which he had suppressed with such violence in Lyons: he became a forger, a black-marketeer, an underground conspirator, and ultimately proffered himself as a willing collaborator. His accomplices were the *Kamaradenschaft*, the masonic fraternity of former SS officers who enjoyed a unique bond of loyalty.

Barbie's first contacts were made around Christmas 1945. According to a Swiss-born CIC agent who penetrated the group, Barbie's associates were similar fugitive SS men who saw themselves as the nucleus of a new Nazi movement, the spearhead of a Fourth Reich. Rather in the manner of *Freikorps*, the right-wing military groups which had sprung up after Germany's 1918 defeat to challenge the new socialist government, and which became the embryo of Hitler's stormtroopers, Barbie and his associates began constructing a German resistance movement. Amongst Barbie's first contacts with the group was Frau Erika Loos, a former SS office staffer, whom Barbie had last seen during the final days of the war in Essen. They met at least three times in Marburg during February 1946. Other members were more high-ranking, including a former SS Major General and senior officials from the former Ministry of Propaganda. The group, at least sixty strong, efficiently divided itself into three parts: policy, propaganda and procurement. Barbie was head of the third section, responsible firstly for setting up an intelligence network throughout the American and British zones, and secondly for organising the production of forged forms, mostly Wehrmacht discharge papers which former SS officers needed to disguise their wartime military service. Later he was to deal in authentic Allied forms stolen from Munich. The forgeries provided the funds for their more serious task, resistance to the Allies.

As their numbers grew, however, the group leaders reluctantly accepted that the combination of oppressive Allied control and the disinterest of the exhausted German population had extinguished any possibility of active resistance. Ever the opportunists, they began discussing a reversal of tactics: if their network could not fight the Allies, why not join them in the fight against Communism. The group leaders decided to approach senior Allied officials and offer their services. Taking part in those discussions was the CIC agent infiltrator. In May 1946, he 'discreetly disclosed' an acquaintance-ship with a high-ranking British Foreign Office official who was a secret Nazi sympathiser. A meeting was arranged and the British official seemed to be suitably impressed. What he needed before he could transmit the proposal to Washington and London, he con-fided to the SS emissaries, was a more complete picture: names of their members and details of what they could offer. The British agent was not disappointed. The result was predictable.

At the end of August 1946, Barbie was walking near Marburg University with Otto Wolfgang, alias Wenzel, an old SS friend. Wolfgang saw a German woman, riding as a passenger in an American army jeep, point Barbie out to the American driver, Dick Lavoie. Barbie hesitated; he was sure that he was totally unknown in the town. But within minutes the jeep had drawn up next to him. In the front passenger seat was Erika Loos, his early contact with the underground group. He was ordered into the jeep:

> I knew they were taking me to prison. Marburg has very narrow streets and when we reached the post office, we had to slow down to let a tram pass. I then thought, 'It's now or never.' I'd taken a parachute course [in 1941] because for a time I was meant to be sent to Baku [in Russia]. As the jeep slowed down, I jumped out. There was a gasp from the pedestrians, the American looked round, and in his excitement crashed into a tree.

Barbie ran down an alley, Lavoie shooting at him as he jumped over a wall. A bullet nipped Barbie's finger:

> I knocked on a door and asked the woman to hide me. She took me upstairs to a bedroom. In the bed lay an old woman. I hid underneath. I heard the Americans when they came and asked if I had passed. She told them that she had seen me, but that I had gone on, jumping over the hedge. When they'd gone, she hid me in the pigeon coop. I stayed there until nightfall, hearing the Americans looking for me. Then I got away.

A few days later, Dale Garvey at CIC headquarters in Frankfurt issued an urgent message to all CIC offices in the American zone that Klaus Barbie, former Gestapo officer and wanted as a war criminal, had been sighted. All units were asked to be on the alert and arrest him on sight. The next time Barbie met Lavoie it was under different circumstances: 'I met that American again, some time later. He interrogated me. He'd become very fat and I didn't recognise him. He told me that Frau Loos had broken her thigh [in the crash].'

Barbie's greatest fear now was rearrest and identification. A priority was to remove the blood tattoo mark under his arm – a tattoo which every SS man was given so that, if he ever needed a blood transfusion, he would receive the correct Aryan blood type. Karl Schaefer, an SS friend, suggested that they go to a sympathetic doctor in Hamburg whose work and discretion could be trusted. In early November, with two other SS men, Barbie headed north, to Dr Heinz Gloede at 22 Wangelstrasse. To his surprise, Gloede's home was still openly filled with Nazi emblems, making no attempt to hide his allegiances. 'I was suspicious, but I thought my worries were exaggerated. We stayed two days with him and I did my first black-market deal – selling my father's gold watch.'

According to Barbie in 1979, the operation was successfully completed. But in December 1947 Barbie gave a very different, and probably prejudiced, version of his Hamburg visit to the Americans. He explained that he went just to keep Schaefer company while his friend tried to obtain new identification papers. Barbie claimed that Gloede had acted as a provocateur, working for British Intelligence, persistently speaking about his armoury of revolvers, his secret transmitters and sizable funds, all of which were available for the fight against the Allies. British Intelligence, Barbie claims, wanted to recruit him as an informer. But alternatively, the British approach might have been an attempt to penetrate his network. Ignoring Gloede's questions about his own activities, Barbie denied any links with underground organisations and refused to write a list of his contacts. Their conversation was followed by a brief, uncomfortable meal with a friend of Gloede's who behaved suspiciously, and whom Barbie also suspected of being a British agent. After Barbie again refused to co-operate, the three SS men went by tram to the main station to catch a train for Hanover.

Intuitively, Barbie sensed that they had been watched in the restaurant and were being shadowed by a green sedan during their tram journey. Just before the train left, he was suddenly grabbed from behind and within seconds was spreadeagled on the platform.

A green-bereted British soldier sat on top of him, pulling Barbie's scarf tightly around his throat. Barbie alleges that he was then taken into an office and, without a word being said, systematically beaten up. Humiliated and unaccustomed to being the victim of such treatment, he became thereafter passionately anti-British.

Stripped of their possessions, the three were locked in two cells (Barbie by himself) in the hastily converted coal cellars of an old house. Unquestioned, they remained in their cells until the third day, when a British officer bringing food revealed that they would not be allowed any exercise because he was alone on guard duty. Thirty minutes later they heard flute music from above. Using a piece of waste iron found in a cell, they broke the cell locks. Barbie was the first to creep up the stairs. To his surprise, the solitary British soldier was totally engrossed in his flute-playing. Grabbing hold of a shovel, Barbie prepared to hit him over the head but was dissuaded by the others. Quietly, they filed behind the musician's back, climbed over a wall and fled. Unshaven, with poor clothes and without any identification papers, Barbie sought out an ex-SS comrade for help. Finding his way through the bombed streets of Hamburg to the Rotenbaumchaussee, he knocked on the door to receive a warm welcome and the help he needed from the mother of his friend.

His escape and refuge were only temporary. The British had seized his personal notebook in which he had recorded compromising details of his underground activities, and the names of his contacts – an immature bungle for any would-be member of the Resistance, and one which the former Gestapo chief himself had so mockingly exploited in Lyons. Twice betrayed, Barbie's own careless arrogance had now betrayed others. Increasingly, he and the group came under intense surveillance by Allied Intelligence, with British Intelligence even discovering that Barbie had threatened to 'eliminate' at least three people whom he suspected of treachery.

From Hamburg, Barbie and his two SS colleagues set out on foot back to Marburg, only to be rearrested by an armed watchman. Their anxiety at having no papers vanished when the watchman revealed himself to be also a former member of the SS. The *Kamaradenschaft* had intervened once more. Within three weeks they had obtained new false papers through a contact of Barbie's and, just before Christmas, he was reunited with his wife. By then, the CIC in Marburg had itself identified 'Becker' as an active conspirator and had asked CIC headquarters in Frankfurt for available information on Barbie. In reply, on 2 January 1947, CIC Marburg received a copy of the 1945 SHAEF 'central personalities index card' describing Barbie as the head of section IV, Sicherheitsdienst Kommando Lyon – the Gestapo chief of Lyons and a 'dangerous conspirator'. Physically he was described as having a 'relatively large head . . . grey cold eyes' and a toe missing.

By early January, British and American Intelligence had exhausted the time-consuming possibilities of both surveillance and penetration. In their view (which was more a reflection of the inadequacies of Allied Intelligence than of reality), this was the 'last large organised group of Nazis to be formed in the Western zones of Germany' and only intensive interrogation of the SS men would satisfactorily expose the full structure of the group.

'Operation Selection Board', the arrest of fifty-seven targeted Nazis in many towns and villages throughout the American zone, was set for 2.00 a.m. on 23 February 1947. Listed as target number three was Barbie, 'a dominant figure', believed to be living at the Schmidt's house in Marburg using the aliases Becker, Speer and Heinz Mertens. His centres of operation were described as Marburg, Hamburg and Munich. But in the run-up to D-day, the Marburg CIC was clearly confused about how to handle their most important target. To protect a CIC source (presumably Frau Schmidt), the CIC agents were ordered not to raid Schmidt's house. Preliminary surveillance had already shown that he was not there. In fact, on the cold and rainy night of the raids, he was fifty miles away in Kassel, staying with Fridolin Becker, another target. When CIC agents raided that house, Barbie escaped by hiding in the bathroom. More than seventy Nazi sympathisers were nevertheless arrested in the American zone, which the CIC considered a satisfactory outcome.

By then Barbie was hesitantly entering that twilight world between conspiracy and collaboration. Inevitably, it was not an easy transition. Suspicious of his German contacts, he was unwittingly also entangled in an extraordinarily chaotic web of inconsistent and contradictory policies and orders issued by various regions and agents of the CIC itself.

In the weeks before 'Operation Selection Board', Barbie had

been shuttling between Marburg, Kassel and Munich, exploring the authenticity of an alluring offer to join a new intelligence-gathering team set up by two very senior ex-SS officers, SS Brigadier-General Franz Alfred Six and SS Colonel Emil Augsburg. Both had been directly involved in murdering thousands of Jews in eastern Europe. Six had been head of section VII in Himmler's head office, the RSHA, and had served with extermination squads in Russia; while Augsburg, working ostensibly as an academic studying eastern Europe at the Wannsee Institute, was in reality attached to Adolf Eichmann's S-4 department handling the Jewish question. Both were in hiding but claimed to have been approached by American intelligence agents with an offer to collect material about the Soviet Union. Barbie was invited to join the team.

Impressed by the high rank of the officers attempting to recruit him (especially Augsburg), Barbie was keen to accept. But the combination of the CIC swoops on 23 February against his own network and Six's sudden arrest by American war-crimes investigators on charges of mass murder alarmed him that the ex-SS officer, Hirschfeld, who was making the offer, might in fact be a traitor. His fears were justified. Hirschfeld was in fact 'Walter', a German CIC informer involved in 'Operation Flowerbox', another CIC operation aimed at penetrating underground Nazi groups. Unsuspecting, Barbie had already confided his real identity and wartime activities to 'Walter' and had also disclosed that he had only recently narrowly escaped arrest. Nevertheless, despite Barbie's history, 'Walter's' handler, a CIC agent called John Dermer, wanted to use Barbie to penetrate a suspected Soviet spy ring in the small town of Schwaebish-Gemund. On 20 March 1947, he asked his regional headquarters in Stuttgart (responsible for CIC Region III) for permission. 'It is at present believed,' he wrote, 'that a tight enough control over him can be maintained so that his arrest could easily be effected should such action become desirable. Using him for the purpose outlined here would be an excuse to keep him under surveillance.' On 16 April, Dermer's proposal was rejected. Barbie was instead to be arrested 'as quickly as feasible'.

To the north, in Marburg, CIC headquarters responsible for Region I were still, unsuccessfully, trying to locate and arrest Barbie at the tail end of 'Operation Selection Board'. Neither Region I nor Region II was aware that Barbie had, after some effort, contacted an old wartime friend from France who was already working for Region IV of the CIC, based in Munich. Having exhausted any possibility of continuing the fight against the Allies, Barbie was on the verge of accepting the offer to join them.

THE MERCENARY

Barbie began working for the CIC in spring 1947. When he arrived on 18 April for his first interview in the small Bavarian town of Memmingen, sixty miles from Munich, he was a reluctant recruit. Robert Taylor, the CIC special agent who was the first American to employ him formally, was himself not overenthusiastic. He knew that Barbie was a former Gestapo officer and therefore on the automatic arrest list; he even admits that he realised immediately that Barbie was 'one of the chief personalities' wanted in 'Operation Selection Board'. As a preliminary introduction Barbie had sent Taylor a copy of a long article about René Hardy from a German newspaper. To prove his importance Barbie had also typed a five-page summary describing his own part in Hardy's arrest and the result of his successful interrogation. But Taylor needed little persuasion because despite any personal reservations he ought to have had, he trusted the German informer who had brought Barbie to his office and Dale Garvey, his superior in Munich, approved the appointment apparently without hesitation. Neither of them thought it necessary at the time to inform CIC headquarters in Frankfurt that Taylor was not only in contact with Barbie, but also considering employing him.

It was not a routine interview for Taylor. A year earlier, the new recruit would have been prosecuted for war crimes. Since then the divisions in Europe had hardened; the Cold War had started, and any lingering ambivalence in American attitudes towards the communists had simply vanished. Former allies had become enemies, hunted enemies had become friends. All the Allied intelligence agencies were under enormous pressure to discover Soviet intentions and prevent the communisation of western Germany. The personal and organisational chaos within the multiplicity of rival agencies nonetheless led to people making decisions which twenty-five years later they find hard to explain. Today, Taylor says that he cannot remember whether he employed any ex-Gestapo agents, nor can he even remember meeting Barbie. At the time it was just

131

another German with a 'dirty past'. But he accepts the documentary evidence which proves he did.

Taylor's had been a typical CIC career. After fighting with the 84th Infantry Division at the Battle of the Bulge, he was drafted into the CIC because he spoke German and, as a former journalist, was thought to know how to ask questions. He never received special training at the CIC headquarters at Fort Holabird, but got first-hand experience with a CIC detachment travelling at the front of the American advance across the Rhine and up to the Elbe. Taylor, like most other CIC officers, felt that he was part of an elite force. It could count Henry Kissinger and J. D. Salinger amongst its ranks. With special privileges and facilities, the CIC played an unprecedented role for an American army.

Their mission, detailed in SHAEF handbooks and the numerous briefing papers which had been so thoughtfully drafted during the months before the D-day landings, was to spearhead the demilitarisation and denazification of Germany. Armed with unlimited powers, they were to exorcise the Nazi spirit from Germany. Their orders were to arrest any German who might pose a threat to the Allied occupation; to arrest nearly all Nazi Party officials and any member of a paramilitary force which was part of the Nazi regime; and to dismiss from public office anyone who had been a supporter or had profited from the Third Reich. It was an enormous task which was compromised from the outset.

Towards the end of 1945, many of the more talented CIC officers clamoured for demobilisation and the chance to return home. 'The rush was so great,' remembers one official, 'that the American military machine just melted like butter in the sun'. It was the less able, who had nothing to return home to and could make better fortunes as members of an occupation army, who remained. While most of the original core preserved their professional approach, the new recruits were distinguished for their ignorance, laziness, inability to speak German, misunderstanding of the situation in Germany, unsuitable backgrounds and tendency to outright corruption; these men were less willing to remove incriminated Nazis from sensitive or profitable positions.

Earl Browning was one of those who took the chance to return home. As a CIC officer moving just behind the front line, he had seen a lot of action: Aachen, the Ardennes, Remagen, and then down to the south of Germany where he was among the first to enter Dachau concentration camp. By the time he left Europe in September 1945, he had 'seen enough to convince me that many Germans were not very nice people. I had been appalled by what I saw. Dachau had been a great shock.' In early 1946, Browning was asked to return to Germany as a senior CIC officer. The CIC had lost too many skilled officers and there was no one in Germany to replace them. Browning accepted and returned in April 1946 as the regional CIC commander in Bremen.

The mood had noticeably changed. 'The Germans were no longer our enemies. Denazification was no longer so important. People were more suspicious of the Russians.' All the same, to his astonishment Browning found the CIC sharing their Bremen offices with the local Communist Party. So far it had been an amicable arrangement and at first Browning did not alter it; after all, it gave him an unbeatable opportunity to see the communists at work. But as he watched the Russian reparation teams move around the city, he decided that the war-time allies were also spying. The CIC asked the communists to leave and in June 1946 Browning submitted a proposal to Colonel Inskeep, the head of CIC in Frankfurt, that he be allowed to penetrate the local Communist Party. General Burriss, the head of G2, the US Army's intelligence section, rejected the idea. In Browning's view, Burriss simply reflected Headquarters' naivety about communist intentions. He began collecting more information to resubmit his proposal.

Little irritated Browning more at that time than the procedures to be followed when handling Russian deserters. Many arrived with valuable intelligence material in the hope that it would sweeten their reception and guarantee them asylum. On the contrary, Browning found himself compelled to obey the agreement signed between General Clay and his Russian counterpart, General Vassily Sokolovsky, according to which the Russians were to be returned as deserters. 'I knew that we were sending them back to be executed, and that was terrible.' Before they went, Browning analysed their intelligence reports and used it to convince Burriss finally that the communists did have 'aggressive intentions towards the US'.

By then the Frankfurt headquarters needed little convincing. The four powers' regular negotiations in Berlin had been totally obstructed by the Russians, who had also subverted the elections to the Berlin city council. The western governments were alarmed that the Communist Party had merged with, or in their view swallowed up, the Socialist Party in the Soviet zone. The new SED (East German Socialist Party) was under Soviet control: there could be a serious threat to Allied security if the Communist Party did the same in the western zones. At the time, the American command was receiving no reliable intelligence whatsoever about communist activities and intentions, whether in Soviet-occupied Europe, or indeed in their own zone. Any hard information, even from the very lowest echelons, was a valuable addition.

'Operation Sunrise', Browning's own name for the penetration of the Bremen Communist Party, began in September 1946. Browning believes it to have been the first covert operation of its kind in the US zone. His best recruits were members of the Bremen Communist Party whose loyalty he knew to be weak. 'I wanted to know what they were telling the KPD [West German Communist Party] in our zone. We didn't learn very much, but considering our total ignorance it was better than nothing.' Within weeks he extended his operation and persuaded his informers to join the SED in the Soviet Zone. Once again, they only returned with trifles, but it was, Browning felt, a good start.

In the autumn of 1946, Browning remembers that he received a telex from Garvey, who at that time was the CIC chief operational officer at headquarters in Frankfurt. Garvey's message had been sent to all regional commands. It alerted CIC detachments that a senior Gestapo officer wanted for many war crimes had been seen in the US zone. If seen, said the telex, he should be arrested. The Gestapo officer's name was Klaus Barbie.

On 1 March 1947, Browning replaced Garvey in Frankfurt as operations officer for the whole 7970 CIC. Garvey had just completed 'Operation Selection Board' and was sent to Munich, officially to 'reorganise' the CIC in Region IV – Bavaria. In fact, his major priority was to root out the blatant corruption among undisciplined American officers which had severely compromised the American military government. Surveying what he had inherited from Garvey, Browning concluded that CIC operations had become hopelessly chaotic. The 700 CIC agents were insufficiently supervised; their information was too often valueless; and German informers were able to sell the same erroneous information to several CIC agents in succession because no one at headquarters was monitoring the sources and the information. As a serious consequence, the same erroneous information coming apparently from two different souces would be used to confirm itself. Browning immediately began reorganising the central index system in Frankfurt and ordered all regions to submit a complete list of the names of their informers. They were to be registered and given a code name for security and future reference. Joe Vidal, described by those who know him as a 'super-cool spook', was in charge of the informants registry, known within the CIC as the 'Tech Spec'. Garvey's list reached Vidal in September. It included the names given to him by the Augsburg detachment which, through an office in Memmingen, was responsible for the area down to the Austrian border. Vidal, who later joined the CIA, noted that not all the informants listed were suitable under existing regulations. He sent the suspect list to Browning:

> I was sitting in my office when Jim Ratcliffe, my deputy, came in holding some paper. It was the Region IV informants list we'd received from Garvey. I read down it and saw the name Klaus Barbie. I couldn't believe it. I remembered very clearly that was the same German whom Garvey had said we should arrest when I was in Bremen, and here he was using him. Ratcliffe began running around the walls in excitement shouting that Garvey was double-crossing us. I immediately sent Garvey an order to arrest Barbie.

It was the beginning of a bitter feud between Browning and Region IV, who were determined to protect the former Gestapo chief. He had become, they insisted, one of their best agents. Browning was told that Barbie had 'disappeared'.

Garvey is quite insistent today that he cannot remember Barbie or anything about the case, but he too accepts the documentary evidence. He says that he had spent his time struggling with 'organisational problems' and that, although his name appears on the messages, he was just 'signing off' what others had written. Indeed no-one who worked at headquarters in Munich can, or wants to, remember Barbie. That is not the case of those who worked in the Augsburg detachment itself. For them, Barbie became a very special source of whom they were increasingly proud.

Taylor's memory after seeing his old files is, however, quite clear about who brought Barbie to his Memmingen office in April 1947. It was Joseph 'Kurt' Merk, a former Abwehr officer from Dijon. Merk and Barbie had together been running one of the most successful penetration operations in occupied France, code-named 'Operationa Technica'. Over a long period Merk had used his French girlfriend, Andrée Rives, to uncover the plans of Charles Merlen, a Dijon Resistance chief. As Merlen's niece, Rives had infiltrated his and many other networks with ease. Merk and Barbie divided the information between them.

Taylor had recruited Merk in April 1946. Although Abwehr officers were still on the automatic-arrest list, there was little stigma attached to employing them. There had been mutual war-time respect between the Allied and German intelligence services. Very soon after the German surrender, Reinhard Gehlen, the head of *Fremde Heere Ost* (the section of the German General Staff which, through the Abwehr, specialised in eastern Europe), had made a deal with an American intelligence officer, General Edwin Sibert, to hand over all his invaluable records to the Americans. Microfilmed and photostatted precisely in preparation for that sort of deal, Gehlen had hidden them in drums underground on a remote Bavarian farm. Sibert's distrust of the Russians was still a minority view among Americans in summer 1945. As late as 10 December 1945, when Gehlen had been in Washington for four months being debriefed on his archives, the War Department sent Sibert a telex refusing him permission to use Germans to gather intelligence about the Russians. Sibert ignored that directive. It was the US Army's view in Europe that they needed intelligence and that only experienced Germans could provide it. Merk was one of those.

Taylor remembers Merk as an ambitious, totally committed intelligence officer who was frustrated by the very limited role that he could perform in Augsburg. His speciality was intelligence, not counter-intelligence which he felt was too passive. But that did not prevent Taylor enthusiastically describing Merk to CIC headquarters in Frankfurt as 'one of the best counter-intelligence men in France during the German occupation', to justify the German's employment. For the moment Merk had to be satisfied. Diligently he had found informers in refugee camps, among demobilised soldiers and former SS officers, and in the bars and shops of nearby villages. These people kept him supplied with news tit-bits and comment about their feelings towards the Allies and their own politicians, the state of the rampant black market and whatever they had heard from friends, relatives and recent arrivals from the Russian zone. All of this was included in Merk's weekly report for Taylor who paid him with cigarettes, chocolate and other food – the currency of the period. It made life comfortable for him and Andrée Rives who, fearing execution as a collaborator, had left France with her mother and lived with Merk under the name Annamarie Richter.

Merk met Barbie by complete chance in February 1947. Travelling by train on a procurement mission, he saw Barbie standing forlornly on a station platform. After the mutual congratulations on surviving the war, Merk revealed the identity of his new employers and suggested that Barbie should also join. Barbie was reluctant. Unlike Merk, he knew that he faced a certain death penalty if he was ever handed over to the French. Merk persuaded him that times had changed and that the Americans were by then quite uninterested in war crimes. This was not quite accurate; a minority had objected when Gehlen, on his triumphant return from America, began recruiting some of the most notorious SS officers for his new agency. Those objections had come from CIC officers who were looking for the very same SS men as internationally-wanted war criminals. But they were a fast-dwindling minority. The American war-crimes trial programme had become completely discredited. Their investigation of the Malmédy massacre had itself become the subject of an intense investigation, and the victim of an extraordinary and vicious political campaign to deny that the Nazis were in fact guilty of any crimes. Many American officers, especially those who had not fought in the war, were opposed to any further American involvement in prosecuting Germans for crimes against non-Americans: with Europe edging towards a new confrontation, it no longer made political sense. Straight and the JAG office had been ordered to wind up the war-crimes trials immediately and release as many suspects as possible without trial, even where the evidence was convincing. Knowing that, Barbie hesitantly agreed to meet Taylor.

Merk had already discovered that his American masters were not very demanding. Taylor's commanding officer, Captain George

137

Spiller, had won two silver stars for outstanding bravery during the campaign in Italy; but he had also lost a lung and suffered another severe wound, so was unfit for active service. His wartime record guaranteed him continued but unstrenuous employment in the military. Heading a small CIC detachment in a Bavarian backwater seemed an ideal posting and Spiller did not complain. Intelligence work did not interest him, so he left those chores to his staff. His routine rarely changed. On Thursday afternoons he would leave his office, collect his German girlfriend and enjoy four days of hunting, love-making and good food. It was all paid for by profits he earned selling American PX stores on the black market. On Tuesday morning he would return, crack the whip and submit the accumulated reports to headquarters without comment. For the time being no one at headquarters queried his output, which was just as well because Merk consistently exaggerated the value of his information.

Barbie's description of his introduction to Taylor suggests a rather pleasant encounter. Taylor assured him that 'he had nothing to fear' and that he would not be arrested. All the American wanted, he said, was to have a few words with him about his past. Taylor did not query any part of Barbie's concoction of lies, or refer to the SHAEF description of Barbie as the Gestapo chief of Lyons or the CROWCASS listing of Barbie as wanted for murder. He automatically accepted that Barbie was a straight, clean intelligence agent and immediately offered him a job and a room at the local station hotel pending his superior's approval. Eight days later Taylor was given the go-ahead. The only condition on Barbie's employment was that he agree to break off all contact 'with other SS or German intelligence personnel' except on the direct orders of the CIC. Without any reflection Barbie agreed to the conditions, and then immediately broke his undertaking.

Merk and Barbie convinced Taylor on three counts that, together, they could provide him with vital intelligence.

Firstly, their wartime experience fighting the French communist Resistance would aid the Americans in their own penetration of the German Communist Party and in the detection of Soviet agents. This should not have been very convincing since the French Communist Party was very weak in Lyons and the German communists were not fighting an underground war, nor did they have much in common with the French party. But for the two Germans and the Americans it was the same enemy.

Secondly, they claimed that they could satisfy the American need for information about trends and events in the neighbouring French zone. It is most unlikely that they actually dared cross into the zone to collect their information, and questionable whether they had reliable sources supplying them; but they definitely gave their American handlers the impression that they had penetrated the French command in Baden-Baden and were drawing on prime sources in French intelligence. Surprisingly, no one in Region IV seems to have been aware that spying on an Ally was strictly forbidden.

Thirdly, Merk persuaded Taylor that they had access to an enormous network of agents stretching from Lisbon to the Soviet border. This last claim, although exaggerated, was partly true in 1946/7. Using his own wartime contacts with Abwehr agents and those he inherited from other Abwehr officers whose speciality had been eastern Europe and the Balkans, Merk began to supply intelligence about the persecution of German minorities, about the Resistance movements still working against the Russians, and about general political trends in those countries and the other zones in Germany. Frustrated by their own ignorance and pleased to be receiving any information, the Americans were undaunted by their inability to verify the accuracy of Merk's information.

Barbie's contribution was his privileged entrée to the *Kamaradenschaft*. At the beginning he looked for those former SS officers who had served in eastern Europe. Their archives and memory, combined with the information brought by the floods of refugees, could, with careful analysis, provide important pieces of the jigsaw. To the CIC in Munich it seemed as if they had finally produced an important team. It was what both Spiller and Garvey wanted to believe; under Spiller's indulgent regime, Taylor accepted with gratitude anything the Merk network delivered. Yet they were involved in operations that were completely contrary to the CIC's official mission, namely counter-intelligence – checking any threat to American occupation within Region IV.

From his office at 36 Kaiser Promenade in Memmingen, Barbie handled his agents with commitment and serenity; an unspoken understanding about his loyal services to the Third Reich was automatically assumed by both his agents and his paymaster. Both became deferential. His agents, according to Barbie, submitted both oral and written reports which were rewritten before being passed on to Taylor. Merk was given between 10,000 and 15,000 Reichmarks per month to run the network, plus food and cigarettes. Most of his agents, including Barbie himself, were paid 500 Reichmarks per month (about 50 dollars) plus supplies of coffee, cigarettes and other scarce but very valuable commodities. Taylor never queried but only praised Merk's work. Regularly, Taylor and Merk spent their weekend recreation together in the picturesque Bavarian village of Marktoberdorf. The American's relationship with Merk had become, according to a later CIC report, 'a firm friendship . . . between two equals, rather than . . . between the American CIC agent and his informant'.

Barbie's use, like that of many former SS officers, might have passed unnoticed at CIC headquarters in Frankfurt had Captain Robert Frazier, reading through a routine Region IV report, not requested on 22 May some more information about a German named Emil Hoffmann. Hoffmann had been an 'Operation Selection Board' target but, according to Barbie, was in fact a British informer who had in January 1947 approached him with an offer to work for British Intelligence – an advance rejected by Barbie because he feared a trap. Frazier's inquiry placed Taylor in an embarrassing predicament. Until then, all Barbie's information was passed on by Taylor, giving Merk as the source. Now feeling somewhat vulnerable, Taylor felt the need to explain Barbie's existence formally and also persuade headquarters of his value to Allied Intelligence. With apparent sincerity, Taylor wrote:

> Barbie impressed this agent as an honest man, both intellectually and personally, absolutely without nerves or fear. He is strongly anti-communist and a Nazi idealist who believes that he and his beliefs were betrayed by the Nazis in power. Since Barbie started to work for this agent he has provided extensive connections to French Intelligence agencies working in the US Zone, to German circles, to high-ranking Rumanian circles and to high Russian circles in the US Zone.

Having established Barbie's importance, Taylor pleaded for Barbie to remain free: 'It is felt that his value as an informant infinitely outweighs any use he may have in prison. Control over Barbie's activities is obvious . . . This opinion is based on this Agent's personal contact with Barbie and the trust which Barbie has placed in this Agent.' Endorsing Taylor's argument, Region IV headquarters in Munich commented, 'It is emphasised that Subject's value as an informant cannot be overlooked.' Their arguments were answered from Frankfurt by an inexplicable silence. Without further instructions, Taylor allowed the network, code-named 'Buro Petersen', to grow from fifteen to at least sixty-five informants on the payroll. By the time Taylor returned to America in August 1947, his successor, Special Agent Camille Hajdu, immediately diagnosed that his predecessor had lost control over the two Germans. He resented what he later described as the 'bosom-pal' relationship between Taylor and Merk which was beginning to cause a 'great deal of embarrassment to Region IV', not least because Merk and his girlfriend had been the witnesses at Taylor's wedding. Yet Hajdu admitted that ninety per cent of the information his office received came from Merk's network and at the beginning, like his predecessor, he too was grateful.

When Browning finally heard about Hajdu's special informant, he was neither grateful nor prepared to tolerate Barbie's continued use. He asked for an explanation. Garvey formally admitted on 17 October that Region IV was employing Barbie and asked 'what disposition should be made' of him. Browning replied twelve days later that he should be arrested immediately. Browning insists that the only reason for that order was that Barbie had been a member of the Gestapo. He admits that even he had used 'Gestapo types' in Bremen, but insists (although he knew nothing about Barbie's wartime service) that they had first-hand experience of the German Communist Party because they had actually worked during the war inside Germany itself, which Barbie had not. Browning wanted Barbie's continued use independently assessed. Garvey was ordered to send Barbie for 'detailed interrogation' to the US European Command Interrogation Center at Oberursel. ECIC was staffed by G2, Army Intelligence, which was not connected with the CIC. Browning hoped that its unbiased, trained interrogators could produce honest replies to a detailed list of questions which he had drawn up, to 'complete his [Barbie's] history' and establish Barbie's post-war contacts with Nazi groups. Garvey and Barbie's handler, Hajdu, resented that order and prevaricated.

Through October and November, Browning sent increasingly acrimonious messages to Garvey saying that Barbie should be arrested, only to be rebuffed by claims that Barbie's skills were invaluable and that there was no one to replace him. According to Hajdu, Barbie was producing 'extremely good material' and was 'exceedingly successful'; his arrest 'would damage considerably the trust and faith which informants place in this organisation'. Instead of arresting Barbie, Hajdu wanted any questioning done informally by local CIC agents. Naively, Hajdu added that Barbie would volunteer to co-operate with that sort of interrogation. In November, Garvey was replaced by Lieutenant Colonel Ellington Golden who argued even more strongly than his predecessor that, if Barbie's arrest was unavoidable, he should at least be given 'some type of preferential treatment' during his interrogation. Hajdu was concerned that if Barbie was mistreated he would defect to British Intelligence; Golden was equally concerned that the CIC would lose its most valuable source of information about activities in the French Zone.

After reading Region IV's pleas, both Browning and Vidal were more than irritated. Vidal especially queried Barbie's activities in the French zone. These were maverick and unauthorised and suggested that the two Germans were continuing the war under different auspices. On 1 December Browning rejected Golden's suggestion of preferential treatment and ordered Barbie's immediate arrest; but his position was suddenly undermined.

Irked by Browning's attitude, Golden had appealed to the CIC commander, Colonel David Erskine, and found a sympathetic ear. Erskine agreed that Region IV's task was hard enough without losing key informers. Humiliated, Browning was compelled to include in his final order for Barbie's arrest an assurance that, 'Upon completion of his interrogation, providing the interrogation provides no information which would demand Subject's imprisonment, he will be returned to your custody with instructions for future disposition.' Browning claims that he was performing a near-impossible balancing act. He had both to comply with Erskine's orders and simultaneously not annoy Golden. Browning promised Munich that Barbie would be kept in prison not because of his own 'subversive activities' before his recruitment, but just to discover what other information on the SS groups he possessed. As a guarantee, Vidal instructed the ECIC interrogators not to question Barbie about his work for the CIC.

Today, Browning insists that his only motive was simply to remove a Gestapo officer from the CIC. 'Everyone knew he was ex-Gestapo,' claims Browning. 'It's just that Region IV wanted to ignore it.' If Browning is correct, then he must have been sorely disappointed with Barbie's interrogation at Oberursel which started in mid-December.

Barbie claims that on arrival he was given rough prison clothes and locked in a solitary cell to await interrogation. Within hours of his arrival, his interrogator appeared, only to be ignored. He left, but returned the next day with a typewriter. Barbie was ordered to write an account of his war record. Left alone for weeks in his cell, Barbie admits that he became desperate and depressed. With nothing to do except throw a coin he had found at the wall, he says that he twice tried to commit suicide. Finally, fearing that he would otherwise be handed over to either the French or the British, he began to write. In 1979 he claimed, 'I didn't tell them any more than I could write on one-and-a-half sides of paper.' In fact it was more, but it was certainly not the complete truth. Later he admitted that it had been a catharsis ('I finally got it off my chest') and that he enjoyed it.

His first interrogation, completed on 28 January 1948, was indeed worthless. It was an unsubstantiated account of an invitation in February 1946 from a former SS officer to work for Soviet intelligence, which he had rejected: nothing else, and it was a good ploy to make his interrogators nervous. Browning's hopes of a definitive report from his professional interrogator were dashed. After stating incorrectly that Barbie had been a captain in the Waffen SS (the SS's elite army group), the interrogator's report concluded that 'Barbie has co-operated willingly. It is not believed that he has wilfully withheld information.'

In return for his co-operation, Barbie was now allowed access to the prison library. To his surprise, these were the same books as had been provided for the Allied pilots imprisoned in the camp during the war. The Nazi books had not been removed. Suddenly, the line of questioning also changed. 'I was asked what I knew about communism. Then it all became much clearer.' To meet Vidal's increasing dissatisfaction with the Merk–Barbie network, the new

Region IV commanding officer, George Eckman (Golden's successor), had sent a new, detailed list of questions to Oberursel about Barbie's work for Region IV itself, and also a detailed questionnaire about the offer of employment by Hoffmann on behalf of British Intelligence. Vidal added that headquarters was still expecting Barbie's 'complete history'.

Two of the three interrogation reports dated 15 April 1948 were extensive descriptions of Hoffmann's recruitment efforts and Barbie's arrest and escape from the British in Hamburg. They reflected Vidal's concern that the CIC should have adequate information should their British allies accuse them of duplicity in shielding Barbie from arrest. To the CIC's satisfaction, Barbie insisted that he would never work for the British: 'owing to the unjust treatment he received from the British after his arrest in Hamburg . . . he lost all interest in the British as well as faith in the many promises they made him.' Without any prompting, he added how happy he was working for the Americans and that he hoped to return to Memmingen. No one disbelieved him since the alternative to his privileged lifestyle was, inevitably, imprisonment.

The third report contained Barbie's own account of his career in the Third Reich. It was an unchallenged cover-up. Claiming that throughout the war he had remained a member of SD's Section VI, he concealed his membership in the Gestapo, made no reference to Lyons and invented a record of service in Italy. Once again the interrogators revealed their inexperience and ignorance, not even mentioning that CROWCASS listed Barbie as wanted for 'murder' in Lyons. Concluding their recommendations, they wrote:

> Because of Barbie's activities with CIC Region IV during 1947, it is not deemed advisable to intern him for his affiliation with the Waffen SS. His knowledge as to the mission of CIC, its agents, sub-agents, funds, etc, is too great. If Barbie were interned, it is the opinion of the interrogator that upon his release or escape . . . he would contact either the French or the British Intelligence and work for them.

The Americans had wittingly confessed that their informer possessed the power of blackmail. On 10 May Barbie was deemed to be 'of no further CI [Counter-Intelligence] interest' and returned to work for Region IV.

It was a defeat for Browning, which he admits was partly his own fault because he had failed to brief the ECIC interrogators about Barbie's Gestapo record. More importantly, he was frustrated by Colonel Erskine's support for Region IV. Says Browning, 'I just had to obey my orders.' But he claims that Barbie's future use by Region IV was subject to 'strict limitations'; principally, that his employment had to be reviewed every three months and all his activities closely supervised and reported. Even before Barbie returned, Browning had already asked for a 'plan for approval by this headquarters' for the future use of the German team.

By the beginning of 1948 there was nothing unusual about the use of incriminated Germans. The Allies had condoned the wholesale reinstatement of former Nazis to their old jobs. Teachers who had lectured on the glories of Nazi race theories were again teaching in the schools and universities; judges who had passed death sentences for trivial offences in the notorious People's Courts were once again dispensing justice; doctors who had knowingly condoned and contributed to the euthanasia programmes were practising medicine; government officials who had without compulsion implemented the worst measures during the Third Reich were once again powerful bureaucrats; and the industrialists who had used slave labour and earned enormous profits during the war were on the verge of re-amassing their wealth and power. In that context, the use of one insignificant Gestapo officer who could give some help against the communist threat seemed, to many, utterly acceptable.

As France reeled from a series of communist-inspired strikes which threatened its fragile return to democracy, American intelligence, in a state of alarm, now added the French Communist Party to its list of urgent targets; and that included its activities in the French zone. It was not particularly difficult to convince Barbie that he was ideal for the task. To Barbie it now seemed that, because the Americans had cleared him, they would also automatically protect him, principally to save themselves embarrassment.

In his absence, Merk's star had waned irreversibly. He had been unable to establish with his new CIC handler, Camille Hajdu, the intimacy that he had enjoyed with Taylor. Hajdu resented Merk's high-handedness, his embarrassing and increasingly unauthorised activities, and he was critical of his deteriorating performance. Hajdu was not alone in strongly suspecting that much of Merk's information was valueless. But just before Barbie's return, Hajdu was reassigned. Dick Lavoie, the man who had tried unsuccessfully to arrest Barbie in Marburg in 1946, was promoted to 'Tech Spec' for Region IV. Eager to prove his mettle, he wanted to exploit his inheritance and refused to share Hajdu's scepticism.

On his return, Barbie's position was reassessed. Spiller was ordered to find a new handler and new accommodation for his elite team, since their cover as 'Buro Petersen' in Memmingen had been exposed. He chose thirty-one-year-old Erhard Dabringhaus who had arrived in March. Theoretically, Dabringhaus was a good choice. Born in Essen, Germany, he had emigrated with his parents to the United States in 1930 and returned to Europe as a major and trained interrogator with the 1st Infantry Division. Leaving the army in 1946, he reapplied at the end of 1947 and was appointed a civilian special agent in the CIC. He reported to Spiller on 1 March 1948. Neither was impressed by the other. Spiller disliked Dabringhaus for having a more senior war-time rank, while Dabringhaus was unimpressed by Spiller's slipshod, inadequate operation. Spiller gave his new recruit a list of German informers with orders to build up his relationships quickly. It was only four weeks later that he was ordered to Memmingen to help two German agents move their belongings to new quarters in Augsburg.

Dabringhaus arrived at 7 Schillerstrasse on 15 June in a small US Army truck. Aware that Merk and Barbie were considered important informers, he helped them carry their belongings out of the house. With them were Andrée Rives and her mother, and Dr Emil Augsburg, who had formerly worked for Adolf Eichmann: he had become a key informant for the Merk–Barbie network. Dabringhaus drove them all to 10 Mozartstrasse, a large corner house in the pleasant leafy Stadtbergen suburb of Augsburg. Soon after their arrival, their new German neighbours protested to the local authorities. The house had been requisitioned from an anti-Nazi family who had thought it was going to be used for Americans. It was infuriating that they had been evicted to make way for ex-Nazis. Inevitably the protest was ignored. Merk lived downstairs with Andrée; the Barbie family lived upstairs, but the Barbie children could often be seen playing in the garden.

Dabringhaus now found himself in a very peculiar position. Two Germans of nearly the same age, both from the Rhineland, who had fought against each other during the war, were now expected to develop a relationship in the service of an occupying power to spy on their fellow countrymen. Barbie clearly had the advantage. He was an experienced, totally ruthless intelligence officer, whereas Dabringhaus had been no more than a field interrogator. The American was never in a position to do other than serve his informant and their relationship remained brittle.

Dabringhaus's initial task was to formalise the Merk network. Their targets were clearly set out by Lavoie. Besides reporting on the activities of the Bavarian Communist Party and Soviet agents, they were to maintain their penetration and surveillance of French Intelligence, both in the American and French zones. Barbie, using the aliases Becker, Behrends, Speer and Mertens, was put in overall command of the network's anti-French activities. Truly it must have seemed that the war had never ended. A proper office was obtained for the two Germans on the first floor of the US billet next to the town's swimming pool. They brought their own secretary, the widow of a former SS officer killed in Russia, who was provided with a rare luxury, her own typewriter. At 9.00 a.m. daily, the four would assemble at the office to discuss the day's operations. Dabringhaus is convinced even today that Barbie had a network of between sixty-five and a hundred informants throughout west and eastern Europe and claims as his own achievement that he cut it down to twenty-five, 'because the rest were giving us nothing and we were stupid enough to pay for it'. Munich headquarters objected, says Dabringhaus, because they wanted more information not less. Barbie and Merk 'had gone way beyond their original mission, which was to penetrate the French zone, French intelligence and the French Communist Party. Instead they had sub-agents in Czechoslovakia, Yugoslavia and Romania, and were getting information from the SS General Gunther Bernau in Stuttgart, who sold information supplied by 125 former SS officers.' Among that valuable intelligence, according to Dabringhaus, was the information that the Czechs were mining uranium (which was commonly known before the war) and reports on the condition of the Romanian economy. According to the Danish journalist Christian Zarp, who had specialised in the Romanian economy for the SS, Barbie had obtained that material from himself and Emil Augsburg. Its value was dubious.

By November 1948, at the end of the first three-month trial

period, Captain Max Etkin, Region IV's Operations Chief, was just the latest American pleading that the two Germans should not be dropped. Headquarters, however, was convinced that the network was too big, too expensive, and definitely compromised, not only in British and French eyes but also amongst the Nazi fraternity. To deflect that criticism, Etkin reported that the team's contacts with Emil Augsburg, Gunter Bernau and every informant not living within the region's boundary, had been severed. Informants of 'dubious character', involved in black-marketeering, robbery and smuggling, had also been dropped. 'The net,' reported Etkin, 'is no longer being employed merely to keep them from being used by an undesirable foreign power.' The 'Merk Empire' had collapsed. It was now, allegedly, just a small six-man agency, working on local surveillance. Barbie and Merk, wrote Etkin gullibly, would not break the new ground rules because they 'feared being left out in the cold, and they are firmly convinced that the US authorities are going to help them in the event of trouble, as they have in the past.' Etkin was reflecting one of his own agent's memoranda: 'Barbie is concerned about the French and realises that if the French were ever to get control over him, he would be executed.' Clearly, there were no doubts about the nature of Barbie's wartime record.

Nevertheless, Browning again argued that the team should be dropped, not least because, as he correctly perceived, despite their promises, Barbie and Merk would never sever their contacts with the *Kamaradenschaft*. But once again he was forced to compromise and agree to another three-month trial period.

'Merk's biggest coup,' says Dabringhaus, 'was to produce two double agents who confided that the French were trying to penetrate US intelligence. That's why we lost confidence in the French.' It is a strange assertion, not least because Barbie's role was exactly the same, only in reverse. It also confirms the extraordinary naivety which prevailed amongst the intelligence community, which Barbie himself soon noticed – especially about communist affairs. On several occasions he took Dabringhaus to local Communist Party meetings, once even at two o'clock in the morning. Dressing in German clothes so that he would not seem out of place, Dabringhaus could thus submit impressive eyewitness reports on communist agitation which even he admits amounted to little more than underpaid workers protesting.

It was in the very nature of the American operation, and Dabringhaus's position within it, that both he and headquarters took everything that Barbie told them on trust. Dabringhaus knew the names of 'no more than a dozen' of Barbie's paid agents, and he rarely met any of Barbie's informants. Instead, he regularly supplied Barbie with up to twelve different forged identity cards at a time and handed over a regular yellow envelope with his wages and expenses. His original claim that the envelopes contained $1,700 per month, has now been revised down to $500 per month. Every other CIC officer has derided this account, insisting that they never used real American dollars, but the military scrip especially issued for the occupation. In fact, Merk and Barbie were already supplying information to other American agencies that were not prevented from using dollars. Nevertheless, Merk consistently complained that he was not paid enough, once telling Dabringhaus that he could not support his network on 8,000 Deutsche Marks ($2000) per month. Dabringhaus, who was nothing more than a cossetter, passed that complaint to Dick Lavoie who in turn passed it on to Browning at the CIC's new headquarters in Stuttgart. It reinforced his view that the net had outlived its value.

In 1979, Barbie was surprisingly silent about his work for the Americans. However, he was proud to have been able to use his position to help so many SS men leave Germany with officially prepared ID papers and money. This was just one of Barbie's many rackets, prompting him to brag to Dabringhaus on repeated occasions about how easy it was to fool the Allies. Dabringhaus could only agree. 'Barbie always told Merk that I was too weak. "When you've got an enemy in your hands," he would say to Merk, "you've got to crush him."'

Dabringhaus now says that he was appalled by Barbie's past, but there is no contemporary record to support that. After five months he was summarily told that he was to be moved away from Augsburg. His successor was twenty-eight-year-old Herbert Bechtold, who had also been born in the Rhineland and had emigrated to America in 1935. Bechtold had spent the war fighting in northern Africa and through Europe from the Normandy landings to the Rhine. When he finally reached Berlin and was eligible for priority demobilisation, he applied to remain in the army because he lacked qualifications for other employment. For a time he was allowed to work in the Army's CID investigation department, but was then compulsorily demobilised. Re-engaged, he was posted to Munich in 1948 under Colonel Aaron Banks. According to Bechtold, he immediately impressed Banks by uncovering a homosexual ring run by an American soldier whom Bechtold revealed to be a Soviet agent. As a reward, Master Sergeant Bechtold was posted as a CIC agent to Augsburg in September 1948. Bechtold's briefing left him in no doubt that he was taking charge of the region's top agents who had become disgruntled. 'A choice assignment which needed tact, patience, diplomacy and skill,' remembers Bechtold. 'My first task was to sort out their problems and get them happier.'

It was Dabringhaus who introduced Bechtold to the Germans. 'Barbie was wary like a fox, scenting a new quarry. He had to figure me out, because he was going to live off me and they hadn't been getting their money.' Within days the two Rhinelanders had taken to one another. In Bechtold's view, Barbie realised that he was different from the normal, bossy American. There was a chance of a real friendship. Nostalgically, Bechtold remembers that they broke the ice at an Augsburg nightclub. As they sat listening to the live band, surrounded by girls and dancing, Bechtold ordered a bottle of champagne and they toasted each other and their future work. 'He opened the window to himself and his personal life. He trusted me and began to reminisce about other champagnes he had drunk.' Notably Barbie spoke about drinking real champagne in France served by distinguished waiters in what he called 'the good old days'. They were to speak a great deal about France over the next twenty months. But first Bechtold had to solve Barbie's problem, which eventually proved to be Spiller himself.

Investigation of Barbie's complaints over money had revealed that Spiller had been using his fund in a currency deal with his German girlfriend's husband. 'Spiller was only interested in his pleasure and profits. Stuttgart was never satisfied with his briefings and then he'd take it out on his staff. He'd always be screaming that whatever we gave him was not conclusive enough, and then throw it in the basket.' Stuttgart at that time wanted information about the activities of General Friedrich von Paulus, who collaborated with the Russians after his capture. They were also interested in how the 6th Army was being used by the Russians, and any news brought by the refugees from eastern Europe. 'Spiller just did not understand the work and irreversibly exposed himself.' He was removed and returned soon after to the United States.

His replacement at the beginning of 1949 was Major George Riggins who, soon after his arrival, was joined by an operations officer, Eugene Kolb. It was now that Barbie began what the Americans considered to be his most effective but also most sensitive work – the monitoring of communist activities in Bavaria. Senior officers in Stuttgart realised that he now knew more about American intelligence than most CIC officers. There was no alternative, they felt, but for the Army to protect him from the French. Kolb, who directed the detachment's work, was initially responsible for that protection.

Kolb was born in southern Germany and had emigrated to America aged seven in 1925. His war had ended at the Elbe and he was then attached to a 'T-force' to search for Nazis and documents – work which, he says, he did not like. He became much happier when the order came down that the intelligence priority was to discover the intentions and activities of the communists. Kolb believes himself above all to have been a professional intelligence officer and the intelligence priorities of the immediate post-war months disturbed him. There was excessive exaggeration of the danger of a Nazi conspiracy which then switched to an obsession with a potential communist conspiracy. What cemented his relationship with Barbie was their mutual understanding, 'a common psychological community of interest' between professionals about intelligence work. Kolb sentimentally remembers that 'meeting of souls' between himself and Barbie, where both recognised the communist danger but derided those who interpreted everything as a communist conspiracy.

Kolb's first task was to assess the output of the Augsburg detachment. After scrutinising all the files, his ten-page memorandum concluded that the Merk network had become expensive and worthless, 'It dawned on people at all levels that it was all hogwash. His system did not really exist. We were getting false information, like a paper mill.' Kolb recommended that the network be dissolved while retaining some of its best assets, of which Barbie was one. Browning ordered its disbandment in April 1949. Only Barbie was to be retained to recruit informants. Their mission was officially restricted purely to counter-intelligence. Headquarters were soon to decide that American CIC agents and not the Germans should be in charge of the networks. Intentionally, it led to greater control but also closer involvement between Bechtold and Kolb, and Barbie. At the height of the cold war, with the blockade of Berlin by the Russians, the employer/employee or victor/vanquished relationship had simply vanished. They were now equal partners in a common struggle. Yet according to Earl Browning, Barbie's use, both in scope and importance, was severely limited by directives sent from headquarters. Those directives were rejected by Munich and according to Kolb did not exist.

Neither Kolb nor Bechtold were concerned in any moral or legal sense about Barbie's war-time crimes. Bechtold openly admits that during the one-and-a-half years in which he became a friend of Barbie, they discussed his brutal methods on many occasions. He still admires Barbie as an intelligence officer and has no qualms about events in Lyons. 'The way he explained it, when they caught Resistance people in the act, there was just no time to lose. They needed the names of the others fast and in war anything goes.' For Bechtold that was an understandably pragmatic approach which he too adopted when asked how he could work so closely with a known, notorious Gestapo officer: 'I was just obeying my orders.' Kolb, on the other hand, completely denies that anyone knew about Barbie's war crimes, 'If we'd known, we wouldn't have used him.' Yet he admits that Barbie was known to be a former Gestapo officer. 'You've got to make a sharp distinction between fighting the Resistance and the Jewish thing. Deporting the Jews was a war crime and we didn't know about it. Nor did the French ever mention it.'

'He struck me,' says Kolb, 'as the sort of interrogator who didn't need torture, and he indicated to me that he subscribed to the theory among all good interrogators that you don't use torture. We probably suspected on one or two occasions that he might have used the rubber-hose technique, but he denied all that and frankly I was even sceptical of the French accusations.' Surprisingly, Kolb even denies that he ever knew that Barbie's name featured on a CROW-CASS list. Coolly, Kolb explains how the CIC in 1949 calculated the problem about Barbie's continued use as, 'Cost = minimal, benefit = enormous.'

Their respect for Barbie stemmed from observing his method of interrogation. Like apprentices watching a master artist, they saw, as Kolb put it, 'how to milk a source'. After discussing the content of his reports during their regular meetings in a safe house, Kolb and Barbie would discuss the techniques of interrogation. Kolb, like many Americans, had been through a British interrogation course in the Cotswolds and was confident about his expertise, 'but Barbie knew it all. He was shrewd, extremely intelligent, good in manipulating human beings, too good.' When Kolb was confronted with a few cases where he had made no progress, he summoned Barbie. 'In one case I was convinced the suspect was a communist agent. Barbie told me I was wrong. Of course I accepted his judgement. He always said use guile not duress . . . except where a bit of duress is needed.'

Beneath this respectful attitude, the two expatriate Germans undoubtedly shared a feeling of kinship with Barbie and also a desire to understand their own country. At dinner in Barbie's house with the family and his mother, Bechtold would listen intently to Barbie's accounts of Nazi life, his admiration for Kaltenbrunner, and the problems of fighting the Resistance. Kolb, in contrast, believes that Barbie was neither anti-semitic nor a fervent Nazi, 'He was just a fellow traveller.' As far as Bechtold was concerned, Barbie had applied to join the judicial branch of the civil service and had just found himself in the 'security services'. Bechtold never calls it the Gestapo.

Under Kolb's direction, Barbie's work changed dramatically. Combined with the new directives to disband the German networks, headquarters had issued orders about new targets. The CIC was to work exclusively on direct penetration of the extremist parties in the American zone, which in reality meant the Communist Party. According to Kolb, although CIC agents were forbidden to cross the border, the regulation was ignored when 'operational requirements' demanded. It was an extension of the new 'positive intelligence' policy adopted in 1947. To emphasise the new aggressive approach, the 7970 CIC was renamed the 66th Intelligence Group, and Augsburg was no longer a sub-station under Munich but the self-governing Region XII.

With new orders came new tactics. Using blackmail, money, offers of sex, and exploiting people's greed, Barbie directed those antenna so admired by Kolb to attract informants inside the Bavarian KPD. In another change of tactics, Kolb also took the initiative and ordered Barbie to try and win over specific targets. As there was no longer any use for Merk, the new team was confined to Barbie and Bechtold, normally working from a safe house and not an American billet. Their secretary was Hans Müller, a former Gestapo officer wanted by the German police for murdering the 'Gebrüder Scholl' – two famous anti-Nazis whose speeches before their execution became an inspiration for post-war Germans, including Beate Klarsfeld. Müller's assets, according to Bechtold, were that he could act on their behalf when they were away and that he had 'excellent contacts with the local police and could always get them to help us'.

As Bechtold quickly discovered, one of Barbie's greatest assets was the *Kamaradenschaft*. With the lamentable failure of denazification, former high-ranking Nazis could be found in nearly every senior position, especially in the German police and security services. Repeatedly, Bechtold stood by in amazement as the unobtainable was secured by Barbie approaching a former SS officer. For example, with tighter German controls over the issue of identity and registration cards, the two found travelling through Bavaria with false identities increasingly difficult: immediately, Barbie sought out a former SS officer who had become chief of a local police force and gratifyingly provided everything. With one set of papers they posed as employees of a research bureau, with another they posed as journalists visiting Bavaria's leading politicians. As Bechtold looked on in wonder, Barbie engaged the latter in lengthy but polite off-the-record arguments, discovering their precise intentions. Considering the intelligence vacuum at the time, it was unique material, eagerly awaited by the highest levels of the American military government in Frankfurt. Neither they nor Bechtold were ever concerned that their whole operation depended on SS and Gestapo officers who had been intimately involved in appalling crimes.

Bechtold is quite honest about Barbie's power and influence. He relied on Barbie's judgement to decide whether a former SS man should be used or not, regardless of his past. Barbie, after all, was a good penetration expert: 'He had served his apprenticeship in other assignments before he arrived in France. In France he got the final polish.' Morality is not a known commodity in the intelligence world. The task at hand was always overriding. As Bechtold says of

Barbie, 'He was a man capable of genuine human emotions, as long as they did not interfere with his mission.' Sentiments which he easily understood. 'In working with him,' says Bechtold, 'I was just obeying orders.'

Their major success together was the penetration of the head-quarters of the Bavarian Communist Party. Kolb says that it was at the relatively low level of secretaries, chauffeurs and office staff, but Bechtold claims that Barbie successfully penetrated the highest ranks of the Bavarian Party. In Augsburg, Barbie had discovered that the secretary of a senior official was unhappily married, profes-sionally frustrated and in need of extra finance. With Bechtold's help, he convinced the woman to deliver regularly the minutes of the Party committee's weekly meeting which included the directives it was receiving from KPD headquarters in Frankfurt. Regularly she left an envelope at a dead-letterbox to be collected by Barbie. Communication between the two was by prearranged innocuous telephone calls followed by other letters. Disappointingly, the minutes revealed little more than might have been expected – arrangements for May Day parades, election manifestos, and de-mands that the Americans should leave Germany. But since few other CIC agents were delivering anything at all, the head of the 'communist desk' in Stuttgart, Daniel Benjamin, joined in support-ing Barbie's protection.

The next stage of the operation was, in Bechtold's view, a greater success. To ensure that their informant was not a double agent, Barbie insisted that they check the source in Berlin itself. Officially, the CIC was not allowed to cross the border, but inevitably these orders were ignored. Barbie selected 'Laib', an SS officer wanted for war crimes by the Norwegians, to organise the mission. 'Laib' brought back not only confirmation, but a bonus – the identity of a Czech agent in Bavaria. Spellbound with professional envy, Bech-told watched as Barbie interrogated the Czech, slowly and skilfully enmeshing their suspect in a web of self-contradictions until, con-fused and exhausted, he confessed and agreed to become a double agent. But that too turned out to be a disappointment when the Czech proved to be a triple agent and tried to ensnare them into Czechoslovakia.

Other approaches were blatantly unsuccessful. One senior KPD official approached by Barbie was threatened that failure to co-operate with the Americans would result in publication of documents showing that he had been a Gestapo informer during the war. This was just one of many 'dirty tricks' with which the American intelligence agencies were experimenting. Three days later the approach was exposed in the local communist newspaper, and the official disappeared shortly after.

Nevertheless, both Vidal and Lavoie at Tech Spec were convinced that Barbie was indeed proving his worth and that increasing French pressure on account of his war crimes should be ignored. They, like other Americans, were concerned with the future and not the past. To them it seemed that European obsessions with such sentimental irrelevancies could only harm the security of the west. Gehlen's new German secret service (BND) had quite blatantly recruited SS officers wanted for mass murder, and that had been approved by Washington. Among the many was General Bömelberg, the senior Gestapo officer in Paris. What distinguished him and the others from Barbie was that, although many of their victims were also Jews, with few exceptions their crimes had been committed in countries now ruled by the communists. Most important of all, they had not murdered Moulin. France was an important American ally and by the beginning of 1950, political pressure in Paris forced the government to intensify their demands for Barbie's extradition.

THE DECEPTION

The French investigation of German atrocities in Lyons began very slowly. After the Germans finally evacuated the town in the first days of September 1944, Lyons, like most other newly-liberated towns in France, burst into an orgy of lawless celebration and bloody recrimination. The immediate victims were collaborators who had somewhat foolishly not fled with the Germans. Throughout the region, cowed groups of terrified Frenchmen awaited the dispensation of justice. Those fortunate enough not to be summarily executed were incarcerated in Montluc and the other prisons where their victims had suffered. But after those heady days had passed, the problems facing the administrators were enormous. Not only did the physical damages of war have to be repaired, the administration of the country had to be reconstructed. Complicating these tasks was the war itself, which continued for a further eight months.

The Lyons police faced an unique problem. To purge their ranks entirely of collaborators would decimate them. To make matters worse, the town was suddenly confronted by an unprecedented wave of robberies and police who might otherwise have investigated German crimes were immediately diverted to prevent domestic banditry. There was also a political problem. The Gaullists were locked in a bitter power struggle with the communists and were unwilling to allow communist police officers the authority to initiate investigations. Since many police officers were former Vichy sympathisers, there was little to be expected from their investigating German crimes.

The examining magistrates were also handicapped by acute legal confusion. The French judicial system needed to be completely reorganised and purged before warrants could be issued; charges could only be made once French law had been considered and retrospectively altered by a new parliament. Many months passed before magistrates knew which new laws would be enacted giving them the powers to prosecute. Only adding to the turmoil, there was a continuous change of personnel, undermining any hope of persistent investigation.

In Paris, responsibility for war-crimes investigation was divided between the Ministries of Defence and Justice. Their agencies, the DST (the French MI5 or FBI), the Direction Générale des Etudes et Recherches (DGER), later the SDECE (MI6 or CIA), and the Police Judiciaire's 'Brigade Anti-Gestapo' all began nominal investigations in 1944. But even in the limited work which they did manage, there was little co-operation with other branches of the various police and security forces, with the examining magistrates or with the special commissions established nationally, departmentally and in each town. The proliferation of investigations hindered effective police work and coordination. In the ensuing chaos much evidence was lost, mislaid or never even collected.

The purging and reconstruction of the Lyons police and judiciary was only partially completed at the beginning of 1945. By then various agencies and officials had started their own uncoordinated investigation into Gestapo crimes. They all faced innumerable problems. With very few exceptions, all the Germans had disappeared, the victims who had survived often did not know the name of the German responsible, while the best informed were the collaborators whose evidence was clearly prejudiced, not least because they were about to be executed. The greatest obstacle was the immaculate destruction by the Gestapo of all their records before their departure.

Gradually the police and examining magistrates in towns and villages across the region collected statements and reports. Corpses were exhumed, massacres reconstructed and eyewitnesses found. (Much of this material was destined for Professor Mazel's *Mémorial de l'Oppression*, a horrific catalogue of Gestapo crimes.) Confounding the police investigation was their ignorance of the Gestapo's structure and chain of command. For four months Inspector Chandon of Brigade Ten sifted the limited evidence to produce, in June 1945, the first schematic explanation of power and organisation in the Ecole de Santé. With all its inadequacies, it still remains the definitive study and clearly shows that Barbie was the Gestapo chief working directly under Knab.

On 31 August 1945, exactly a year after Barbie left Lyons, the city's military tribunal issued a warrant for his arrest on charges of illegal arrests and murder. On 12 September another examining magistrate charged him with murder and arson. The charges were based on the murders in the Ecole de Santé, the deportations of members of the Resistance in Montluc, and his campaign around St Claude. There was no mention of Moulin, nor of the Jews. In fact it was merely a formal procedure. Thousands of warrants were being issued throughout France against Germans who were just faceless names, very often wrongly spelled. The Lyons magistrates could only hope that an Allied soldier would see Barbie's name on one of the many wanted lists and notify the French government representative at Baden-Baden. There was nothing else to be done. The American and British governments had consistently refused to allow French investigators to be attached to the Allied armies, and, because of the chaos in France, no French teams could be expected to operate in Germany for the foreseeable future. There the matter might have remained until today – with Barbie, like so many other officers of the Lyons Gestapo, living a prosperous life safe from prosecution in West Germany. His misfortune was the trial of René Hardy.

Until Hardy's first trial, very few Frenchmen had heard about Moulin and the events at Caluire. Moulin was after all dead, just one of many dead Resistance heroes. After Hardy's second escape, he fled to North Africa where some of the Resistance leaders were less convinced by the allegations made in France. After serving the Free French government, he returned at the Libération and was appointed director of the repatriation department in Frenay's new Ministry of Prisoners, in clear recognition of his services to the Resistance. The Caluire survivors were determined, however, that Hardy's treachery should not remain unpunished and with little effort initiated a secret investigation resulting in his arrest on 12 December 1944. Hardy's trial started on 20 January 1947 and ended four days later with his acquittal in the absence of any conclusive evidence. Aubrac and others were furious but helpless.

Just weeks later, the situation changed dramatically. The godfather of Roger Wybot, the head of the DST, was an administrator of *Wagons Lits*, the railway sleeping-car company. An employee told him that he had been the conductor on Hardy's train and actually saw him arrested by the police. As evidence, the railman produced the duplicate reservation slip for Hardy's couchette.

Hardy's whole defence was rendered worthless. His own lawyer described the trial as a 'legal fiction'. Hardy had insisted that he had jumped off the train after seeing the collaborator at the Perrache station. After Wybot's revelation, he admitted that he had lied and that he had in fact been interrogated by a Gestapo officer for eight hours; but he claimed that he had outbluffed the German and was allowed to leave Gestapo headquarters without compromising himself. Asked why he had lied, Hardy explained that, while in custody, he had learned of General Delestraint's arrest and feared that he might be blamed. Suddenly Hardy's fate was transformed from an internecine dispute between Resistance personalities into a national sensation. He was rearrested just two months after his acquittal. Moulin rapidly became a legend whose betrayal and death had to be avenged, and only one man could prove the betrayal – the Gestapo officer himself.

Responding to pressure from Resistance leaders in the government, several police and military agencies began looking for Barbie. One agency even spent considerable time finding a 'Paul Barby' in East Germany. Others confused Barbie with a French *milice* collaborator called Barbier who worked in Grenoble. It was in early 1948, after Barbie's release from interrogation, that an unknown American leaked Barbie's presence in Germany to the French. After lengthy secret negotiations between the DST and G2 in Oberursel, the Americans agreed that the French could question Barbie about Hardy in secret, on condition that they did not embarrass the Americans by either asking for Barbie's extradition or publicising the interrogation. The French, just anxious to discover the truth and apparently unconcerned about whatever crimes this particular German had committed, were quite prepared to accept any conditions.

The first session was held near Frankfurt on 14 May 1948. There were four Frenchmen present: Commissaire Louis Bibes, the examining magistrate, Major André Gonnot, the magistrate of the Paris military tribunal, Inspector Charles Lehrmann of the DST, and Lieutenant Jean Whiteway, a Canadian-born French liaison officer from Baden-Baden. Two further sessions followed on 18 May and 16 July in a house near Augsburg. During all three sessions, Americans remained in the room. The transcripts of the interrogations have so far not been released, but there is no doubt that Barbie told the French that Hardy was a traitor. They were, however, as much puzzled by the numerous contradictions in Barbie's account as French historians are today. Significantly, Barbie was not questioned about his war crimes or his wartime activities.

Despite the guarantees, news of Barbie's discovery had been quickly leaked to Capitaine Michel Poignet, the Lyons military magistrate responsible for the Barbie case. Innocuously he wrote on 16 April to the DGER wondering whether there was any news of Barbie. The reply on 3 May conceded that Barbie had been found, but did not say where. Over the next weeks, Poignet pressed Gonnot to ask the Americans to extradite Barbie, but on 23 August Gonnot formally wrote that there was no hope of American help, on the grounds of 'interests of American security'. As consolation, he sent Poignet a photograph of Barbie. Poignet was not so easily placated. Considerable pressure had built up locally demanding punishment for the Gestapo officers, not least because so little had been done by the police during the four years since the end of the occupation. Poignet therefore completed a file on Barbie, listing the evidence of his known crimes, and sent it on 25 November to Baden-Baden, where Whiteway was based, with a request that they submit a formal request for Barbie's extradition. On 10 January 1949, the war-crimes investigation office in Baden-Baden replied to Poignet that Barbie was believed to be hiding in the Russian zone of Germany. But just eleven days later, on 21 January, Lieutenant Whiteway and another French officer interrogated Barbie yet again in Munich about the Hardy case. Vidal had refused to hand him over as a witness because he was convinced that he would be 'interrogated in the usual French manner' to reveal his CIC activities in the French zone. After two more interrogations, the French declared themselves as satisfied as was possible. Again, there was no mention of Barbie's war crimes. This was all of little comfort to Poignet, who thereafter was to have little confidence in the French ability to find Barbie. He nevertheless urged his fellow countrymen to submit the application for extradition.

Had the Allies still observed the solemn declaration signed in Moscow in 1943, Barbie's extradition to France would have been completed within at most a few weeks; but the change in the political atmosphere had affected the rules governing the handing over of war criminals. In the weeks after the war, the British and Americans had delegated individual extradition decisions to the unit on the spot. The only proviso was that the requesting nation had to produce a plain statement of facts (without even producing evidence of a prima facie case). The only exceptions were for the more important or valuable Germans. But despite the ease of obtaining suspected criminals, in the months following the war there were very few requests because of the chaos in each of the previously occupied countries. The demands for extradition only began in 1946 and by then the western Allies had become both suspicious and reluctant. The east European countries were asking not only for Germans but for their own nationals who had collaborated with the Germans. In the case of Yugoslavia, it was sufficient that the suspect was simply opposed to Tito. Nevertheless, extraditions continued, but with tighter safeguards.

By the beginning of 1947, the Allied military governors were under considerable pressure both from their own armies and from Germans to end the trials of war criminals. It was a natural progression that, if there were to be no further trials in the western zones, then Germans should not be dispatched to the hostile communist block where their chance of a fair trial seemed increasingly remote. In June, the British announced an end to trials and severe restrictions on extraditions. Six weeks later, on 30 July, Clay went even further and announced not only a complete end of trials, but also the end of extraditions after 1 November. Exceptions would only be made in cases where countries could convincingly explain why the request could not have been made before. Like many other countries, the French government immediately protested, claiming that their list of twenty thousand wanted criminals was growing daily and that their investigations had only just started. Clay, although severely criticised for unilaterally breaking an international obligation, rejected the complaint. He had after all retained the right to make individual exceptions personally, but that was for purely cosmetic reasons to forestall the charge that the American zone had become a sanctuary for war criminals.

For France to obtain Barbie's extradition, it now had to submit in English a very full and convincing dossier on Barbie's crimes and, after June 1948, the case had to be submitted to the Germans who required a formal extradition trial to judge whether there was a prima facie case. The biggest hurdle was the American regulation that the French, like all the other countries, had to provide the address where the suspect could be found. The French had been allowed to retain a mere six-man war-crimes team in the American zone and, as Poignet had already discovered, their head office in Baden-Baden was singularly incompetent.

It was just a few days after Kolb arrived in Augsburg in early 1949 that an acquaintance rang with the news that a French team was in town looking for Barbie. It was not the first time that the French, frustrated by American obstructions, had launched their own search party. Once, during Dabringhaus' stint as Barbie's handler, Barbie had escaped down the back steps as the French walked into the office through the front door. This time, Kolb ordered Barbie to stay hidden in his safe house for a week. 'I did that,' says Kolb, 'on my own initiative. I don't think we informed headquarters what was going on, but as I recall there were no directives from headquarters on this.' The 'bewildered' Americans pleaded ignorance and the French left.

There are three reasons given by Kolb and other CIC officers to explain why the CIC decided to protect Barbie. Firstly, they genuinely believed that his work was valuable. Secondly, they felt that his alleged crimes against the Resistance were in reality acts of war and that the French were in pursuit of revenge and not justice. Most of them also insist that they never had any idea of the atrocities of which Barbie was accused. Thirdly, and most importantly, they did not trust the French. France was, in the American view, riddled with communists and the Americans were in little doubt that the real reason behind pressure for Barbie's extradition was that the communist wing of the French security services wanted to interrogate Barbie about the extent of American penetration of the German Communist Party. 'If the French had got Barbie,' explains Kolb, 'I have no doubt that he would have been in Moscow within a few days.' For Barbie's part, he was more afraid that he would not even survive the interrogation on his return. His appearance at a trial, he ingeniously told his American friends, would have been too embarrassing for the French. Secretly, he feared charges of mass murder.

In May, on the eve of Earl Browning's final return to the United States, his unease at employing a former Gestapo officer appeared to be vindicated. On 14 May, a Paris newspaper briefly reported protests to the American ambassador by Lyons Resistance groups about the employment of Barbie. The piece summarised Barbie's terror tactics in the region, including the use of an acetylene torch in interrogations. Ten days later, Browning's office sent the small clipping to Major George Riggins, the commander of the newly named CIC Region XII based in Augsburg, for whom Kolb and Barbie now worked. Riggins was ordered to interrogate Barbie about the torture allegations, but without revealing the newspaper article. Riggins was told that headquarters had known about Barbie's 'successful missions' against the Resistance but had 'interpreted [them] as mere performance of his duty. It was not however known that such barbaric methods had been employed by Subject to obtain confessions from his victims. This headquarters is inclined to believe that there is some element of truth in the allegations.' Anticipating the worst, Browning ordered Riggins to drop Barbie 'administratively as an informant' but to maintain relations until the State Department and the Department of the Army had decided what to do. Kolb admits that, when he read Browning's orders, he was both 'puzzled and unhappy. It just didn't make sense.'

Eight weeks later Kolb reported that Barbie had been 'discreetly interrogated'. Barbie had admitted using 'duress during interrogations, such as interrogation over a long period of time . . . but has never implied or indicated that he used torture.' After again eulogising his work, Kolb concluded that Barbie 'is intelligent and skilful enough to accomplish a successful interrogation by use of his head and consequently did not require the use of his hands.' On balance, Kolb believed Barbie rather than the French. But, for the record, headquarters was told that Barbie had been (or would be) 'dropped . . . as an informant'. It was a purely cosmetic statement and, to minimise the dangers of future embarrassment, communications inside the CIC about Barbie were to be kept strictly 'Top Secret'. Obsessively fearing that Barbie might still offer his services to another government, Kolb was ordered by Vidal to make sure that Barbie remained unaware of all the problems, especially by continuing the payment of his regular allowance. Until then, the CIC could justify Barbie's use on grounds of their own self-inflicted ignorance. Although they knew he was a former Gestapo officer, and the organisation's record was by then well-documented, they deliberately denied themselves even a glimpse at the wealth of unconcealed evidence of his crimes. Their predominant concern was their own convenience and the fight against Communism.

On 7 June 1949, the first formal French request to the Americans to help find Barbie was sent to the US Military Government (OMGUS) in Frankfurt. Significantly, it mentioned that Barbie was wanted for 'war crimes', the first time the charge was officially made. OMGUS, who knew nothing about Barbie, forwarded the request to the Munich police. With typical efficiency, the reply from the chief of Munich's criminal police department arrived two weeks later. Barbie, he wrote, had not registered in the Munich area; but he added helpfully that Barbie's name would be included in the police wanted list as a murder suspect. When Region XII discovered the listing in April 1950, they tried unsuccessfully to get it removed. Before the German police had replied, the French had already written to the US Military Government in Munich asking for their help to find him.

Poignet, increasingly frustrated, went even further and asked the political adviser in the French zone to appeal for assistance to HICOG (the American High Commission, successor to the Military Government in the US zone). His approach was eventually answered by an expression of regret and a plea of ignorance, very puzzling for Poignet since the Americans had produced Barbie at least three times for interrogation. A year earlier Gonnot had told him that the Americans were protecting Barbie; now it was to be spelled out in greater detail.

On 28 July 1949, M. Schmelk, the head of the Justice division in Baden-Baden wrote to the French Government Commission for German and Austrian Affairs enclosing Barbie's address in Memmingen, which unknown to him was long outdated. He ended his letter thus:

> I feel I must respectfully point out that Barbie is protected by the American authorities and it is possible that these authorities will not help our inquiries, so preventing us completing the formalities for a valid application for extradition. The application must include not only the real identity and description of the person concerned, but also a residence certificate which can only be authorised by the Public Safety Officer in the region. You should be aware that the security division, the political adviser and the liaison services, are all involved in this affair.

Poignet was given Barbie's outdated address a month later.

The pressure for Barbie's extradition again increased but it was still primarily motivated to ensure his appearance at the forthcoming second trial of Hardy. Several members of the French parliament, anxious for Hardy's conviction, urged the government to raise the issue with the Americans in Washington. The government hesitated. Ministers were unwilling to embarrass the Americans on something relatively minor when Washington's urgent help was needed on a whole range of major issues affecting France's very survival. Moreover, in Paris, there was still only scant concern about a possible trial for Barbie's crimes against the people of Lyons and the region; there was no mention whatsoever of charging him with the deportation of the Jews to Auschwitz, although the telegram signed by Barbie announcing the deportation of the forty-one children from Izieu had actually been produced and cited by the French prosecutor at the Nuremberg trial in 1946. Nevertheless, urged on by Poignet, the Ministry of Foreign Affairs finally asked the French ambassador in Washington, Henri Bonnet, to approach the State Department and ask for Barbie's arrest and extradition. His request was passed on to the office of John McCloy (Clay's successor, now called the American High Commissioner, at HICOG) who cabled back to Washington: *We have no record of request for extradition of Barbie Klaus by French*. An accurate but inevitably unhelpful statement. At that stage no US organisation other than the CIC knew about Barbie. On 6 December the ambassador described to Robert Schumann, the Foreign Minister, the result of his efforts: the State Department had been told by the High Commission in Frankfurt that they had no knowledge of Barbie and had therefore suggested that the French should contact HICOG in Germany.

Yet just two days later Inspector Aimé Ferrier, an officer of the Police Judiciaire, interrogated Barbie near Augsburg about a collaborator, Lucien Doussot, who was charged with treason. Supporting his former colleague, Barbie formally denied that Doussot was involved in fighting with the Gestapo and Ferrier sent his report to the Lyons magistrate. Bechtold remembers that because Barbie was more concerned than usual for his safety, Captain Hugo Sandford was brought specially from Munich to 'babysit' him. Sandford's credentials were impressive. He had been awarded the Légion d'Honneur, which he wore in his lapel, and spoke fluent French. The interrogators were apparently sufficiently intimidated and did not stray from the agreed questions.

Bechtold also remembers why Barbie was suddenly offered to the French on this occasion. 'The army was embarrassed because the French had been given the run-around in Heidelberg. McCloy's office brought pressure on us to admit his presence. So we had to allow the interrogation.' Yet, the US Department of Justice investigation in 1983 into the American connection with Barbie reported that, at that time, HICOG was completely ignorant about Barbie's existence. After that interrogation, Region XII asked CIC headquarters what it should do with Barbie in the future. Its orders were to stay in contact with Barbie, to pay him from the Confidential Funds, and to have him available either for further interrogation or for extradition.

The scenario was now set for an extraordinary farce which would play for the next fourteen months. On the one hand, the State Department, HICOG in Frankfurt, the army command in Heidelberg, CIC headquarters in Stuttgart and the CIC office in Augsburg were all performing a charade of denials; on the other side, the exasperated French were trying to use every channel available to discover Barbie's elusive custodian.

The play started with a letter from SDECE to Colonel Camadau, the government commissioner at the Paris permanent military tribunal. Camadau had asked whether SDECE could negotiate Barbie's appearance as a witness in Hardy's trial. On 13 February 1950, SDECE replied that the Americans would be willing to release him as a witness on condition that he would only be in France for a limited period and that the French would guarantee his return to Germany. After three weeks' thought, Camadau's superiors, not unreasonably, rejected the offer because, 'The witness is a war criminal . . . wanted by the French authorities.' To fulfil the American conditions would be 'impossible and at least inopportune'. Hardy's second trial started on 24 April 1950 without the star witness, and ended on 8 May in a sensational acquittal. Many more Frenchmen were infuriated than had been over the first acquittal because they were now all aware that the Gestapo officer was enjoying a protected existence in Germany. To the French officials it now seemed impossible for the Americans to deny any knowledge of Barbie's address, especially because of the December interrogation. Pride and honour now demanded that the Americans be forced to extradite Barbie.

The Counsellor for Judicial Affairs at the French High Commission in Baden-Baden, M. Lebegue, sent two letters at the beginning of March emphatically establishing the French demand. On 2 March he wrote to Elizabeth Lange in HICOG's justice division, setting out at length Barbie's wartime crimes and French efforts for his extradition. He concluded, 'Public opinion in France, and especially in Lyons and its vicinity, is now aware of the presence of Barbie in the US zone, and if this individual were not brought to trial, it would not fail to create a strong and legitimate emotion among the population.' In his second letter, on 6 March, to Robert Bowie, HICOG's general counsel working in McCloy's office, Lebegue emphasised the importance the French now attached to the issue and asked Bowie to use his influence to find a solution. The initial American reaction was to disbelieve the French assumption of Barbie's presence in the American zone. The allegation was, wrote James McGraw, the Chief of HICOG's Public Safety Branch, rashly, 'unjustified and unwarranted'. He refused to initiate any inquiries without more information. A draft order alerting all American law enforcement agencies to arrest Barbie was left unsigned by Bowie. The only concession Lebegue won was that HICOG was prepared to consider the application, without the French providing Barbie's address. It was clearly a near-worthless concession. On 25 April the chief of the justice division replied to Baden-Baden asking in whose office Barbie had been interrogated by the French in 1946 (*sic*), the names of the Americans present and information about Barbie's address and his date and place of birth.

The unsatisfactory American reply arrived in the middle of the Hardy trial. Maurice Garçon, Hardy's lawyer, had just launched an emotional attack against the Americans for protecting Barbie and preventing him personally giving evidence in the court. The French press immediately demanded an explanation from EUCOM, the American army command in Heidelberg which was in overall command of the CIC. EUCOM did not know about Barbie at the time. It was natural that it should fall to Joe Vidal to give EUCOM's press office a 'Top Secret' background briefing. He knew more about Barbie than anyone else.

168

After explaining that Barbie had ceased to be employed by the CIC as an informant exactly a year earlier (which was untrue), he summarised Barbie's career, and the series of French interrogations of Barbie which had been willingly arranged by the CIC, and concluded that Garçon's accusation that the American army was protecting Barbie was, 'a malicious distortion of fact'. The same day, 3 May, Vidal handed Colonel Erskine a detailed five-page history of Barbie's relationship with the CIC. After again criticising Garçon's distortions, he suggested that Barbie could be extradited to France without endangering American operations because his network in the French zone had been liquidated. The following day, Vidal's recommendation was rejected by Erskine at a top-level CIC meeting. Erskine decided that Barbie should remain under American protection. As far as he was aware, after all, the French had still not asked for his extradition and he comforted himself with the suspicion that they feared that on his return he would denounce important Frenchmen as collaborators.

Until then, the CIC had been relatively immune from direct pressure, but only the previous day, 2 May, HICOG was suddenly faced with demands from the American embassy in Paris for help and information. HICOG replied the same day that the French accusations of American protection were 'unjustified and unwarranted'. Yet, the very next day, HICOG sent another urgent cable to Paris stating that new information had been discovered which made the previous day's cable 'possibly . . . inaccurate or incomplete'. Clearly someone at HICOG had spoken to an informant at Army headquarters, EUCOM, and heard that there was some truth in the French allegations. At issue now was, what should HICOG say to the French government and press. HICOG's files for the days immediately after 3 May contain urgently redrafted letters to Lebegue referring to 'recently received clues which may enable us to find him'. But the letters were not sent.

Politicians in Paris were now concerned that the irksome failure of the authorities in Baden-Baden might reflect on them. Summaries of French attempts to locate Barbie were submitted and considered, but there still seemed to be no easy solution other than to find Barbie, despite American protection. A final effort by the war-crimes bureau in Baden-Baden was attempted at the end of May but the agent's terse and coded telegram report from Munich spelled failure, *Durand not found*. Incompetently, the French investigators had failed to exploit another lead from a sympathetic American: the address of Barbie's mother in the French zone itself.

Fearing that the formal request for extradition would once again be ignored by HICOG, the Ministry of Foreign Affairs decided to submit the application at the beginning of June through their embassy in Washington. But once again they were stonewalled. The hapless Bonnet reported to Schumann on 21 June that the State Department, 'have just replied that they do not have in their possession any new information permitting the discovery of the present residence of the party concerned. But they have contacted the American High Commission requesting any new information.' The French could now draw only one conclusion: not only were the Americans lying to them, they were also lying to one another.

What remains uncertain is whether HICOG was ever told the complete truth of Barbie's relationship with the CIC until, or even after, 3 May. According to the official documents so far declassified and produced by the US Department of Justice in 1983, HICOG officials were told that the CIC's relationship with Barbie was completely broken on 28 April, the date when negotiations for Barbie's possible return to France as a witness collapsed. HICOG officials, according to the Department of Justice report, unquestioningly believed the CIC's account that the agency had lost all contact with Barbie after that date. It is an assumption based solely on the absence of documentary evidence to prove the contrary. It deliberately excludes any possibility of verbal agreements which were not recorded. Considering the disappearance and loss of other equally crucial documents, the report's conclusions that HICOG was innocent of any participation in a cover-up, and that the CIC was exclusively culpable, raised more questions than it answered – principally, whether HICOG officials were so naive and incompetent as to believe that the CIC would lose complete contact with an agent whom the CIC admitted was better informed than most about its operations, and an agent whom they had long feared as a possible cause of considerable embarrassment. Relying on flimsy documentary evidence, the report assumes that HICOG officials unquestionably accepted that, after a three-year relationship, CIC officials had simply lost contact with Barbie after a few days. Even James McGraw, HICOG's Chief Public Safety Officer, did not

170

believe that and decided on 5 May 1950 to renounce all responsibility for the case. There is no evidence, either oral or documentary, that any of McGraw's agents actually went to the CIC in Region XII and asked Kolb or Bechtold about Barbie's whereabouts. McGraw's legacy was that the only available explanation which HICOG's political and legal sections could give the French was that Barbie had 'disappeared' from his last known address.

The ultimate responsibility for Barbie's protection is John McCloy's. He was the senior American official in the zone and his office indisputably dealt with the problem. But both McCloy and his assistant, John Bross, not surprisingly deny any recollection of the French demands: there were, they claim, thousands of telegrams and files passing through the High Commissioner's office daily. Nonetheless, the policy guidelines for handling a case such as Barbie's had been very carefully set out by McCloy. On his arrival in 1949, he had inherited from Clay the problem of reviewing the convictions of 104 defendants at the subsequent trials in Nuremberg. Among them were some of the architects of the Final Solution – the leaders of murder squads, senior officers from concentration camps, some of Germany's most prominent industrialists and the SS officers who had ordered the execution of the American POWs at Malmédy. McCloy had arrived in Germany with an attitude of antagonism towards the already deep-rooted German desire to minimise responsibility and even dispute the occurrence of atrocities. Yet within a year German pressure, the intense division of Europe, the fear of a communist coup in Italy and the developing threat of war in Korea had forced him to adopt a more pragmatic approach. The West now urgently needed the support of German industry and its military experience. The price McCloy would have to pay included the reprieve and release of most of the 104 Nazi mass murderers. In that context, the French demand for a Gestapo captain who was obtaining useful information about the communists, would not be pursued with excessive energy.

In June, McCloy was under pressure both from Washington and Paris to produce some answers. Ben Schute, director of HICOG's Office of Intelligence, was ordered to 'smoke EUCOM out'. McCloy wanted a full account of the Barbie saga from Brigadier General Robert Taylor, EUCOM's Director of Intelligence. Schute met Taylor and Browning's successor, Major Wilson, on 16 June.

He was allegedly told that Barbie's employment with the CIC had ceased on 24 May 1949 (on Browning's orders), and that the CIC had lost contact with Barbie in late April 1950. Schute's report was written five days after the meeting. He claimed in 1983 to have completely forgotten his involvement in the affair: 'I probably just wrote down whatever Taylor told me.' The Department of Justice Report states that Taylor and Wilson lied outright to Schute and that Schute, in his honest ignorance, simply accepted their assurances. It would, however, be quite ridiculous for HICOG's Director of Intelligence not to have queried the extraordinary coincidence of Barbie's disappearance just days before the sensational attack at the Hardy trial. But there was apparently no pressure on him from either McCloy's office or HICOG's political section to look into the glaring inconsistencies. On the contrary, in June 1950, Allan Lightner, the deputy political director (who ignorantly persisted in referring to Barbie as 'Barbier'), proposed to continue the inactivity in the 'hope that the whole business will blow over'. That inactivity included an undocumented but nevertheless official veto on any actual search for Barbie.

Confirmation of Schute's and HICOG's implicit awareness and approval of the CIC conspiracy to protect Barbie surfaced on 30 August. The CIC had received what seemed a routine request from HICOG asking whether it objected to Barbie's extradition, if found. The CIC knew the French were pressing for extradition but believed that the result of the meeting with Schute was that Barbie would not be handed over. Joe Vidal, who had heard about the 'agreement' from either Erskine or Wilson, queried this request with his superiors; but, after rapid consultation, the CIC headquarters realised that while it was important to be seen to agree to Barbie's extradition, it would in practice be meaningless.

At the top governmental level there was little more that could be done. When Schute reported to McCloy that the American army had lost all trace of Barbie, McCloy passed the message on to Washington, and in turn to the French ambassador. As a polite palliative, he was also told that the search for Barbie was continuing.

Those officers in army headquarters in Heidelberg who had allegedly given Schute the deliberately blurred 'negative' answer were now growing concerned at the stream of inquiries about

Barbie. They were irritated by reports that a senior CIC officer in Stuttgart had become drunk at a Saturday night party and loudly declared to his French guests that he would never surrender Barbie. A senior official in McCloy's office told the army that HICOG were now finding it practically and politically impossible to resist telling Washington the truth. Something had to be done so that everyone was covered. The message was passed down and reached Kolb that Barbie should be 'taken off the books'. When he queried the order, Kolb was told that Barbie should still be used, but that his name and fees should be laundered through another agent's file. 'I told them it was ridiculous, and it was ignored.' Bechtold had been told in June that he was to be reassigned. The reason, which he was ordered not to pass on to his friend, was that Barbie's career with the Americans was coming to an end. With very little notice, Bechtold handed Barbie over to Lieutenant Joe Strange and an apprentice agent, Leo Hecht. A few weeks later, Bechtold phoned Hecht and asked about Barbie. 'The whole family,' replied Hecht, 'are learning Spanish.'

During the autumn of 1950, Barbie continued to ply his trade, obtaining information on the Bavarian KPD and passing it on to Strange. CIC positive-intelligence operations were by then being taken over gradually by the newly formed Central Intelligence Agency. With the CIC acting as temporary agent for the CIA, Barbie had two masters, the CIA vetting all his work at Stuttgart headquarters. The targets, however, remained the same. Nevertheless, it was now just a matter of time. Fearing a French snatch, even Barbie wanted to leave for South America. Shortly before Kolb left Augsburg at Christmas, he took an urgent phone call from Stuttgart: 'Get rid of Barbie. No more contacts.' French pressure, says Kolb, had become too strong. 'It was an absolutely sudden reversal, a reversal in just a space of a week or two. It must have come because of high-level pressure from headquarters.' Although still an asset, Barbie had become a liability. The escape plan had already been finalised; Kolb bid Barbie goodbye, believing that he would never hear about him again. Meanwhile, HICOG's Legal Division wrote several polite letters to the French, regurgitating yet again the various listings of Barbie as a wanted man, and in the meantime ponderously arranged a formal extradition hearing, concluding with a letter on 31 January 1951, '. . . concerning Klaus Barbie, whose extradition to France as a war criminal is desired. We take this opportunity to advise you that continuous efforts to locate Barbie are being made. Very truly yours . . .' Five weeks later Barbie and his family had left Augsburg, escorted by George Neagoy, who was about to join the Central Intelligence Agency.

THE RAT LINE

Barbie and his family escaped from Europe down the 'Rat Line', an efficient, well-funded route, established with official approval by the US Army's 430 CIC in Austria. The Rat Line had been set up in 1947 by Jim Milano and Paul Lyon, to help American agents and sympathisers out of the Russian zone in Vienna down to safety in Salzburg in the American zone. The 'shipments' were mostly Russian defectors and valuable contacts who had worked for the Americans in Soviet-occupied Europe and were suddenly vulnerable. According to Milano, 'As a reward for services, we settled them in different parts of the world.'

Once in Salzburg, Milano and his three-man team would put the 'body' in a safe house, known as the 'rat house', and set about processing. Invariably the safest destination for the 'body' was South America, especially certain countries with ports – Chile, Peru, Brazil and Colombia. The only potential obstacles were the documents, passports and visas necessary for safe passage through the many checkpoints and borders of Europe and thence into South America. But these were not a problem for Milano. At his disposal was a laboratory where his experts forged and altered documents, passports and identity cards of every nationality, including American. Milano is insistent that forgery was not always necessary: 'documents could be bought. One of our good sources was in the Italian State department. Bribery was a key element in this business.' Another important supplier in Rome was an American diplomat in the International Refugee Office who eventually became an alcoholic and an embarrassing liability. Finance was supplied to Milano, with his superiors' approval, from the intelligence fund.

Every Rat Line operation was meticulously rehearsed, step by step, to prevent any embarrassment to the American government. 'We would never let a Rat Line product out of our sight,' says Milano. When the paperwork was completed, his three-man team, with the 'body' dressed in an American uniform, drove in an army jeep down to Bad Gastein and proceeded, with the jeep, by train

175

through the Alps to the Italian border. There a 'friendly' customs official waved the party through and the four headed for either Naples or Genoa, depending on the availability of the next ship across the Atlantic.

The contact in Genoa was Krunosla Draganovic, a Croatian priest whom Milano called 'the good Father'. Draganovic had been discovered by Lyon on one of the earliest Rat Line operations in Trieste and had proved to be enormously valuable for the American operation, not least through his good contacts with displaced persons organisations managing quotas for emigration to South America. At the time, the South American countries were eager to attract skilled labour. Draganovic briefed the Rat Line team on the particular skills needed by each country: it was then a simple matter of filling in the 'body's' profession on the documents. Draganovic's fee was about $1,000 per person (half-price for children) and there was a special rate of $1,400 for VIP treatment. Invariably there were delays in the port, so a small hotel was selected where no questions would be asked: 'The escort would babysit in the hotel, not letting the shipment out of sight until the ship's departure. Then we would walk him right up to the gangplank, turn him over to somebody aboard the ship who knew that this was a special person who had to be taken care of, and that was the end of the Rat Line.' No one left Europe with less than $1,000 and some left with as much as $8,000, in recognition of their services and to help them start their new life. Barbie is said to have been given $5,000, although he was later to admit to the Bolivians that he possessed only $850.

Who it was who actually decided to put Barbie onto the Rat Line is still unknown. The key CIC documents recording the decision, according to the Justice report, 'disappeared' apparently just before the file was microfilmed in 1951. Amnesia has severely afflicted all those who are still alive and were directly involved in the decision in Augsburg, Stuttgart and Frankfurt, including the CIC commander, Colonel David Erskine. Many files have not been declassified, not only those of the CIC but also files from EUCOM and HICOG. According to the available evidence, EUCOM gave the final approval on 25 January 1951.

Barbie's entry into the Rat Line was with George Neagoy, from 430 CIC's B detachment, based in Linz. Leo Hecht, a twenty-three-year-old German-born Jew, had been ordered by Kolb's successor

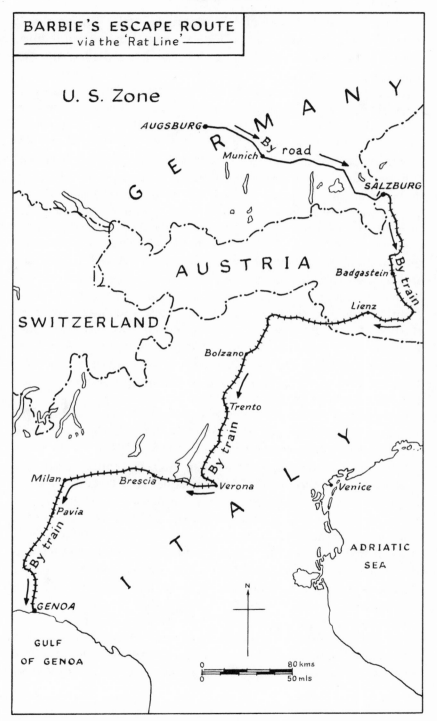

BARBIE'S ESCAPE ROUTE
— via the 'Rat Line' —

U. S. Zone

GERMANY

AUGSBURG

Munich

By road

SALZBURG

AUSTRIA

Badgastein

By train

SWITZERLAND

Lienz

Bolzano

Trento

By train

Milan

Brescia

Verona

By train

Pavia

Venice

By train

ITALY

ADRIATIC
SEA

GENOA

N

GULF
OF GENOA

0   80 kms
0   50 mls

at CIC Region XII, Wasel Yarosh, to help the Barbie family prepare for evacuation: at Neagoy's request, he now procured passport photographs of Barbie and the family, provided suitcases and other minor necessities for the journey from Augsburg and arranged a meeting between Barbie and his mother for their final farewell. Fearing that French agents might be following the mother to find her son, the meeting was arranged with all the finesse of a top-secret operation. Barbie's mother was ordered to take a circuitous route from Trier to Augsburg; Hecht, dressed in civilian clothes, met her at the railway station; he used a specially procured undercover car, and was ordered to be present throughout the farewell to ensure that Barbie did not reveal his future plans. According to Hecht, Barbie was 'looking forward to and rather expectant' about his new life. When Neagoy had finally collected the family (Yarosh himself drove them to an autobahn restaurant and handed them over), Hecht remembers feeling that, 'without Barbie, Augsburg was rather empty. He'd made such an enormous contribution. And we had no idea then what he'd done in France.' Both Milano (who left Europe in 1950) and his successor, Jack Dobson, who authorised Barbie's 'evacuation', insist that they would never have approved use of the Rat Line for 'shipping' Gestapo officers. But by then CIC in Augsburg and Stuttgart was quite proficient at lying about their star asset.

Neagoy had returned to Augsburg with Jack Gay, another CIC agent, on 9 March. He brought with him a temporary travel document for stateless people, no. 012,145,4, issued by the Combined Travel Board at the American High Commission office in Munich on 21 February 1951. It was either forged by 430 CIC or obtained under false pretences. In it Barbie was described as one Klaus Altmann, born on 25 October 1915 in Kronstadt, Germany, a mechanic by trade. His children, Ute and Klaus, were stated to have been born in Kassel on 30 June 1941 and 11 December 1946. He was also given a transit visa, no. 1,507, allegedly issued by the Italian consulate in Munich, which allowed the family to travel to the Italian port.

Neagoy loaded the family onto an American army truck and drove them across the border to Salzburg. From here, two days later, since it was impossible with two children to travel as American soldiers, the family continued by train for Genoa. Their destination, according to their travel documents, was the American port at Trieste. The only complication arose at the Austrian border, where the customs official queried the documents. According to Barbie, 'I said to him, "Look, I've got children . . ." and he shouted at me, "Get going, and I don't want to see you again." I replied, "You can be sure of that."'

The meeting with Draganovic in Genoa was like a natural homecoming for Barbie. Before the war, Draganovic had been professor at the faculty of Catholic theology in Zagreb. During the war, he was one of the leading clerics who favoured the forced catholicization of orthodox Serbs. With the rank of Lieutenant Colonel, he became a chaplain in the concentration camps to which the Serbs were sent. For those Serbs who resisted catholicization, the Ustachi, who collaborated with the Germans, used methods of torture which even very few Germans practised during the war. The domestic holocaust between the nationalities in Yugoslavia was a sideshow of which the world was largely ignorant but the casualties were staggering. Hundreds of thousands died at the behest of Catholic priests and, many have suspected, with the cognisance of the Vatican.

At the end of the war Draganovic, like many other senior Ustachi leaders, disappeared into western Europe, protected by the ignorance of the Allies and their growing distrust of Tito's government. Draganovic fled to the Vatican, was given sanctuary, and was then appointed to care for Croatian Ustachi imprisoned in Allied camps. While in the Vatican he met Bishop Alois Hudal, the representative of the Deutsche Nationale Kirche. Hudal, like many other clerics, had sympathised with the Nazis and other fascist governments because, in his view, only they could protect the Church against Russian communism. Following the collapse of the Third Reich, Hudal personally helped hundreds of incriminated Nazis, including senior Gestapo officials from Berlin and the officers of extermination camps, to leave Europe for South America on what has become known as 'the Vatican route'. Draganovic obtained from him the necessary introductions, firstly to the Red Cross officials who could provide an internationally accepted passport for Europeans anxious to leave the continent for a new life, and secondly to the network of consular, port and shipping officials who, for a bribe, could smooth the fugitive's path. In his original briefing to Milano, Lyon had described Draganovic as 'a Fascist, war criminal, etc.'. Nevertheless, the CIC still called him 'the good Father'.

According to Barbie, Draganovic was waiting for the family at the Genoa railway station holding a photograph sent ahead by Neagoy. He took the family directly down to a small hotel by the harbour whose other occupants, as Barbie would discover later, were all Nazi fugitives – among them Eichmann himself. George Neagoy travelled with the family to Genoa, supervised the travel arrangements and waited with them until their departure.

Over the next few days, according to Barbie, Draganovic organised their departure. Barbie's original intention had been to live in Argentina; he had obtained a letter of introduction to the government to ease his entry. But Draganovic convinced Barbie that, with its oil prospects, there was a better future in Bolivia. 'Draganovic knew a priest in Cochabamba and people on the way here also told me that it's always spring in Cochabamba.'

There were several matters for Draganovic to settle. The next ship leaving Genoa, the *Corrientes*, a converted liberty ship, was already full, with room only for Barbie. Draganovic bribed the shipping clerk with a large raw ham to cancel a previous reservation, freeing a cabin for the Barbie family. Their next call was to the Bolivian consulate: here Draganovic arranged a cabled request to La Paz for a residence permit. As a testimony to Draganovic's influence, the approval was granted within two days. Then they visited 38 Via Albaro, the Argentinian consulate. The officials greeted the visitors with 'Heil Hitler'. Barbie, naturally cautious, feared a trap but to his surprise they seemed genuine. He waited in an outer room while Draganovic took his five-year-old son, Klaus, into the official's office. They emerged shortly after with entry visas, dated 19 March. Their final call in this labyrinthine paper-chase was to the International Red Cross Commission who, seeing the Croatian priest, automatically granted a temporary passport for the Altmann family.

During that time Barbie established a friendly relationship with Draganovic. There were trips to nightclubs and restaurants. When Barbie asked why Draganovic was helping him, the answer was gratifying. '[His reasons] were purely humanitarian. He helped both Catholics and Protestants, but mostly they were SS officers, about two hundred in all. Anti-communists. He said to me, "We've got to keep a sort of reserve on which we can draw in the future." I think that was the Vatican's motive as well.'

Amongst hundreds of Italian immigrants, the family sailed in a third-class cabin from Genoa on 22 March, arriving in Buenos Aires exactly three weeks later. It was a pleasant journey. There were many other Nazi fugitives aboard, some of whom Barbie had glimpsed at the hotel: here was a chance to discuss the old days and the future. After six days in Argentina, the family set off finally by train for Bolivia. As a professional and dedicated intelligence officer, Barbie was to remain silent thereafter about his American connection.

The arrival in La Paz, in June 1951, was a depressing experience. At 12,000 feet above sea level, Barbie and his wife immediately succumbed to altitude sickness. Worse, most of his money had been spent in Buenos Aires or on the journey and he had less than one thousand dollars left. The family moved into one of the capital's dirtiest and cheapest hotels and Barbie set out immediately to walk the streets, looking for work: 'It would have been no use being a qualified lawyer in that situation. My only asset was what I had learnt in the Hitler Youth and afterwards.'

They had arrived in Bolivia just two weeks after the country's 169th change of government. Since winning independence in 1825, the poverty-stricken country has experienced 182 coups and 193 presidents. Its three million inhabitants, eking out their living from agriculture and tin mining, were ruled by a rich oligarchy many of whom were the children of German emigrants. Although very few Nazi fugitives went to Bolivia, most preferring the comparative wealth and comfort of the bigger South American states, a newly arrived German need not feel a complete outcast. Some sixty per cent of the country's economy was owned by the German community; German nationals trained and led the national army during the Thirties; and there had been many Nazi sympathisers in the provincial towns of Santa Cruz and Cochabamba during the war, often parading in Nazi uniforms. 'The Phalangists,' said Barbie twenty years later, 'were a comforting sight. It did me a lot of good to see them.' As in most other South American countries, the military in Bolivia played an important role in the nation's government and could but welcome the advice of someone with five years' experience of war in Europe.

181

The few people who remember seeing Barbie on his arrival describe a dirty tramp, doing the daily rounds, begging other Germans for enough coins to buy himself and his family the next meal. 'The first offer of work I got,' he says, 'was to repair twelve bunsen burners; I was really proud that I could do it.' His salvation was Hans Ertl, who had heard of a job as manager of a remote sawmill, high in the Los Yungas. Despite his complete ignorance of woodwork, Barbie left his family in the city and drove for two days in a truck up perilously winding rough mountain tracks, through the Cumbre pass, 4,650 metres above sea level, and down into the tropical mahogany forest at Caranavi, 2,000 metres above sea level. In the deep ravines below lay the rusting chassis of trucks which had missed one of the thousand bends. 'I never thought we would arrive; I knew nothing about wood, diesel engines or sawmills, and couldn't speak Spanish.' The estate was a hunter's paradise, filled with wild fowl, wild turkeys, deer and black bears. 'I spent three years there and recovered from the war.'

Barbie's immediate problem was to establish his authority over the eighty local Indian workers. 'I had to decide whether I should shout at them Prussian-style or say nothing because I couldn't speak Spanish.' He decided to say nothing but to impress them by working with them, setting himself apart, and instituting what he calls, 'some of our good National Socialist ideas'. Injured workers were given first aid, Barbie personally cleaning their wounds with alcohol and ointment. 'That really impressed them. They never forgot it, and I never had any problems.' Once he had established himself, his family joined him from La Paz; his wife managed the estate's grocery store.

Barbie had been hired after a two-question interview with Herr Riess, the general manager – 'Why do you want to work?' and, 'Where do you come from?' There were no questions about why Barbie had left Europe. It was not until a month after he was hired that Barbie met Ludwig Kapauner, the German estate owner, who had emigrated to Bolivia before the war. He arrived with four other people: 'A jeep drew up and five beautiful Jews stepped out . . . One day Kapauner came up to me and said, "Herr Altmann, do you know anyone else like you? I need them because I can't trust my own people." ' The appalling irony of this moment reduced Barbie to tears and laughter when he recalled it in 1979; and there was more

183

to come. Phalangists had daubed Kapauner's trees with Swastikas in his absence. Kapauner ordered their removal, and Barbie obediently obliged. Until Barbie's exposure in 1972, Kapauner never suspected Altmann's background and even promoted him to be his representative in La Paz. 'Altmann,' he told friends, 'is probably one of those unlucky Germans.'

As Barbie was settling into his new life in South America, the permanent military tribunal in Lyons was hearing eyewitness evidence of his crimes during the April 1944 campaign in the Jura and especially St Claude. By a majority verdict, on 29 April 1952, the seven judges sentenced him to death in his absence. A second trial started two years later, on 15 November, to judge the crimes committed by twenty-two Gestapo officers in Lyons. Barbie was again charged in his absence. Amongst the crimes mentioned were the massacre at St Genis-Laval and the shootings in Montluc. By a majority verdict, Barbie was found not guilty on various technical charges, but was convicted and sentenced to death for his crimes in Montluc. When the news reached him from Germany, he felt untroubled but realised that he would need to take some precautions for his safety.

In 1957 he was still using the temporary Red Cross documents obtained in Genoa as identification papers. Moving to La Paz had made it important to regularise his status, both for living in the city and so that he could leave Bolivia if necessary. The first and natural solution was to apply to the German embassy for a passport. Barbie's application was handled in the customary way, with requests for six photographs and birth and residence certificates. Herr Altmann's excuse, that they had all been lost during the war, was unacceptable to the consular official. Sensing potential danger, he quickly applied for Bolivian nationality.

Under Bolivian law, an applicant has to live ten years in the country before qualifying for naturalisation. But in Bolivia, as in all countries, laws are subject to flexible interpretation. As his Spanish had improved, Barbie had forged contacts with officials of the MNR party, a group which previously had been pro-Nazi, but more recently had swung to the left. Local party officials were delighted to meet an authentic ambassador from the Reich. After the embarrassment at the German embassy, Barbie quickly appealed to his new contacts for help and with little effort the statutory ten-year rule was ignored. The documents granting the Altmann family Bolivian nationality were signed on 7 October 1957 by Dr Hernán Siles Zuazo, then President of Bolivia. Twenty-six years later, when he returned to the presidency, he denied that his executive order was valid.

By 1960, Barbie was not wealthy but he had sufficient income from a sawmill which he founded in 1960 in Cochabamba, with a partner, for the family to live quite comfortably. A thoroughly sanitised version of his wartime services to Germany was common knowledge amongst the town's German community. At their small but racially exclusive German club, Barbie often spoke about the glories of the Third Reich, rousingly led the singing of the Nazi Party's *Horst Wessel* song, and gradually let slip that he had been more than a nominal supporter of the Third Reich. As the months passed, the crestfallen refugee recovered his old, bellicose self-confidence and blatantly displayed his former allegiance. Europe, the war and Lyons seemed far enough away.

The news from home was that, thanks to the Economic Miracle, Germany was booming, and the only memory of the wartime years was tinged with nostalgia. Prosecutions for war crimes in Germany had effectively ceased in the early Fifties, the new German government conveniently assuming that the occupying powers had cleaned up the mess and fulfilled the needs of justice. Bolivian newspapers in 1956 did not report the trial and conviction of eleven former Auschwitz guards in Ulm, not far from Augsburg, and no-one told Barbie. The evidence of their participation in the mass murder had horrified many Germans who, after the war, had been too concerned with their own struggle for survival to take notice of Allied propaganda about German atrocities. Surprisingly, until their arrest, the eleven had been living normal, exemplary lives, just like any other ex-servicemen. Their discovery had been an accident but their testimony, and their self-confessed effortless ability to avoid criminal investigation, embarrassed West German politicians. In the anguished debate which followed, Bonn was convinced, reluctantly, that most German war criminals had not fled to South America after the war, but had stayed and prospered in the Federal Republic. In 1958, the State Ministers of Justice agreed to create a central agency in Ludwigsburg to investigate German war crimes.

Ponderously, yet with characteristic methodical efficiency, thousands of Germans suspected of war crimes were listed for investigation. Every German police force was sent a list of suspects whose last known address was in their area. Barbie was listed automatically. One of Ludwigsburg's first inquiries was addressed to the American Army in Germany. It replied curtly but revealingly that all contact had been lost in 1951 'and his present whereabouts were unknown'.

In April 1961, police in Kassel went to 83 Eichwaldstrasse, the home of Carol Bouness, a relative of Barbie's wife. Unusually for this sort of inquiry, the police were not met by deliberate unhelpfulness but instead given a vital lead, and even more. Bouness did not like Klaus Barbie and told the police without hesitation that he had worked for the Americans in Augsburg and that Regine had written to her from Bolivia. As a throwaway line, she added that, according to Barbie's mother, the Americans had even helped the family escape. Having exhausted their own powers of inquiry, Ludwigsburg passed the case on to the prosecutor's office in Kassel. Despite Bouness's assertions of American help, this was still Barbie's last-known place of residence. This was the beginning of that bureaucratic process which has suffocated most West German investigations into war crimes. With some notable exceptions, the state prosecutors' lethargy, lack of interest, political prejudice and outright incompetence has left most of their 83,000 investigations unresolved. The Barbie file was set to share the same fate.

After a year's investigation, the Kassel police concluded that Barbie had been employed in Munich by the Americans as early as 1945, under cover as a tradesman. According to their investigations, Barbie had arrived in La Paz only in 1961 or 1962, and his wife had joined him only recently. They believed that he was still employed by both the CIA and the BND, the German secret service, and that he was in direct contact in Germany not only with his mother and aunt but also with his daughter, whose address was fully enclosed. It was a lamentable piece of investigation.

After months of inactivity, the Kassel prosecutor passed the file to the Augsburg prosecutor, because that was Barbie's last-known address; the Augsburg prosecutor decided that he could do nothing because Barbie was believed to be living in Bolivia, a country with which West Germany had no extradition treaty.

On 7 November 1963, a memorandum marked 'secret and confidential' and containing the results of the Kassel inquiry was sent from the French Sécurité Militaire (FSM) in West Germany to the investigation bureau at the Army Ministry in Paris. It concluded with the request that the Bureau ask the two French secret services to find Barbie in La Paz, but at the same time advise them of his use by the CIA and BND. The FSM also requested permission to intercept the Barbie family's mail and to tap their phones. They received no positive reply. General Jaquier, then head of the French Secret Service (SDECE) in Paris, denied in 1983 that he ever saw the memorandum: 'If I had, I would remember it.' The following year, on 28 September, General de Gaulle paid an official three-day visit to Bolivia. Whether or not he knew that the country was harbouring the murderer of his wartime delegate to France, we do not know; but there were more important matters on his mind.

Twenty years after the war, de Gaulle's visit reinforced Barbie's sense of security. Despite the spectacular kidnapping in 1960 of Adolf Eichmann from Argentina by a Mossad squad sent specially from Israel, Klaus Altmann was convinced that his real identity was truly buried. When the German ambassador came in March 1966 as an honoured guest to the German club, the former Gestapo chief stood up during the toast to Germany's continuing prosperity and shouted 'Heil Hitler'. It was just the latest in a series of Nazi slogans and anti-semitic taunts with which he had amused the club members. But the ambassador reacted with honest horror, demanding Barbie's immediate expulsion. As he was hustled out of the club, he is alleged to have shouted, 'Damn you, ambassador. I was an officer of the Gestapo.' By now, however, Barbie was too important in Bolivia to be seriously affected. After the 1964 military coup by General René Barrientos, Barbie's relations with influential army officers rapidly intensified. He did not participate openly in military operations, but they shared a common language and shared their experiences.

Overnight, Barbie became not only influential but rich. 'For the first time, I was a war profiteer,' Barbie told General Wolff. The war in question was in Vietnam; Barbie's profits came from selling chinin – a wood bark used for the manufacture of quinine – to Von Böhringer, the German chemical company in Mannheim. For Eberhard Büttner, Böhringer's South American representative,

Barbie's sawmill in La Paz was an ideal base for stripping wild chinin trees. Büttner's contract was with Herr Hochhauser, the mill owner, but the profits were divided with Barbie, who by then possessed considerable expertise in wood. Alone, or by mule with Büttner, Barbie drove into the Bolivian wilderness to negotiate with wood dealers for a regular supply of bark to his mill in La Paz, for shipping via Chile to Germany. As the American casualties in Vietnam increased and demand for quinine grew, Büttner returned to La Paz and suggested that Barbie and Hochhauser try to cultivate chinin trees. Seed and saplings were shipped from the Congo and planted 300 kilometres from La Paz. Barbie claims that the project was a great success – 'Only two of the 200 trees died.' Von Böhringer said that the project was a disastrous failure and that the plants died of disease. In the early Seventies, as American involvement in the war diminished, the chinin business slowly disappeared. Barbie's claim that he earned 'hundreds of thousands of dollars every week', is derided in Mannheim but there is no doubt that substantial amounts were paid into an account which he had opened in the Bahamas. He had earned enough 'to pay for all my legal bills'.

Unknown to Barbie, in 1965 he was also being considered for re-employment by the US Army as a special agent. The Office of the Assistant Chief of Staff for Intelligence (OACSI) wanted to mount an intelligence-gathering operation in Washington. On the intelligence staff was someone who had been involved with Barbie in Germany, and knew that he had gone to Bolivia. After clearance with the CIA, the OACSI asked its liaison officer at the American embassy in La Paz to confirm that Klaus Altmann was in La Paz. The reply was positive. But, according to the documents so far released, Barbie had still not been approached when, in mid-1966, the prominent Jewish US Senator Jacob Javits passed on to the State Department a letter from a constituent, Sandra Zanik.

Zanik had just watched an NBC television programme in which Alfred Newton, who by then was very ill, had complained that his Gestapo torturer was now a prosperous businessman living in Munich and working as an American and French agent. Zanik asked Javits to find out 'why a man can go free after killing and torturing. This is a very odd situation. I am wondering how many more people such as this are on the United States payroll or getting rich from us.'

The State Department asked the Army about Barbie and received a relatively honest account of the German's background and
the American connection. But the State Department's short reply
to Javits was completely deceptive, suggesting that Barbie was just
one of many informants and that an investigation into his past had
been found to be 'inconclusive'. To the bureaucrats' relief, Javits
did not pursue his inquiry; but it had been a salutary warning for the
CIA. As the Bolivian situation worsened over the next two years
and Barbie's importance grew, Javits' inquiry was used by the CIA
as a reason to veto the Army's persistent interest in re-enlisting their
man. But the CIA did not consider telling the US immigration
service, or the French and German governments, who Klaus
Altmann was and where he could be found.

By then Barbie's second major business venture, which started in
1966, had confirmed him as a prominent Bolivian citizen and had
introduced him to crime on a scale which, until then, even he had
neither experienced nor imagined.

In 1879, Bolivia lost the maritime Antofagasta province in a war
with neighbouring Chile and the country was suddenly landlocked.
Bolivia has ceremoniously mourned this shattering consequence
every year with processions and a dedication at their naval ministry,
which is based on an inland lake. In 1966, President Barrientos
announced that a public fund would be launched to buy a cargo ship
which would fly the Bolivian flag, the only ship of its kind in the
world. The presidential appeal to national pride failed to stimulate
enough donations; only $50,000 were collected, while four million
were needed. Suddenly a German emigrant appeared with a possible solution. Barbie described himself as a maritime engineer and
said he would be proud to use his expertise to arrange the purchase
of not just one boat, but a whole fleet. Relieved of the embarrassment, the President handed over to Barbie the $50,000 fund and
guaranteed him a state loan. 'Transmaritima Boliviana' was born.
Ownership was divided: 51% for the state and 49% for Barbie and
his business associates. In theory Barbie was working for the state,
but in practice he rapidly excluded the state representatives from
supervisory control.

Even for Bolivia's traditionally turbulent political life, the up-
heaval following the discovery in early 1967 that Che Guevara was
at large in the Bolivian countryside, attempting to foment a Marxist

revolution, was tempestuous. With the Vietnam war at its height, Washington was convinced that Fidel Castro had sent his faithful lieutenant there as part of Moscow's planned international aggression and policy of encirclement. The CIA and an elite jungle warfare unit, the 'Green Berets', were rapidly deployed to hunt down and destroy the Cuban revolutionaries. In October 1967, Guevara was captured and killed in the Bolivian jungle, but his death plunged the already brutalised and corrupt country even further into spiralling political anarchy. Politicians disappeared or were killed, while the country's government swung between right-wing and left-wing military dictatorships, the latter determined to remove American military and economic domination. Relations with Washington were stretched to the limit. The American government, uncertain in late 1970 about the new left-wing government led by General Torres, was suddenly hesitant about arms supplies and economic aid. The differences between left and right hardened. On the verge of civil war, factions in the army vying for power and planning a coup against the Torres government began searching for a secure and secret supply of arms.

No group was more concerned about the country's instability than the powerful German community. Their candidate in the military was Colonel Hugo Banzer, an American-trained cavalry officer whose rich landowning family had originally emigrated from Germany. To stage his coup he needed weapons. One obvious source was the German in La Paz with a shipping company, who had often boasted of his long and distinguished military career, and whose political views were unquestionably favourable to a right-wing military group. After twenty years in the wilderness, Barbie could once again offer his services in the fight against communism.

Every businessman has a characteristic method of trading. As manager of the Transmaritima, Barbie's was to 'buy' or 'rent' equipment, but not pay. For five years he chartered, but never bought, four cargo vessels. He appointed friends as managers and his son Klaus as company representative in Hamburg. Most important of all, as an important state employee, he secured a much prized diplomatic passport which gave him privileged facilities to travel. In quick succession he went during the late Sixties to Peru, Brazil and Argentina. More significantly, using a visa issued on 17 July 1969 by the American embassy in La Paz, he flew to Miami twice on 19 July and again on 21 January 1970. On both visits he flew for one-day trips to Freeport in the Bahamas to deposit money in secret bank accounts. Besides Miami, he is known to have visited New Orleans, Houston and San Francisco. His business in New Orleans seemed innocent – Barbie even claims that he was presented with the keys of the city by the Council in 1970. Captain William Ayres, president of the Ayres Steamship company, clearly remembers Klaus Altmann using his agency to carry general cargo between the Gulf ports and South America. The relationship lasted only a few months because of an argument with an Ayres representative. But suggestions that the cargoes were foodstuffs are derided by Barbie's acquaintances in La Paz. George Portugal, a long-established Bolivian arms dealer, insists that Barbie had become an arms supplier to a military faction.

The international arms trade is by nature plagued by secrecy, spurious denials and especially rumour. Disentangling fiction from truth, fifteen years after the event and without eyewitnesses, is often impossible. Yet there are substantial and verifiable events to suggest that, by the late Sixties, Barbie, as general manager of Transmaritima, had established close relations with the various military leaders by offering vital services. The cheap and unmonitored supply of arms was one such service.

Amongst the arms Barbie is alleged to have imported into Bolivia over the years are 50,000 rounds of .38 calibre bullets, Ingram sub-machine-guns, Israeli-made Uzi and Galil sub-machine-guns, and German-manufactured Heckler and Koch A3 sub-machine-guns. In the Seventies he is alleged to have arranged the purchase of 100 light tanks from Austria, although both the manufacturers, Steyer, and an alleged Austrian middleman, Evelyn Krieg, deny all knowledge of the deal. The most sensational of all these arms deals is his alleged purchase in 1967 of small arms from Belgium, ostensibly for Bolivia, which were then diverted to Israel, which was, at the time, cut off from its usual sources of supply by an international arms embargo. The use by Israel of a German of uncertain origin for services concerning its very survival, is not unusual.

It was in the course of arranging these deals that Barbie, using his diplomatic passport, flew to Germany. (Sometimes he claims to have visited France and laid flowers on Moulin's tomb, but there are grave doubts that Barbie has ever returned to France. He did, however, fly on an Air France plane in South America, spending the flight with his head hidden behind newspapers.) His visit to Hamburg ended in a bizarre mystery which led to one of many colourful but unsubstantiated allegations surrounding Barbie's Bolivian life. The purpose of the journey was to meet representatives of Hapag-Lloyd to negotiate contracts on behalf of Transmaritima. During his stay Barbie heard that the Bolivian consul in the city, Roberto Quintanilla, had been shot dead in his office. Back in Bolivia, Quintanilla, an aggressive right-wing policeman, had investigated a series of apparently related murders following the mysterious helicopter crash in April 1969 in which President Barrientos was killed; but his notoriety stemmed from his close proximity to the hunt and murder of Guevara. Quintanilla's assassin was Monika Ertl, the daughter of the man who had arranged Barbie's first job and who had remained a close friend. Monika Ertl was a member of a guerrilla movement determined to avenge all those associated with Guevara's death. It is alleged that either Barbie or his son made the arrangements and accompanied the body of the right-wing policeman back to Bolivia. On his return, Barbie was asked by her family to persuade Monika Ertl to surrender. He failed, and Ertl, when caught, was executed on the spot to avoid any diplomatic complications. Barbie used his influence to minimise the Ertl family's suffering, pleased that he was not plagued by the same problems with his own children.

At the time, Barbie had some business problems but he found life otherwise very pleasant. Despite their long separation during the war, his relations with his wife were very good. In 1969, his daughter Ute, then twenty-seven years old, was living in Kufstein, Austria. Barbie had arranged through Manfred Rudel, a wartime pilot and infamous post-war neo-Nazi, to find her a suitable school there: he had not wanted his daughter to mix with the local boys. Later, she married an Austrian teacher and lost close contact with her family. Barbie's son Klaus, then aged twenty-two, studied law in Barcelona but had returned to Bolivia. Neither knew about their father's past until 1971.

On 5 June 1968, the Barbies celebrated their son's marriage to Françoise Craxier-Roux, a French girl whom Klaus had met in Europe. To legalise the marriage according to French law, Craxier-Roux informed the French embassy in La Paz. Yet, although the

Barbie's American handlers: Herbert Bechtold (*Bower*), Eugene Kolb (*Bower*), Erhard Dabringhaus (*UPI*), Earl Browning (*Bower*) and Dale Garvey (*Bower*)

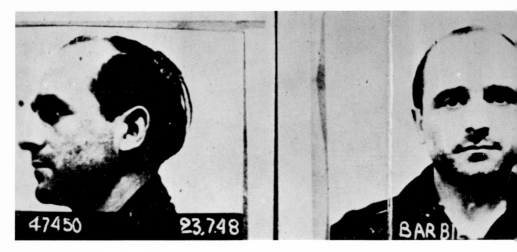

Barbie in 1948, when he was interrogated by US Army Intelligence (*Klarsfeld*)

The 'Rat Line' organisers: George Neagoy and Jim Milano (*Bower*)

VISAS
CONSOLATO D'ITALIA MONACO DI BAVIERA

VISTO DI DOPPIO TRANSITO PER L'ITALIA Nr. **1507**

conosco a **ALTMANN Klaus**

con diritto a 6 giorni di sosta per ogni transito.

Il viaggio di ritorno dovrà essere effettuato entro sei mesi
dalla data del primo transito.

Monaco di Bav., **21 FEB 1951**

R.P. **1683**

art. 57 T.C.

L. oro **3.—**

D.M. **4.10**   II CONSOLE

The 'Rat Line' documents used by Barbie and his
family for their passage through Italy and into
Bolivia (*McFarren*)

INFORMA:

Los inmigrantes Klaus Altmann Hausen su esposa Regina Wilhelms y
sus hijos menores María y Jorge, tienen sus documentos personales
en orden y han llenado todos los requisitos pertinentes para in-
migrar al país. Sus certificados acreditan su moralidad y capaci-
dad de trabajo.

JORGE ARCE P.
Consul General

La Paz 24 Mayo de 19..

Legalizada la firma y rúbrica del señor

Barbie under American protection: with his
wife, children, and Herbert Bechtold in
the garden of their house in Augsburg

Klaus Barbie in 1969, as managing director of the Transmaritima Shipping Corporation (*Sygma*). Beate Klarsfeld demonstrating in La Paz in 1972 (*Gamma*)

The 1972/3 attempt to kidnap Barbie (*Klarsfeld*)   Regis Debray, who helped in the attempt

Barbie released from prison in 1972 (*AP/Wide World*) and with his
permanent bodyguard, Alvaro de Castro (*McFarren*)

The Fiebelkorn Gang in 1982 (*McFarren*)

Barbie en route from La Paz to Montluc prison, February 1983 (*McFarren*)

Justice and investigation. Allan Ryan, US Special Investigator (*UPI*) Christian Riss, the Lyons
examining magistrate (*UPI*) and Alain de la Servette, Barbie's first defence lawyer, with
Ute Messner (*Gamma*)

French had known since 1963 that Barbie lived in La Paz, neither the embassy's vice-consul, Dominique Colombani, nor the ambassador, Joseph Lambroschini, even considered comparing the birthdates of Altmann and Barbie. Lambroschini says that he had never even heard of Barbie or of Altmann when he served in the embassy.

The reaction in the German consulate in summer 1969, on the other hand, when Ute applied for a visitor's permit, was considerably different. The embassy had already been alerted by an angry Bolivian Jew that Altmann was Barbie's cover name, and were immediately suspicious when Ute described her father as Polish. The ambassador asked Bonn to check the discrepancies in Ute's and Klaus's dates of birth. The reply was that, while there was no record of the birth of Ute Altmann on 30 June 1941 in Kassel, the birth of Ute Barbie was registered on the same day in Trier. Klaus-Georg Altmann was allededly born on 11 December 1946 in Kasel, near Leipzig, which had no record of his birth. Klaus-Jörg Barbie's birth was registered on the same day in Kassel, near Frankfurt.

Comparison of their parents' details also produced remarkable similarities. Klaus Altmann was born on 25 October 1915, whereas Barbie's date of birth was 13 October 1913. There was also a similar coincidence about Mrs Altmann's maiden name, given as Regina Wilhelms. Barbie's wife's name was Regine Willms.

On 20 September 1969, the West German foreign minister sent his colleague, the minister of justice, a short summary of Altmann-Barbie's post-war history. It concluded, 'We advise you to make only discreet inquiries, because Klaus Altmann has close relations to important people in the Bolivian government, and to former Nazis now living in South America, such as Fritz Schwend in Lima.' Attached to the note was a photo of Altmann, published in a Bolivian newspaper, showing him as a prosperous businessman in the centre of a group of similar people. It had been sent through an intermediary the previous year to a German public prosecutor by Herbert John, a German journalist and publisher living in Lima, who believed that Altmann was in fact another Nazi war criminal, Theodore Dannecker.

Dr Wolfgang Rabl, the public prosecutor in Munich, had inherited the Barbie file from Augsburg in 1971 when the Bavarian state government decided to concentrate all Nazi war-crime prosecutions in the state capital. Rabl did not try to hide his lack of interest in war-crime prosecutions, and, despite the initial evidence of Barbie's possible address, was disinclined to take the matter further. After perusing the file he noted simply that the case should be dropped. His reasons, he felt, were legally justifiable. He ignored the possibility of public repercussions.

Rabl knew that German courts could not try cases involving Nazi crimes against the French. According to a 1954 agreement between the Allies and the new German government, German courts could not prosecute Germans for war crimes while a prosecution was still pending in France. The French negotiators had insisted on this provision, fearing that German courts would be too lenient with their own countrymen, but they had ignored the provision in the new West German constitution which forbade the extradition of German nationals to stand trial in any other country. The 'catch-22' was finally acknowledged by the two governments to be benefiting only Nazi criminals living in safety in West Germany, but negotiating a new agreement was proving difficult. Rabl wanted to hand the case over to the French.

Rabl's second reason for wanting to drop the case was also, in his view, legally sound. The only alleged crime with which Barbie could still be charged was the arrest and deportation of the children from Izieu. It was the only known crime for which he had not yet been tried. Some would consider the case quite watertight. Barbie's name was on the telex to Paris and the text was unambiguous. But Rabl was not convinced that the telex alone was sufficient evidence for a successful prosecution: 'The mere fact that, on 6 April 1944, the defendant arrested forty-one children who were obviously not destined for the labour camps and had them shipped to the concentration camp at Drancy, cannot be interpreted to mean that he knew the eventual destination of those children. Not one sure piece of evidence of his subjective interpretation of his act can be produced.' Rabl doubted whether anyone could prove conclusively that Barbie actually knew that he was sending the children to be murdered. He believed that in 1944 Barbie was either still completely unaware of the Final Solution or that his knowledge could not be proven. On 22 June 1971 he formally submitted his summaries to Manfred Ludolph, his departmental chief, suggesting the case be dropped. Ludolph nodded his assent.

Hugo Banzer attempted his first coup in Bolivia in January 1971.

Ill-prepared, it failed and ended in strikes and violent fights between the military and the students and workers. By June, Banzer had strengthened his position. Secretly-acquired weapons and ammunition were airlifted clandestinely from Brazil to Santa Cruz, and for the next two months, with direct American support, the Banzer forces pushed south towards the capital, killing hundreds of students and workers. On 22 August, Banzer moved into the presidential palace, proclaiming that his regime was dedicated to destroying communism and trades unions. At his disposal was a police force which rapidly developed ruthless techniques of questioning which had not been used in Bolivia before; the same type which the Germans had found useful thirty years earlier in Europe. The new junta was grateful for the help and services of 'Don Klaus', a man to whom they felt indebted for his supply of arms.

Professional gamblers weigh the odds before committing themselves, considering their assets and then taking a calculated risk based on their experience; those who play the game rashly are called punters, and they usually lose. Barbie's venture into shipping falls into the latter category. By 1970, Transmaritima was 10,000,000 pesos in debt, eight-and-a-half times the initial capital. The following year, its foreign creditors became alarmed when the Bolivian government removed Barbie from the company board. To protect their debts, the creditors issued writs in Panama and Hamburg to seize the company's assets, only to find that they were the victims of a clever confidence trick. Transmaritima had no assets. Barbie had milked the company for his own purposes, a bitter disappointment to thousands of Bolivians who had contributed to the national fund – but not enough in a country like Bolivia to put Barbie at risk. In 1969, Barbie might have been embarrassed by the investigations of three journalists in La Paz into the Transmaritima saga, but they had been mysteriously murdered. There were good reasons to suspect Barbie's involvement, but there was no proof and his position remained unaffected.

Nevertheless, soon after the company collapsed and Banzer became President, Barbie decided to move to Lima, Peru, to continue work in the shipping business. According to Barbie, his wife was suffering from La Paz's high altitude and they left on medical advice. Others are convinced he left for his own safety and with the President's blessing in the wake of the Transmaritima scandal. He arrived in Lima with enough money to buy a Swiss-type chalet, with large grounds and swimming pool. The cost, he said, was $22,000.

Barbie had an acquaintance in Lima, Fritz Schwend, a former SS colonel and also a fugitive. Schwend had masterminded 'Operation Bernhard', Hitler's audacious plan to flood the world with forged British currency: the notes were distributed to German agents throughout the world with orders to spend them as fast as possible. After murdering one of his accomplices in Italy, Schwend had fled Europe but, unlike Barbie, arrived in South America with considerable wealth. His presence in Peru had never been a secret. He lived in an enormous house, surrounded by a high wall which encouraged speculation that he was the financier of the Odessa network, or even the Fourth Reich, in constant communication with all the important Nazi politicians who were not killed or captured in 1945. Martin Bormann, Josef Mengele and Gestapo chief Heinrich Müller were just three of the infamous Nazi fugitives said to have passed through his home. Barbie had met him for the first time when he passed through Lima in 1968 and soon after his arrival in October 1971 he called on Schwend again.

At first the Barbies were very happy in Lima. The climate was much more pleasant and the city more cosmopolitan. Schwend was a perfect host and, over many days and nights, the two former SS men talked about the past and even planned joint business ventures for the future. Among the many entertaining people to whom Schwend introduced him was Herbert John, a collaborator of Luis Banchero Rossi, known as the 'guano king'. Schwend was negotiating a deal with Rossi, a multi-millionaire fishing magnate and one of Peru's richest businessmen. On New Year's Day 1972, however, Rossi was found dead. He had been murdered and Schwend was the prime police suspect. Barbie, who was working with Schwend on the deal, was also automatically under suspicion. The Peruvian police were convinced of a Nazi conspiracy.

Barbie's new-found happiness was suddenly clouded. He did not know that in Europe Rabl's decision to drop his case had been vigorously challenged by a young German woman whose efficiency and fervour matched Barbie's own, and who was determined that he should be brought back to Europe to stand trial for his crimes of forty years ago. A Protestant, born in Berlin, Beate Klarsfeld was just three years old when Barbie arrived in Lyons. The 'Butcher' could be forgiven for not foreseeing that, after a lifetime of manipulation, evasion, deceit and monstrous crime, he would eventually be doomed by a young woman.

THE NAZI HUNTERS

Beate Klarsfeld is an internationally mobile protester and pro-vocateur, who has ingeniously exploited the world's media to embarrass any government or politician who deliberately or by omission has protected Germans involved in the extermination of French Jews. Born Beate Künzel in Berlin in February 1939, 'just three weeks before Hitler entered Prague', she grew up suffering most of the material deprivations of defeated Germany. After her family home was bombed, she lived in cramped conditions in the countryside. Back in Berlin after the German surrender, she grew up disillusioned with the city, her parents and her secretarial job. Anxious to break away, she became an au pair in Paris. In May 1960, waiting on a platform for the metro, a Frenchman asked her whether she was English: three years later, still a Protestant, she married and became Mrs Serge Klarsfeld.

The Klarsfeld family were victims of the Holocaust. During the first three years of German occupation, Serge lived in Nice, with his parents and sister, having abandoned their home in Paris just before the German army entered the city. During the night of 30 Septem-ber 1943, the Gestapo raided their house, searching for Jews. Serge's father, anticipating the threat, had already built a false back in a cupboard to hide the family. Motionless and terrified, the four cowered in their cramped refuge, listening to the blows and screams as other Jews were grabbed and bundled into lorries waiting outside in the street. When the Gestapo burst into the Klarsfeld flat, they wilfully broke the nose of a neighbour's young daughter, who was refusing to cooperate. To help her, and to distract the Germans' attention from his own family, Serge's father squeezed out of the hiding place and surrendered. He died with all the others arrested that night, in Auschwitz.

Although a Zionist, Serge Klarsfeld had not considered reveng-ing his father's death before he met Beate. He was naturally interested in the circumstances of the German deportations but had not considered the fate of those Germans and Frenchmen who had masterminded the operations. When he met Beate, he was just finishing his higher education at the School of Political Science and about to be employed by ORTF, the French state broadcasting corporation. Similarly, until meeting Serge, Beate had never considered Nazi Germany's treatment of the Jews. In Berlin, it had not been mentioned either in her home or at school. Deeply in love with Serge and the Klarsfeld family, she became exceptionally ashamed of her own country's immorality.

In early December 1966, French newspapers reported that the conservative West German politician Kurt-Georg Kiesinger, had declared himself as a candidate for Chancellor of Germany. The reports added, without details, that during the war Kiesinger had been a senior official in the Foreign Ministry responsible for Nazi propaganda broadcasts. As a young German now determined to atone for her country's history, Beate Klarsfeld seized on the announcement as the beginning of an astonishing personal campaign to expose the total failure to denazify post-war Germany. With Serge and a few friends, she proved that Germans who had been directly and indirectly involved in mass murders were living comfortable, secure and prosperous lives in the new Federal Republic. Kiesinger was just one of many who had effortlessly buried his past and reached prominence without anyone questioning his wartime activities. Kiesinger was elected Chancellor on 12 December 1966.

To uncover Kiesinger's wartime activities, Serge searched through Third Reich documents stored in archives in East Berlin, Washington and London. With little difficulty, but at tremendous personal cost, he discovered memoranda and orders either addressed to Kiesinger, or actually signed by Kiesinger himself, which proved conclusively that the newly-elected Chancellor was an outright supporter of Hitler and of Nazi policies, including all Himmler's anti-Jewish measures. During the war he rose to the position of deputy head of propaganda broadcasting to foreign countries.

The next step was to publicise the results of their investigation. 'Kiesinger the Nazi' had the basic ingredients of a good story, yet nearly all the newspapers approached by Beate seemed uninterested. Without any training, but with enormous motivation, the Klarsfelds learnt very quickly the subtle art of news management. Essentially, it is to present journalists with an apparently original and well-researched story which they will try their best to get published. Beate's second discovery was that, however good the story, journalists need a 'peg' or an event to capture not only the public's attention but their editor's interest. Publicity stunts, she discovered, are the recipe for launching 'difficult' stories. Posing as a journalist, in cooperation with a German magazine photographer, Beate Klarsfeld stalked Kiesinger from meeting to meeting, seeking the opportunity. On 7 November 1968, at the CDU Party congress in Berlin, she finally manoeuvred herself behind Kiesinger. Shouting, 'Kiesinger, you Nazi!', she smacked Germany's leader across the face. This led to the first of many arrests of Beate and, as intended, huge banner headlines in newspapers around the world.

Over the next year, during West Germany's election campaign, Beate Klarsfeld hounded Kiesinger remorselessly in towns and villages throughout the country, heckling him during his meetings with taunts about his Nazi past. His eventual defeat and disappearance into obscurity was due in part to the success of the Klarsfeld campaign. Their next targets were Germans directly associated with the Final Solution in France: the Gestapo officers and embassy staff who had organised the arrests and deportations of Jews such as Serge's father.

Attracting media attention was the key to the Klarsfeld campaign. Newspaper and television journalists were lobbied either in person or by phone, and personally handed massive folders containing photocopies of original documents which always provided seriously incriminating evidence against their target. The Klarsfelds either called their own news conferences or infiltrated other people's; politicians were approached, called or harassed to win their support; speeches, demonstrations and 'incidents' were arranged to ensure maximum publicity; no day passed without considerable expenditure on telephone calls or photocopying machines. From the outset, it was a family at war to reverse what they considered an outrageous failure of justice. Even their baby son travelled with them and joined the campaign.

After Kiesinger's demise, their next target was Ernst Achenbach, another member of the West German parliament. During the war, Achenbach had been a member of the German embassy in Paris, directly involved in organising the Jewish deportations from France. His nomination by the German government to be the country's representative at the European Commission in Brussels was blocked after a Klarsfeld campaign. His own campaign in the German parliament to prevent the continuation of war-crime trials, and to prevent the ratification of the 1971 Franco-German treaty which reversed the 1954 agreement, was destroyed by the Klarsfeld exposures of his past. He too was forced to retire into obscurity.

Next were Kurt Lischka, Herbert Hagen and Ernst Heinrichson – three Gestapo officers, based in Paris, who were directly involved in the arrests and deportation of French Jews to Auschwitz. None of the three had been prosecuted for these activities and all were prospering as businessmen or lawyers in Germany. The Klarsfeld campaign started in July 1971 with an unsuccessful attempt to kidnap Lischka outside his home in Cologne, for which Beate Klarsfeld was subsequently arrested and prosecuted. At her trial in 1974, the courtroom was invaded by noisy supporters and the embarrassed judge had no choice but to suspend the hearing amidst the chaos. Her subsequent conviction and imprisonment, contrasted with Lischka's freedom, forced reluctant prosecutors to bow to media outrage and charge all three with first-degree murder. In 1979 they were convicted and imprisoned.

Just three weeks after the abortive kidnapping, the Klarsfelds heard that the Munich prosecutor proposed to drop the Barbie case. All their future campaigns would collapse if Rabl's decision were upheld. The Klarsfeld publicity machine went into action. Energetically, the archives were scoured, eyewitnesses and survivors sought, and press dossiers collated for distribution.

Tactically, the Klarsfelds realised, the campaign was best launched in Lyons itself. On 28 July, the Lyons *Progrés* carried the story prominently with banner headlines. The response from the survivors of the Resistance was, predictably, outrage. Dr Frédéric Dugoujon, the owner of the Caluire villa where Moulin was arrested, wrote to the newspaper, 'I have prayed to Heaven to give me the grace never to sit in judgement, but if I were a judge or a member of a jury, I would sentence Klaus Barbie to death.' Other papers were filled with similar reactions. The media campaign had started. The next obvious step for the Klarsfelds was to organise a demonstration at the courthouse in Munich to get the case reopened. But despite the cause, wartime divisions had already split their potential supporters. Non-communist veterans' groups did not want to be seen with communists, and Dugoujon and others in Lyons, while welcoming the Klarsfelds' initiative, were unwilling to be associated visibly with aggressive, Jewish protestors. Dugoujon wanted to be part of a delegation, not a demonstration. Twenty-five years after the war, he was more concerned with Barbie's crimes against the Resistance, not the Jews. After consultations with government and consular officials, he thanked Beate Klarsfeld for her help but implied that they would be better off without any troublemakers present. He had been reliably assured that diplomacy was the best route, not publicity stunts.

Undeterred, Klarsfeld sought out Mme Benguigui, one of the mothers of the children of Izieu. Mme Benguigui had herself been deported to Auschwitz, but lived in the hope that her three children were safe in the isolated village. In May 1944, sorting through the clothes of people recently gassed, she was shattered to see the sweater of her son, Jacques. The martyred mother, Klarsfeld felt, would be a good symbol on the Munich courthouse steps. But once in Munich, Klarsfeld found that her tactics were completely unacceptable to the Resistance veterans. In the immediate interests of unity, she momentarily accepted exclusion from the delegation visiting Manfred Ludolph, Rabl's chief, and the department's leading prosecutor.

Ludolph had told the forty-strong delegation before they left France that he would only reopen the case if the French could provide new evidence. The Resistance delegation had brought nothing, but vigorously protested that the Munich prosecutors had closed the case without sifting through the documentary evidence available in France, or having even questioned one single eyewitness. Ludolph greeted them politely but gave them no assurances; they returned to Lyons, criticising Beate Klarsfeld for planning a press conference. Klarsfeld, however, had already prepared a dossier containing an affidavit from Kurt Schendel, the Jewish liaison officer in Paris, who had heard Raymond Geissmann's account of Barbie's comment, 'Shot or deported, there's no difference.' In his absence, she left it on Ludolph's desk.

Convinced that only public protests would win the argument, at 9.00 next morning, Klarsfeld and Madame Benguigui, who was severely incapacitated after her release from Auschwitz, stood in the rain on the courthouse steps. Beate's placard read, *Prosecutor*

Rabl is rehabilitating war criminals. Madame Benguigui's read, *I am on hunger strike for as long as the investigation of Klaus Barbie, who murdered my children, remains closed*. By the end of the day the cause was won. Ludolph agreed to meet the two women, read the dossier and promised to reopen the case if Geissmann swore an affidavit about Barbie's aside. If true, it would prove that Barbie did know the real fate of the Izieu children.

Back in Paris, the Klarsfelds successfully searched for Geissmann and secured from him an affidavit confirming what Barbie said in 1943. They flew back to Munich and obtained an official under-taking on 1 October from Ludolph that he would reopen the case into Barbie's deportation of the Jews. 'Once he had the affidavit, Ludolph completely changed his attitude,' recalls Beate Klarsfeld. 'He gave us two photographs of Barbie taken in 1943, and a photograph of a group of businessmen taken in La Paz in 1968. Pointing at one of the businessmen, he said to me, "Why don't you help me identify this man?"' The source of the photo was Herbert John. Ludolph had decided to work with the Klarsfelds. Mean-while, the Resistance veterans who had shunned the Klarsfeld campaign had still not fulfilled their assurance to Ludolph that they would send him new evidence which would persuade him to reopen the case.

Charged with new enthusiasm and new hope, the Klarsfelds realised that they now had to discover the assumed name under which Barbie was living. Paris newspapers were unwilling to publish the 1968 photograph naming the businessman as Barbie, in case there was a mistake. The next option was recourse to an anthro-pometric, a scientist who by minute analysis of facial features of the two photographs could determine the similarities. With customary audacity, Beate Klarsfeld doorstepped the government expert and persuaded him to carry out an immediate comparison. The result was positive. When Ludolph heard, he immediately invited Klars-feld to return to Munich, at his expense, to discuss the case. In the meantime, he submitted the same photographs to the anthro-pometrical department of Munich University. German experts confirmed the French results, and a friend of Herbert John revealed to the Klarsfelds in November 1971, what Ludolph already knew, that Barbie was using the name Altmann. The next step was for the French government to ask for Barbie's extradition. 'I phoned an important official in the Prime Minister's office and briefed him on the situation,' recalls Serge. 'But from the reply, it was obvious any response would be slow and cautious.'

More inquiries by Klarsfeld revealed that 'there was a blockage at the level of the Minister of Defence' which amounted to bureaucratic lethargy. The Minister at the time was Michel Debré. As always, the Klarsfelds opted for direct action. On 19 January 1972, the Paris newspaper *L'Aurore* published the pictures and the story and challenged the French government to demand Barbie's extradition. That night a French journalist rang on the door of Barbie's home in Lima. Barbie had just returned from a weekend by the sea with his wife and the Schwends. 'The Frenchman said he had something important to tell me,' recalls Barbie.

> I told him to go away because we were just getting ready for bed. Then he rang a second time, and I told him that I didn't know what he was talking about. He left saying that I would get a surprise the next day. The next morning I drove into town and bought a newspaper at a kiosk as usual and there it was, the whole front page. That was the beginning. I just don't know if it was Schwend's fault and all his gossip with Herbert John. I never told Schwend anything and he didn't know me during the war.

Barbie did not realise, even in 1979, that the first convincing confirmation about his real identity had been obtained from his own children.

Over the next days, Barbie doggedly denied to journalists that he was anyone other than Altmann: 'I am not Klaus Barbie, but Klaus Altmann, a former lieutenant in the Wehrmacht. I've never heard of Klaus Barbie, and I've never changed my identity.' But just as public interest was beginning to wane, news agencies from Paris reported that Beate Klarsfeld was about to fly to Peru with the conclusive documentary evidence. According to Barbie, at 2.30 a.m. on 26 January 1972, a squad of Peruvian police burst into his house and arrested him:

> They wanted to take me to the Interior Ministry. I refused to leave the house because I was afraid that they would kidnap me. But I went with them the next morning. An official told me that a Beate Klarsfeld was coming and that there was going to be a lot of trouble, so I had to leave the country. They wanted to fly me out, but I had my car, a Volkswagon Cabriolet, and I suggested that I drive to the border, under escort.

The ministry agreed. Barbie drove out of Lima on 27 January, heading for the Bolivian frontier, a two-day journey. Beate Klarsfeld flew in the following morning. Her first twelve hours were a continuous press conference. The next day, with Barbie still driving through Peru, Klarsfeld showed officials at police headquarters and the presidential palace the documentary proof that Altmann and Barbie were the same man, and the evidence of his crimes. It was a fight against time to convince them that Barbie should not be allowed to cross the frontier before an extradition request arrived from Paris – but the French ambassador, Albert Chambon, never received the necessary instructions from the Quai d'Orsay. Paris was more concerned to protect its fragile relationship with Lima, which had only just been patched up following Peruvian protests against the French atomic tests in the Pacific.

As Barbie drove southwards, his escort phoned Lima regularly to report their position. In Arequipa, the last major town before the border, the police escort were handed a telegram from the Ministry of the Interior in Lima, saying that Barbie's expulsion was annulled and he could return.

> I called my wife and asked her advice. She said, 'No, Klaus, it's better that you drive immediately to Bolivia. I've spoken to Schwend and he says the same.' I also asked the Bolivian consul and he said that I should go to La Paz. I spent that night with the police escort getting terribly drunk, and then they took me through Puno to Desaguadero, the frontier town. There they handed me a form to sign and said to me, 'Herr Altmann, you left Peru voluntarily, didn't you?' I replied, 'If it was voluntary, why would I have needed an escort?' But I agreed to sign in the end. I crossed the bridge into Bolivia . . . and there was a fifteen-man military squad under the command of Colonel Navarro waiting to greet me. They drove with me to La Paz.

In the capital, police and Ministry-of-Interior officials advised Barbie to hide, 'because Klarsfeld is coming'. 'I went to my friend Hans and the fifteen soldiers came as well to protect me.'

Back in Lima, acknowledging the setback, Beate Klarsfeld caught the next flight to La Paz. She arrived to a very cool reception, from both the Bolivian government and the French embassy. Three days after her arrival, she was arrested and then expelled; but the journey had achieved its purpose. Barbie was now an international issue and the reluctant French ambassador, Jean Louis Mandereau, on instructions from Paris, formally asked for his extradition. The Klarsfelds, having launched the Barbie issue, hoped that with headline reports on both sides of the Atlantic they could now rely on the media to maintain the momentum.

Three days after Beate Klarsfeld left La Paz, on 6 February, Barbie was arrested by Colonel Hugo Banzer's police on charges of failing to pay taxes. For a moment it seemed that Barbie's apparently invulnerable position had disintegrated. Even he was momentarily uncertain and realised that, living as he did under an arbitrary regime, he would have to fight to convince Banzer that his extradition would cost more than his release. It was as part of his strategy that, two days later, he agreed to be interviewed by French television for $2,000, paid by the French consul. Having outwitted and humiliated countless Frenchmen during the war, he convinced himself that his powers of manipulation, distortion and intimidation would once again triumph. Instead, he became ensnared in the very contradictions and inconsistencies in which, in the past, he had delighted to see his victims flounder and destroy themselves. Through ignorance and conceit, he had committed a fatal mistake.

In the interview, he completely changed the previous accounts of his life story. Admitting that he had been a member of the Waffen SS, he said that he had served in Holland, Russia and France. Pushed by the interviewer, Ladislas de Hoyos, he further admitted that he had served in Lyons, but not as Klaus Barbie. The similarities, he insisted, were extraordinary coincidences. At the outset of the interview, Barbie claimed that he could not speak French, but later he suddenly broke off from Spanish and said in fluent French, 'I am not a murderer; I am not a torturer.' Asked at the end, whether he had a good conscience, he replied in German, 'Yes.' The drama of the interview was heightened in France where four of his victims were invited to watch the transmission in the studio: Raymond Aubrac, Frédéric Dugoujon, Simone Legrange and a Lyons policeman, René Fusier. Although, tantalisingly, only Aubrac positively identified Barbie, France was utterly convinced. The following day, 9 February, two French lawyers left Munich with a suitcase of documents given to them by Ludolph, the basis of any French demand for the extradition of Barbie. It was an explicit admission by the French government of their own dismal failure to investigate the crimes commited against their own countrymen.

France submitted its request for Barbie's extradition on 1 February, followed four days later by a formal letter. Officially, the government in Paris declared itself to be 'optimistic', but their request faced seemingly insuperable obstacles. Firstly, France had no extradition treaty with Bolivia; secondly, Barbie was either German or Bolivian, but not French; thirdly, Barbie had in the past enjoyed the protection of President Banzer. The French argued that Barbie was neither German nor Bolivian, but stateless; but any optimism that he had lost the protection was thwarted on 12 February, when, after paying $1,000 of a $4,500 debt, Barbie was released. He went into immediate hiding and persuaded his police bodyguard to 'leak' by a telephone call that Barbie was in Paraguay.

Events in La Paz had become a major issue in Paris. President Pompidou felt politically compelled to intervene and sent a personal letter to Banzer. 'Time wipes out many things,' he wrote, 'but not all. Unless their sense of justice is sadly tarnished, Frenchmen cannot permit crimes and sacrifices to be lumped together and then forgotten through indifference' – sentiments which were shared by most Frenchmen, who were to be very surprised when on 23 November 1971 the same president pardoned Paul Touvier, a known murderer, member of the Lyons *milice* and collaborator with Barbie.

Although France's extradition request had been sent to the Bolivian supreme court, Banzer's prompt reply to Pompidou was emphatically unsympathetic, ending on an unhelpful assurance that Bolivia's independent judiciary would nevertheless consider the case. The Klarsfelds felt once again that the politicians would only respond to direct action. Beate Klarsfeld started raising money for a return trip to Bolivia and, anxious to make the protest newsworthy, began searching for another of Barbie's Jewish victims to take with her.

The Lyons Gestapo, and Klaus Barbie in particular, had ravaged Itta Halaunbrenner's family. On 24 October 1943, she was living with her husband, son and three daughters under surveillance in Villeurbanne, Lyons. At 11.00 a.m, Barbie and two other Gestapo officers walked into the house to arrest her nephew. Pulling out his revolver, Barbie terrorised the family and young children for the next seven hours. When Mme Halaunbrenner's son returned home, both he and her husband were arrested. According to the daughter

Alexandre, 'We all wept and howled, but in vain. Barbie shoved my mother aside as she was trying to yank her son and her husband back, took out his revolver again, and beat her hands with it to make her let go. But all was useless.' M. Halaunbrenner was executed immediately. When they found his body in the morgue, it had seventeen bullets in the neck and chest. Their son Léon died in Auschwitz. Fearing for the safety of the two youngest daughters, Madame Halaunbrenner sent them to Izieu; but this was not far enough from Barbie's grasp. Like the others, they were gassed in Auschwitz.

With considerable difficulties, the two women finally arrived in La Paz on 24 February, to be greeted with threats to their lives from the police and an official prohibition against talking to the press. Undeterred, Beate Klarsfeld held a press conference, followed by banner headlines, arrests and an inevitable expulsion order. Having failed to engineer a confrontation between Halaunbrenner and Barbie, the only recourse was a public demonstration. Chained to a bench outside the Transmaritima offices, Klarsfeld and Madame Halaunbrenner held up a placard: *Bolivians. As a mother I only claim justice. I want Barbie-Altmann, who murdered my husband and three of my children, brought to trial.* Barbie had become a minor embarrassment to the regime.

Soon after Beate Klarsfeld's departure, Barbie was paid by a Brazilian journalist, Dantas Ferreira, to cooperate in his biography. Although notable for its distortions and omissions, it contained some astonishing confessions. In paraphrase, he told Ferreira:

> I am a convinced Nazi who admired Nazi discipline, and I am proud to have held a senior position in the SS, the most valuable troops in the Third Reich. The SS soldier is a superman whose blood is traced back four generations before being allowed to join. Any idiot can't join the SS. I had to study law and philosophy. What I did was normal for war, and I would do it a thousand times again; for Germany and for Bolivia. I had nothing to do with concentration camps or gas chambers. I led a special squad to fight the Resistance. I can't be compared to Bormann or Mengele, while Hitler was a genius.

What happened in France, he explained, was excusable because it was war, and his actions were carried out as a duty to defend his country. Asked whether he had any regrets, he derided the question. 'In time of war, everyone kills. There is neither good, nor evil.'

His confidence that the interview would not harm him in Bolivia was misplaced. The French demand for his extradition had reached the Supreme Court and, despite his connections with the President, it was felt that for appearances' sake, Bolivia had to put on a show.

Summoned to appear before Gaston Ledezma, the Bolivian prosecutor, he admitted that he had used the name Barbie in Lyons, but only as a cover. 'I can't believe,' he told Ledezma, 'that Bolivia is interested in what happened thirty years ago between France and Germany.' Regretfully, Ledezma disagreed and on 2 March 1973 ordered his arrest. Cut off from the world inside the San Pedro prison, waiting for the supreme court to consider France's extradition request, Barbie wanted both to justify himself and to earn enough money to hire a lawyer. He gave more interviews, explaining to select journalists that war crimes do not exist, just acts of war, such as the French had committed in Indo-China and Algeria, and the Americans in Vietnam. The French in 1940, he told a French interviewer, should have behaved as did the Germans in 1945 and just laid down their arms.

His seven months in prison, he explained in 1979, were comfortable, undemanding and very unconventional. He already knew the truth of the saying, 'beware of Chilean women and Bolivian justice', especially if you had no influence or money. Life inside the prison was managed by the inmates, who had to pay for everything themselves. Among the rabble of common prisoners, 'Don Klaus' made sure that he was seen as an important personality; he bought a lock for his cell, turning the key on the inside when he went to sleep at night. His wife, who had returned from Lima, brought food every day and stayed with him in the communal grounds. To pass the time there were football and film shows, and the occasional execution. 'One had the impression that no one in there had done anything wrong. I had a lot of laughs.'

By July 1973, the Supreme Court still seemed hesitant about the case. If Barbie was naturalised under a false name, the judges reasoned, could he still be considered a Bolivian citizen? Their lack of political realism irritated the President. Impatient with their legal qualms, Banzer threatened to dismiss all the judges as 'incompetents' and appoint a completely new court. Five days later, on 5 July, the French demand was rejected on the grounds that there was no extradition treaty between the countries, that Barbie was a

Bolivian citizen and that the Bolivian penal code did not recognise war crimes. Barbie's release was ordered on 9 July; but just before he left the prison, he was rearrested. Peru were demanding his extradition on charges of currency fraud, a charge on which Schwend was already imprisoned. That demand, with Banzer's help, was also rejected. Barbie finally left the prison on 25 October, with two bodyguards provided by the President for his safety. With little money and no home, he and Regine stayed for a short period with a friend in Cochabamba; once he had picked up the threads of his business affairs, they returned to La Paz.

Barbie now owed a debt to the Banzer regime and the military. Its repayment over the next nine years was a pleasure. Banzer's policies and style of government were the closest to Nazi Germany's that Barbie could ever expect. The government's motto or 'holy trinity' was, 'Peace, Order and Work.' Critics were brutally eliminated and, with American support, the labour force suppressed so that the government could direct the economy's recovery without opposition. Banzer called it his revenge against 'communist treason'. Barbie found no difficulty fitting into that atmosphere. His role was not as a permanent paid adviser, but rather as a reliable freelance consultant, always available for fast trips to Europe to deliver bits of intelligence or rumours about what people were saying, and finally as a security adviser to Bolivia's cocaine barons. Dividing his time between his sawmill in Cochabamba, a retreat in Santa Cruz and the remnants of the shipping business in La Paz, he soon knew the country better than most – and there is no doubt that his information would have been passed automatically to the local CIA station chief, who would have known the source and his background.

In the dusty, sloping streets of La Paz, the bald, stocky German was now regularly seen walking, even strutting, between his home and the *Café Daiquiri* or *Confiteria La Paz*, enjoying the public acknowledgement of his growing influence and position. By his side was his permanent bodyguard, the ever-faithful Alvaro de Castro, paid for by the government. Sitting at his favourite table, Barbie freely dispensed advice about the situation in Bolivia, peppering his conversation with distorted references to his wartime experiences. Concealing some of these events was no longer necessary, but to protect the legality of his naturalisation, he insisted that he was called Altmann. His sparsely furnished fourth-floor apartment was dominated by a large oil painting of Hitler, standing, dressed in a black coat with the collar turned up. By the hi-fi, were Austrian records with Hitler's historic speeches, to which the ex-SS captain listened regularly. He was understandably obsessed with the historic events in which he had played a part – an increasingly important part, in his view, as the years passed. He read many books about the war, but was especially interested in Isser Harel's account of how his Israeli secret service unit kidnapped Adolf Eichmann. Barbie had no fears of being the victim of a similar Israeli attempt. He seemed and felt himself to be impregnable, even to those who came to either embarrass or to kill him.

In July 1972 René Hardy was paid by *Paris Match*, the French magazine, to travel to La Paz with one of their staff to confront Barbie. At their first meeting, staged in the Plaza San Francisco, Barbie did not even recognise the former Resistance man who introduced himself as an American journalist. 'I remembered Hardy as tall and thin. There standing in front of me was a fat old man.' Secretly photographed with Barbie, and now fearing arrest, Hardy left Bolivia with the journalist the same day. Some months later Hardy returned with a public challenge for a confrontation. Barbie claims that Banzer forbade him to meet Hardy. 'I got the letter through the Ministry of the Interior. He said that he felt it important that it did not occur. I could not disobey the government.' Hardy left without salvaging his reputation.

Michel Goldberg wrote that he too made the long journey to La Paz to avenge Barbie's deeds. His father, Joseph Goldberg, was one of the eighty-six Jews who were arrested and deported by Barbie in Febuary 1943. Plagued by an identity crisis, an anguished victim of anti-semitism, Goldberg says that he intended to shoot Barbie in a La Paz street: he would thus not only revenge his father's death, but also reassert his own French citizenship. There are serious doubts about his claim that he intended to shoot Barbie but the sentiments are expressed in eloquent prose. Goldberg claims to have sat on a park bench, watching Barbie, a few yards away, talking animatedly to another man; under his poncho he held a fully-loaded gun. He wrote later of the thoughts which passed through his mind at that moment:

There he stands, the presumed instrument of my liberation, of my rebirth, waiting . . . I can kill Barbie almost without risk . . . Something now tells me that to kill is not the right solution . . . Obviously justice will never be done. The man responsible for the death of some ten thousand men, women and children, usually in hideous circumstances, cannot be punished for his crimes . . . What does a quick death mean to a purveyor of slow death? No, justice will never be done.

He left, one of many Jews and others who over the years have threatened loudly to avenge their families' suffering but have always failed to match their words.

Barbie read Goldberg's widely-publicised account some years later. His inevitable reaction was contempt for someone whose 'weakness' precluded killing, and double contempt because the would-be assassin was Jewish (Barbie insists that he has only become an anti-semite since the war). Had he been killed, he was convinced the government would never have allowed Goldberg to leave the country alive. Barbie believed himself to be indestructible. 'I've seen death so often in my life that I haven't cared about my own safety, but only thought about my family, about my wife and my children' – natural sentiments which he did not expect his victims to share.

With Banzer's protection indisputably confirmed, French interest in Barbie disappeared. Even the Klarsfelds acknowledged that, unless they kidnapped or killed him, their campaign was paralysed. In 1976, reports from Bolivia mentioned that a government commission, established to persuade 150,000 white immigrants from southern Africa to settle and farm in the country, included Barbie on its panel. Despite international criticism, bureaux were established in Rhodesia and South Africa. Barbie's role was obvious: as a German, and one who understood the politics of racism, he better than anyone in Bolivia would know how to approach the whites. But despite his advice, the scheme quickly collapsed because the proposed sites did not offer the whites the pleasures and profits to which they had become accustomed.

In July 1978, Banzer was forced to resign amidst political chaos and strikes, and fled the country. Over the next two years, Bolivia was perpetually on the verge of civil war, enduring no less than three elections, three coups and six presidents. Amongst those physically denied office by the military, despite his election victory, was the ex-President, Hernán Siles Zuazo. Despite Banzer's disappearance, Barbie was so firmly established within the inner circles of power that, far from suffering, he actually profited. Exploiting the turmoil, he developed a close relationship with the most ruthless and determinedly right-wing military group who were intent on reversing the various attempts to return to democracy. Just as in wartime Lyons, although this time he was the servant rather than the master, he was associated with a criminal fraternity who were plotting to take over the government of the country. Their purpose was to exploit the fast-growing demand for cocaine in the United States.

Until fashionable New York and Hollywood socialites discovered the use of cocaine as a stimulant in 1977, most of Bolivia's coca crop was used legally in Bolivia, often as part payment of wages for peasants and workers, who chewed the leaf as a normal but essential part of everyday life. The remainder of the crop was illegally exported to Colombia where it was converted in laboratories from paste to white powder, before being smuggled to the northern hemisphere. The potential of the sudden American demand was first recognised by a rich Bolivian landowner and part-time smuggler, Roberto Suárez. He had both aeroplanes and the right connections within the Bolivian military and police to establish himself as the middleman between the growers, the laboratories in Colombia and the importers in America. Building rough airstrips in the remote wooded hinterland around Santa Cruz, he developed, within five years, a business which was estimated in 1982 by the US government to be annually worth no less than $400,000,000. Barbie's contribution to Suárez's boom was the provision of a team of bodyguards.

Joachim Fiebelkorn arrived in Santa Cruz from Paraguay in mid-1978. Then aged thirty-one, he had led a very chequered life. After deserting from the West German army, he joined the Spanish foreign legion and then returned to Germany as a pimp in Frankfurt. He arrived in South America with Nazi uniforms and medals and a fanatical obsession with the glories of the Third Reich. Over a short period, eight other mostly neo-Nazi Germans, all aimless wanderers with squalid military backgrounds seeking excitement and fortune, joined him in Santa Cruz. As the price of cocaine soared, Santa Cruz was transformed into a mixture of Wild West Klondike and Las Vegas. Exuberant lawlessness mixed with vast new riches oozed all over the town. Fiebelkorn and his group sat in the town's *Bavaria* bar, armed with pistols, shooting into the ceiling, singing Nazi songs and advertising themselves as available mercenaries. Their first client was General Echeverria, a local commander, who needed help in procuring and maintaining his weapons. Echeverria was already deeply involved with Suárez in the cocaine trade. Both had become concerned about their inability to prevent consignments being snatched without payment by Colombian purchasers on the airstrips. They needed a private army for protection and Echeverria suggested to Fiebelkorn that his group might consider the proposition. For the Germans, it was like a gift from heaven.

Suárez gave them a luxury villa, cars, guns and lots of money. They became feared in the town as the German mafia, enjoying free drinks and free women. Other fascists in Europe soon heard about this wonderland sanctuary and the wealth that the Germans were enjoying in Bolivia. Among the new arrivals in 1979 were two important and very violent Italian fascists, Stefano Delle Chiaie and Pierluigi Pagliai. Over past years, both had been involved in numerous conspiracies, bombings and brutal murders in Italy. Their most notorious crime was to plan the bombing of the Bologna railway station on 2 August 1980 which killed eighty-five people and seriously injured about 200 more. Amongst those charged with that mass murder by the Italian magistrate was Joachim Fiebelkorn who is believed to have travelled from Bolivia to Italy expressly to plant the bomb in the station.

All these post-war fascists were understandably very impressed by Barbie, a man who had been on the front line, fighting their cause with methods they so much admired. According to one member of Fiebelkorn's group, Barbie visited them in Santa Cruz in late spring 1980 in the midst of Bolivia's turbulent political chaos. 'He was then security adviser to the Bolivian Ministry of the Interior. He said, "The time has come; we must make this government move before this country is turned into an enormous Cuba. With our other foreign friends [i.e. Delle Chiaie and Pagliai] we are putting together a security force. We want you to help, but naturally you have to prove yourselves first." '

Barbie was inviting the German and Italian fascists to help

General Garcia Meza to overthrow President Lidia Gueiler and install himself as the President. Meza was a close friend and ally of Roberto Suárez. Overwhelmed by the billions of dollars flooding into the country, Suárez and some of the generals had become greedy. They wanted the money and no more irritating government interference. That meant taking over the government. Barbie's test for the Germans was the tedious task of acting as guards at meetings. As soon as he was satisfied, Dr Adolfo Ustares, Banzer's lawyer, arranged for Fiebelkorn's group to be given extra military training, shooting practice and new weapons, including a half-track tank.

On 17 July 1980, Fiebelkorn's group took up positions in Santa Cruz, ready to shoot anyone who challenged Bolivia's 189th coup. Unlike other towns, where there was fierce shooting and considerable bloodshed, Santa Cruz was quiet. As the reward for their services, Barbie arranged for the Germans to be hired permanently by the new government, based in a special building near Santa Cruz's airport.

'Our big breakthrough,' according to one of the Germans, 'was at the end of 1980 when Klaus Altmann rang us from La Paz and said that three of us should come to the capital. The President and the Minister of the Interior, Colonel Luis Arce Gómez, wanted to speak to us. Altmann took them to a brick house next to the West German embassy where the Minister of the Interior was waiting for them.' Barbie had a very close relationship with Arce Gómez, who described Barbie to one French journalist as, 'my teacher'. According to a French diplomat, Barbie was even seen at police headquarters in La Paz during Gómez's reign giving orders to interrogators about the questioning of political prisoners, students and labour leaders.

A heavyweight with a round chubby face, Arce Gómez is Roberto Suárez's cousin. His jocular appearance belies his record of brutality and violence. Superficially, it also conceals his notoriously keen interest in the cocaine trade which earned him the epithet, 'Minister of Cocaine'. With his help, Bolivia's cocaine crop tripled in just three years. According to the US Drug Enforcement Agency, he took a hefty commission on each bale of coca leaves that was illegally exported. In Barbie's presence, Arce Gómez asked Fiebelkorn whether his group could carry out 'special, risky assignments'. All three at the meeting jumped up and pulled out their revolvers.

Arce Gómez paled and then laughed, 'You're our kind.' Their task was to end the cocaine operation of about 140 small dealers. Arce Gómez's motive was to re-establish friendly relations with Washington, which had been seriously damaged both by the coup and the phenomenal spread of cocaine use in America. No Bolivian government can survive for long without Washington's approval, and the US administration had both refused to recognise the Meza regime and withheld economic aid. Arce Gómez's task was to convince Washington that the new Bolivian government was cooperating in ending cocaine exports to the United States. Barbie's neo-Nazi recruits were hired for that task.

After a meeting with President Meza, the three returned to Santa Cruz and celebrated their appointment in style. Fiebelkorn dressed up in a black Nazi uniform and, to choruses of 'Heil', christened the newly enlarged group, 'The Fiancés of Death'. Their style of operation was, not surprisingly, reminiscent of Gestapo raids forty years earlier in Lyons. 'In the first months of 1981, we stood Santa Cruz on its head. We burst into one house after another, grabbing hostages. From them we got more names and they were handed over for questioning. But the interrogations were done by Bolivians. Most of us did not like getting involved in those things.' Their profits and pleasure were enormous, but short-lived.

Exposed by American CBS television as intimately involved in the cocaine trade, Arce Gómez was forced to resign on 30 March 1981. Five months later, American pressure forced President Meza himself to resign. Both of them fled with millions of dollars to asylum in Argentina. Fiebelkorn and the 'Fiancés of Death' were forced to leave just weeks later. Bolivia was once again plunged into political turmoil. Klaus Barbie, however, had sufficiently close contacts with others in the army to feel relatively secure, although his personal life was soon shattered.

On 1 May 1981 he left Cochabamba with his wife to watch their son hang-gliding in Tunari. Both had been very concerned when their son Klaus had taken up the sport and Regine had pleaded that it was too dangerous. On the Labour Day holiday, they were watching their son floating in the air when a sudden gust of wind pushed him uncontrollably earthwards, causing him to crash fatally just yards from where they stood. Barbie's problems were now to multiply.

THE RETRIBUTION

Manfred Ludolph was true to his word: in 1972, Barbie's case file was returned to the active list, but little more happened. In 1976, the Lyons prosecutors sent a complete copy of their Barbie file, totalling 3,000 pages, to the Munich prosecutors who began the laborious task of translating and examining the potential new charges not just against Barbie, but against all the surviving members of the Lyons Gestapo. In 1979, police officers were sent to interrogate Stengritt, Floreck, Bartelmus and all the other Gestapo officers who had returned from imprisonment in France. Each was warned that he faced further prosecution, and then was asked for evidence against Barbie. Only Floreck condemned his former chief outright as a brutal murderer. Despite the volumes of testimony against Barbie, there seemed to be no new charge to bring which had a living eyewitness. Then someone pulled out of an old file the sworn statement made in August 1971 by Alfons Glas, the former Wehrmacht soldier, who had actually seen the St Claude Resistance leader, Joseph Kemmler, beaten to death on Barbie's orders. On the grounds of the Kemmler murder, the German government, in May 1982, formally but in secret submitted to the Bolivian government a new request for Barbie's extradition. Anticipating their reaction, the Germans argued that Barbie's Bolivian naturalisation was fraudulent and that he was therefore still a German citizen.

No one in Munich at the time expected that the request would be considered seriously. Bolivia was engulfed in an intense political crisis as the military fought desperately to prevent the liberal President-elect, Siles Zuazo, returning to form a civilian government. But for the first time, Barbie might have felt more than usually concerned about the outcome of the protracted battle for power. Waiting impatiently in exile in Peru, Zuazo had told reporters in mid-July that his government would not continue to protect the German fugitive.

One week later, the Bolivian presidency changed yet again, and General Guido Vildoso became head of state. It had been Vildoso's

217

soldiers who, in August 1981, on Barbie's command, had arrested and intimidated two American journalists in Cochabamba as they attempted to interview him. Eight days after Vildoso became President, he received his first private visitor – Klaus Barbie. As he left the Palace, Barbie told bemused reporters that they had discussed 'legal and administrative questions' concerning Transmaritima. No one believed him. He was at the pinnacle of his influence; now matters could only get worse.

In early August, Washington intervened directly in Bolivia's crisis. An American diplomat promised Zuazo generous loans if he returned to form a government. Shortly afterwards, the German government made public its May extradition request. Questioned about that request, Vildoso's own Foreign Minister, Agustín Saavedra, hinted that Barbie might be extradited to Germany. European interest in Bolivian affairs increased – not, for once, in the yo-yo fortunes of its presidents, but in the fate of Barbie. Other than staying put, where else could he go?

Barbie was now living permanently in La Paz. His wife had been complaining of stomach pains for some time and examination revealed that she was suffering from terminal cancer. Having buried his son only recently in the city's German cemetery, Barbie became depressed at the prospect of a solitary life; but he was not worried about his security. Not even the triumphant election of Zuazo as President on 6 October seemed to shake his conviction that his Bolivian citizenship gave him complete protection. Sipping coffee as usual in the *Confiteria La Paz*, he told journalists: 'I'm not worried about the German extradition demand. Bolivian law rules here.' But over at the presidential palace, the 192nd incumbent was emphatic: 'We will extradite him. We have no interest to protect people like him.'

Zuazo had already demonstrated his urgent resolve that Bolivia should cease to be a sanctuary for neo-fascists. Just three days after taking office, he had agreed that the Italian government could fly a special commando squad from Rome to seize Italy's two most wanted terrorists, Delle Chiaie and Pagliai. The special Alitalia DC10 arrived on 10 October, the same day that Zuazo was inaugurated. Italian anti-terrorist police, supported by Bolivian security forces, drove straight to the Italians' home in Santa Cruz. In the spectacular shoot-out which followed, Pagliai was shot in the neck and paralysed. There was no sign of Delle Chiaie. Pagliai was immediately flown back to Italy, but died soon after his return.

Despite the swift resolution of that particular problem, Zuazo was aware that his international standing had been damaged by this willing compromise of Bolivia's sovereignty. He was determined that Barbie's case should be treated with ostensible legitimacy. He told the French ambassador and Mario Roncal, the special emissary from Paris, that he wanted Barbie out of the country as soon as possible but that it had to seem like an extradition, not an expulsion. Bonn's extradition request had therefore to be subject to the Supreme Court. Not the least of the drawbacks to this solution was that the majority of the court's twelve judges had been appointed by the generals, and they showed no intention of reversing their view that Klaus Altmann was a Bolivian citizen. Nevertheless, in early January 1983, the German request was resubmitted to the court with the support of the Bolivian public prosecutor, who put forward the spurious claim that an extradition treaty between Bolivia and Germany had been signed in 1889. By this time, with international attention focused on the country as a haven for Nazi war criminals, the government was ready to consider any strategy to ensure Barbie's removal.

Regine Barbie died just before Christmas and was buried next to her son in the German cemetery. It was a place which Barbie had visited many times over the years – tending the graves of his friends seemed the closest he would ever come to his Fatherland, for which he had given so much. Some hundred people came to pay their last respects. Afterwards, Barbie moved back to Santa Cruz to live with Klaus's widow and his three grandchildren; an unsatisfactory arrangement which was not to last for long.

In January 1983, Jacques Friedman, the Inspector General of France's treasury, arrived discreetly in La Paz to establish the help his government might offer Bolivia in its efforts to reduce a massive four-billion-dollar international debt. His visit had been organised by the French cabinet's 'Barbie team', coordinated by Jean Louis Bianco, the Secretary General of the Elysée. Bianco, fluent in German, was now in regular contact with Waldemar Schreckenberger, the head of the German Chancellor's office in Bonn.

Until December, it had always been assumed by the French government that the most they would achieve would be Barbie's

219

extradition to Germany: legally, politically and practically, there seemed no alternative, and with this they were satisfied. Justice would take its course in Munich just as well as in Lyons. However, from the outset of their conversations, Bianco began to realise that despite their request for Barbie's extradition the Germans were wary of the full implications of the Nazi's return.

Aware of the French President's personal interest in the matter, the German government feared that the fragile equilibrium between the two countries might be damaged if Barbie was awaiting trial in Germany. French newspapers would certainly begin to criticise Germany's poor record in prosecuting Nazi war criminals. German courts could be proven, in French eyes, to have been too lenient. Several trials in Germany had degenerated into grotesque attempts by sympathetic neo-Nazi lawyers to whitewash the Third Reich and glorify their clients. Bonn was still smarting from the international criticism which had greeted the recent trial in Düsseldorf of fifteen former staff of the Maidaneck extermination camp. The trial had lasted six years and was notable for the startling claims made by the defendants' lawyers – amongst them, that the camp's gas chambers were not used for killing people, but for cleaning clothes. Witnesses, a few survivors of the terrible brutality, had left the courtroom in tears, complaining bitterly that their own credibility was at issue, and not the defendants'.

This was not Schreckenberger's only concern. Chancellor Helmut Kohl was at that time leading an interim right-wing government and was committed to national elections in March. Raking over the Nazi past was always embarrassing for the conservatives and at that very moment Germany was suffocating under an avalanche of events commemorating the fiftieth anniversary of Hitler's accession to power. With luck, any adverse effects of this would have disappeared by election time. Barbie's return and the reawakening of past history would definitely not win the conservative government any extra support and, worse, might result in further tribulations. At the outset Schreckenberger refrained from being explicit but Bianco was sufficiently sensitive to understand that it might be worthwhile considering arrangements for an alternative destination for Barbie.

Towards the end of January, Barbie returned to La Paz. Walking in full public gaze along the capital's main thoroughfare, the Prado, with his bodyguard Alvaro de Castro, he scotched the rumours that he had fled the country. 'Here I am,' he told staring reporters. The French, fearing that he had disappeared forever, were relieved when he returned. 'It would have been so easy,' recalls one of the Ministers, 'for him to have disappeared into one of the enormous haciendas in Santa Cruz. The German mafia could easily have hidden him and then flown him out of the country from one of their private airstrips. But he was old, had lost his family and probably just couldn't be bothered with precautions anymore.' Some felt that there was even a new self-confidence about him and they were probably right.

Barbie was so sure of his position that, when he was summoned to government offices to arrange the repayment of a $10,000 debt incurred by Transmaritima in 1968, he decided not to take his lawyer. The $10,000 were claimed by Comibol, the state-owned mining corporation. Barbie told officials that he was prepared to repay the amount, but began to haggle excitedly over whether the official or black-market rate of exchange should be used to convert the Bolivian pesos. The argument was cut short by his arrest. The following day, 26 January, Barbie was charged with fraud, with contravening Bolivia's immigration regulations and with creating a personal army.

Both the French and German governments had expected Barbie's arrest. As arranged, the German ambassador reapplied for his extradition, and Bianco rang Schreckenberger to discuss how to get Barbie out of Bolivia. The most sensitive issue was Bolivia's insistence that its sovereignty be protected: Barbie must leave the country on a non-Bolivian airline to give the appearance of a legal extradition. Lufthansa, the German national airline, had a twice-weekly flight out of La Paz, flying via Lima to Frankfurt. It was an ideal solution. The French expected that the Bolivians would put Barbie on the flight and Mario Roncal, the Bolivian Minister of the Interior, agreed. On 27 February, Roncal summoned the French and German chargés d'affaires and told them that the Bolivian government had decided not to await the expected adverse Supreme Court decision and wanted Barbie extradited immediately to Germany. The myth that Barbie's fate was to be decided by rigorous examination of the law was finally exploded. But now, after weeks of prevarication, the Bonn government refused outright, under any circumstances whatsoever, to allow Barbie to return to Germany.

The Elysée was staggered. The French knew that Zuazo could not prolong Barbie's imprisonment and that he needed to staunch the embarrassing rumours and leaks now plaguing La Paz. Puzzled and anxious, the Bolivian President urged the Europeans to settle what seemed such a simple matter. Paris urged the Germans just to take Barbie out of La Paz. 'We just asked them to take him anywhere,' recalls the Minister, 'so that we could pick him up. Lima for example. They just stared at us.' The French then proposed a compromise. Bianco suggested that Barbie be put on the Lufthansa flight from La Paz bound for Lima, and then diverted 'for atmospheric reasons' to Cayenne in the French colony of Guiana. On 29 February, Bonn rejected this plan outright. There was no alternative but for Barbie to be expelled to France via Cayenne. The problem now was, how to get him to Cayenne. The DGSE, the Direction Générale de la Sureté Exterieure, was alerted to draw up a rapid plan, in cooperation with the French military, for returning Barbie to French territory without compromising Bolivia's sovereignty. If Barbie could not be extradited on a German plane, he would have to be expelled on a Bolivian one. The unacceptable alternative was that Barbie would be expelled across any border of his choice and then disappear forever.

Barbie's expulsion was set for 1 February, but the failure of Paris and Bonn to agree cast uncertainty over arrangements once again. 'Nobody outside realises how close we were to failure,' is the view of one French negotiator. 'We suddenly realised that we might lose Barbie because the situation in Bolivia became very tense.' Zuazo's coalition partners led by the Vice-President, Jaime Paz Zamora, began arguing that Barbie's trial should be held in Bolivia. Some left-wing members had already withdrawn their support for the government, criticising Zuazo's failure to tackle the paramilitary groups. With his government's fate in doubt, Zuazo became nervous. More so the following day, when he heard that Barbie's lawyer, Carrión Constantino, had paid the $10,000 debt and was demanding his client's immediate release. Carrión was also complaining publicly that he had not been allowed to see his client for the previous forty-eight hours. To add to the President's discomfort, the lawyer was asking him to explain why Bolivia, whose penal code did not recognise war crimes, was suddenly interested in

222

culpability for ancient events in Europe. 'It smells like money in return for my client,' he told anyone who visited his rundown office.

For the next two days, Zuazo prevaricated. Barbie was kept in solitary confinement, not only to isolate him from the arguments about his fate, but also to prevent someone from the German community or from the cocaine trade killing him to prevent him talking. On 4 February it seemed that, again, no decision would be made. The cabinet had travelled 100 kilometres to Lake Titicaca to celebrate the four hundredth anniversary of the appearance of the virgin of Copacabana. Yet, that night, Bolivian television showed a short film about the Nazi extermination camps, with a picture of Barbie appearing between shots. Towards the end was a clip of Adolf Eichmann's trial in Jerusalem – 'The fate,' said the narrator, 'of Klaus Barbie.' The dithering had stopped. It seemed that Barbie's destination was still uncertain. Lima was the conventional first stop for any flight leaving La Paz for the northern hemisphere, but Aeroperu, the Peruvian national airline, had been ordered by its government not to carry Barbie under any circumstances. Lima had given the same instruction to Lufthansa. Zuazo grew increasingly nervous. International attention was forcing him to resolve the Barbie question within hours; Bolivia's sense of national esteem demanded that Barbie leave the country on a Bolivian plane, but Bolivian pilots had launched an indefinite strike. The problem seemed insoluble. The DGSE had for some days claimed to have the answer, but the operation's success depended upon sticking to a precise timetable.

A French military Hercules C-130 would arrive by night at El Alto Airport with its true nationality completely obliterated: instead, it would be disguised as belonging to Lloyds, a privately-owned Bolivian airline. Barbie would have to be brought from the prison just as the plane was landing, and it would take off for its return to Cayenne immediately after refuelling. Several times the Hercules had been about to leave Cayenne but had been held back at the last moment because of indecision in La Paz. Because the attempt could be made only once, the French government would only give the go-ahead when it was convinced that it would be successful. Politicians and officials on both sides of the Atlantic agree that the tension between the two countries at that moment was enormous.

At 9.00 p.m. on Friday 4 February, after several false alarms, two figures shrouded in blankets were rushed from the San Pedro prison and driven towards the airport. Barbie was finally to be expelled for obtaining Bolivian nationality with false papers and a false name. Handcuffed, he was taken to the military side of the airport. The Minister of Information, Rueda Pena, was one of the last Bolivian officials Barbie met. Standing at the foot of the stairs up to the Hercules, Pena told Barbie in German that he was being expelled to Germany. According to Pena, Barbie was quite cheerful about it: 'He only complained that he was cold because he had not been allowed to take any belongings. I ordered a nearby policeman to hand over his parka.'

Barbie was unaware of the plane's true destination. French agents, disguised as crew, spoke to the Bolivians in sign language. At the last moment, a Bolivian television crew had been allowed to board the plane and film Barbie's journey back to France – an unusual privilege, explicable because Ugo Roncal, a member of the team, was the brother of the Minister of the Interior. The camera's continuous observation of Barbie, recorded on film, reveals him as remarkably unconcerned about the return to his homeland: 'He continuously asked questions about life in Germany, and for example the cost of a razor.' In La Paz, the government was asked to explain the legalities of expelling him to French territory. 'France,' said Mario Roncal, 'was the only country who agreed to receive him.'

After seven hours, as it prepared to land at Rochambeau airport near Cayenne, the plane was plunged into darkness. Once it landed, Barbie was taken to the doorway. Below him, in the dim light, he saw the French uniforms of local gendarmes and soldiers. It was a terrible shock. At the foot of the stairs, after a momentary pause, he was formally charged. An hour later, on a French military DC-8 often used by the President, he took off for France, now a very sullen and resentful man. 'The expulsion was illegal,' he told Roncal, once again filming Barbie. 'The Supreme Court refused my extradition several years ago.' For the remainder of the journey, Barbie reminisced about his early days in Bolivia, his first Jewish employer, and how he had always remained neutral in politics. About his service in France, he just quipped, 'The past is the past. Woe to the vanquished.' After some thought he added that two hundred years ago, Napoleon was condemned for his tyranny, yet 'Now he is a hero.' Like Napoleon, he realised, he would never again be a free man.

Long before Barbie arrived in Lyons, at the end of the non-stop trans-Atlantic flight, the Klarsfelds had alerted news agencies and journalists. As his plane landed at Orange military airport, some of his surviving victims were already giving anguished accounts of his deeds, while others rushed to the Lyons municipal airport or to the Montluc prison, seeking by their presence some small consolation for the misery he had caused them. At 10.25 p.m. on the Saturday night, a bright-blue police maria carrying Barbie sped through the crowd outside the prison. He could not have seen the simple plaque fixed near the heavy door: *10,000 imprisoned; 7,000 died*. The heavy symbolism of this return to the very scene of his crimes was deliberately overladen by French television and newspapers with emotional accounts of Gestapo rule forty years earlier. Brimming over with the excitement of the moment, France's Prime Minister, Pierre Mauroy, tried to inject a sense of historical solemnity into the event: 'We did not do this for revenge. First we wanted justice done. And then we wanted to show fidelity to those hours of grief and struggle in which France saved its honour.' It was a triumph for the French left. But the exultation evaporated very quickly.

A small group of lawyers and officials had been alerted about Barbie's arrival, amongst them Christian Riss, the examining magistrate, and president of the Lyons bar association, Maître Alain Compagnon de la Servette, who had agreed, in the interests of justice, to act as Barbie's temporary defence lawyer. In 1954, Servette had defended two Frenchmen accused in the same trial as Barbie. Servette remembers his new (non-paying) client looking 'tired and prostrate – the effect of jet-lag on an old man. Not the man he was forty years ago.' In a two-hour session, Barbie's identity was formally established; he was charged with crimes against humanity and then led to a section of the prison which had been cleared of all other inmates. As he walked across the prison courtyard, he was photographed. The picture's publication was used as an excuse by the government to transfer him later that week, as previously arranged, to an isolation block in the St Joseph prison – for his own safety.

Servette's role was difficult. His normal practice is commercial

225

law, but at the outset he felt honour-bound, by virtue of his position, to volunteer to serve Barbie's interests. In an unassuming way, he enjoyed the publicity and the challenge. Gradually, as he became acquainted with his client on his twice-weekly visits, he admits that he saw a person rather than a monster. Strangely, for some time, Barbie could not come to terms with the fact that he was back in Lyons. 'He forgot that I lived through his reign,' says Servette. 'He even tried to explain to me where the Hôtel Terminus was.' The lawyer was soon the victim of hate mail and even lost clients for his pains. When he saw the case which Barbie had to answer, he realised that preparing the defence would be an enormous task. There was one consolation. Barbie confessed that he could remember very few names of those with whom he had worked, especially the collaborators. His constant threat to create fear amongst Frenchmen collapsed.

Barbie heard the full charges on 24 February. He was indicted on eight separate counts: the killing of twenty-two hostages, including women and children, in reprisal for an attack on two German policemen in 1943; the arrest and torture of nineteen people in 1943; the liquidation of the eighty-six members of the UGIF on 9 February 1943; the shooting of forty-two people, including forty Jews, during 1943 and 1944; the round-up of French railway workers at Oullins on 9 August 1944, during which two were killed and others wounded; the deportation to Auschwitz and Ravensbrück of about 650 people, half of them Jews, by the last rail convoy to leave Lyons on 11 April 1944; the shooting of seventy Jews at Bron on 17 August 1944 and the shooting of two other Jews and two Roman Catholic priests on 20 August 1944, at St Genis-Laval; and the deportation of fifty-five Jews, including fifty-two children, from Izieu in 1944 (fifty-two was the original government estimate in 1945).

According to Riss, each of the charges can be classified as a crime against humanity, a definite legal anomaly in the French penal code. The specific term, 'crimes against humanity', was 'adopted' by Allied lawyers in 1945 as one of the indictments against the leaders of the Third Reich for the main Nuremberg trial. It was a piece of blatant legalistic improvisation to render Nazi atrocities – the extermination camps for example – retrospectively illegal despite their 'legality' under Nazi law. Critics would argue that power had been substituted for principle. Under the Nuremberg Charter, crimes against humanity were defined as, 'Murder, extermination, deportation and other inhumane acts committed against any civilian population, before or during the war, or persecution on political, racial or religious grounds in execution of or in connection with any crime within the jurisdiction of the Tribunal, whether or not in violation of the domestic law of the country where perpetrated.' The Allied lawyers viewed it as a suitable charge against the leaders of the Third Reich, but did not intend that it should be used for crimes committed by individual German officers in the field. These were all charged under the normal laws of warfare. After 1945, none of the Allies included crimes against humanity within their domestic law.

Towards the end of 1964, however, there was a sudden panic amongst French Resistants. According to French law, crimes can be punished only within twenty years of their commission. After that, they are prescribed and the criminal is free of all risk. That prescription was sacred to French criminal law and applied equally to all crimes, including crimes committed by the Germans during the Occupation. To their consternation, the French suddenly realised that SS officers of 'Das Reich' Panzer Division, who had been responsible for such massacres in France as the slaughter of 642 men, women and children in Oradour in June 1944, could in 1965 return to the scene of their crime and, with complete impunity and immunity, parade their 'successes' in front of their children. Under their commander, General Heinz Lammerding, who at the time was head of a construction company in Düsseldorf, they regularly held parties to celebrate their wartime years. None of them, despite being sentenced to death by French courts in their absence, had ever served any sentence. The French suddenly conjured up a revolting image of ex-SS officers, in 1965, taking coach trips to Oradour to celebrate on the spot.

In an emotional three-day debate starting on 16 December 1964, the National Assembly confronted their dilemma. The vast majority of German war criminals had not been punished and were leading prosperous lives in the new Federal Republic. The only legal tool available to maintain their criminal status was to incorporate Nuremberg's 'crimes against humanity' into the French penal code and declare them exempt from the statute of limitations. The proposal was enacted on 26 December by 'taking note' retrospectively that crimes against humanity are imprescribable. This inevitably became the subject of interminable, intricate legal squabbles, not least because it offended the basic criterion of a crime: that it should have defined penalties.

Barbie's lawyers will find it difficult to challenge the legality of that legislation. Paul Touvier, Barbie's wartime collaborator, has already tried and failed. So have Maurice Papon and Jean Leguay, two former Vichy officials who allegedly collaborated with the Germans in the deportation of French Jews to Auschwitz. They were suddenly hauled from apparent respectability into the limelight by Serge Klarsfeld on charges of crimes against humanity – a category, they argue, which was intended for the prosecution of Germans, not Frenchmen. The examination of their wartime collaboration continues.

Whether, in Barbie's case, the eight crimes can be interpreted as crimes against humanity will be open to argument. He would have to prove that those deported or killed were involved in acts of Resistance, and that deportation was not a crime against humanity because special conditions apply in wartime. Barbie's defence, so far, has been to plead, firstly, ignorance; secondly, that he left Lyons for the last time on 17 August 1944 and never returned, and therefore cannot be responsible for anything which occurred after that date; thirdly, that he was only the third-ranking officer in the Gestapo headquarters and therefore cannot be held responsible for general commands; fourthly, that, if anyone was tortured, it was done by subordinates; and fifthly, concerning the Jews, that, in signing the two telexes to Paris, he was standing in for the specialists normally sent from Adolf Eichmann's team. He claims that he sent the telexes as a mere administrative chore. He vehemently denies having been in Izieu; that he said, was 'Wenzel's responsibility' (Wenzel died during the 26 May Allied bombing of Lyons). As proof, he argues that his name on the Izieu telegram is preceded by the letters *IA*, the German for 'Im Auftrage', meaning 'Acting under orders'. It is a weak argument because all Gestapo officers used that format, even Adolf Eichmann. Barbie also denies that he knew the fate of any of those deported, including the children. It is an argument which a French jury will hear with some scepticism, if only because his superior, Werner Knab, was a member of an *Einsatzgrüppe* in the east.

'It was only because of the children of Izieu that I chased after Barbie, and on that he'll be convicted,' says Serge Klarsfeld. 'In 1944, there were lots of refugee homes for Jewish children in France, and the Gestapo knew all about them. Only two Gestapo officers in the whole of France didn't deliberately ignore them, both because it was the end of the war, and they were after all children. That was Alois Brunner and Barbie. Barbie must be convicted because he murdered those harmless children of Izieu.'

At the beginning of June 1983, Barbie changed lawyers. The modest, uncommitted Servette was replaced by the flamboyant, left-wing Jacques Verges. Verges claims that Barbie approached him because he is famous in both Germany and France for championing unpopular causes. His former clients include Algerians fighting against the French army during their war of independence, Palestinian-backed aeroplane hijackers, and German members of the Baader-Meinhof group. Verges only started work again in France four years ago. During the previous ten years, he had disappeared; some suspect that he was in China and Albania, others say that he was in the Middle East. He refuses to reveal his whereabouts. In the early Sixties, he edited a well-financed magazine called *Revolution*, a pro-Chinese monthly devoted to the Third World. One of his earliest contributors was Régis Debray who wrote about the guerrillas in Venezuela. Twenty years ago, the two were comrades for the same cause. Verges does not hide his present disdain for Debray: 'He is now an official, and I am still fighting a cause.' He is clearly delighted at the opportunity to embarrass the unfaithful.

Verges' first objective is to expose the deceptive Hercules flight. He is convinced that, because Barbie was expelled rather than extradited, he will have to be released. 'The key is that the expulsion was the result of connivance between the French and Bolivian governments, and the French courts will refuse to judge a case where an expulsion or extradition is improper.' Klarsfeld laughingly rejects Verges' argument. The lawyers will clash about the interpretation of jurisprudence, but even Verges is realistic about the slim chance of finding a French judge who is prepared to order Barbie's release and face the consequences. 'To release him,' says the Marxist, 'would be a victory for French justice and would halt this appalling piece of theatre. Riss's dossier against Barbie is thin and unconvincing.' It is the natural brazenness of the lawyer for the defence. To Klarsfeld's insistence that Barbie will be convicted for sending the Izieu children to Auschwitz, Verges answers that his client had nothing at all to do with the Jews, 'He was just number three in the Gestapo, obeying orders.' Klarsfeld, delighted that Barbie's lawyer not only speaks his client's language but even seems to believe in his defence, insists that because Barbie's SS written record describes him as 'the dynamo of the department', there will be no doubt that the twelve-man jury will be convinced that Barbie was a ferocious leader rather than a meek subordinate.

On 5 March, Barbie's daughter Ute travelled from Austria to visit him. To the press she said, 'He is still for me my father, a very good father, not a war criminal,' and claimed that the two-hour meeting had been 'very moving'. But those who saw the reunion were surprised by the lack of emotion. The following day, Barbie was rushed to hospital with a strangulated intestine. The medical expert who had made the diagnosis was Dr René Guillet. In 1944, Guillet had been a young doctor in the Ain Resistance, close to both Heslop and Romans-Petit. Among the many brutalities he witnessed was an incident that resulted from a visit by a Gestapo detachment, led by Floreck, to the hospital in Nantua on 12 July. Nine patients, too wounded and sick to be evacuated, were seized and executed in a nearby village. 'It was a shock when I walked in and saw the patient in the flesh, but then I treated him like any other sick man.'

Forty years on, the unforgettable was still unforgivable, but the society which Barbie had tried to demolish had proved that its humanitarianism had more than survived.

AFTERMATH

Erhard Dabringhaus became quite excited as he watched the television news reports of Barbie's return to France in February 1983. He had already tried to contact the local NBC station in Detroit to tell them that he, an obscure, retired professor, had known this Nazi who was now headline news across the world. It was to take another twenty-four hours before anyone in the station's New York headquarters was prepared to take his claim seriously and transmit an interview on the nightly news show. But even as he repeated across the world his story that the Nazi butcher had been a paid US agent, there was genuine disbelief. For the public, the Second World War was a just war, where good had triumphed over evil and the criminals had been punished at such places as Nuremberg. Was it at all possible that the American Army, having fought and sacrificed so much to defeat the Nazis, could actually embrace one of the perpetrators of the worst Nazi crimes? Dabringhaus said it was, but he was an unconvincing witness, even when the Klarsfelds supported his allegations. All the other dozens of Americans who knew the truth held steadfastly to their thirty-five-year-old secret.

In Washington, the US House of Representatives' Judiciary Committee for many years had been investigating and publishing disturbing evidence that many eastern Europeans, who had willingly aided the Germans in the extermination of millions of Jews and others during the war, had been smuggled illegally into the USA, had been granted American citizenship and were leading peaceful, prosperous lives. Investigation had revealed that their presence in America was the successful result of an extraordinary criminal conspiracy between the CIA, the FBI and the US immigration services. The Committee's current chairman, Peter Rodino, and other politicians followed Dabringhaus's claims with interest and waited for further revelations. The few which appeared shed little extra light but confirmed the need for an official inquiry. The initial reaction of William Smith, the Attorney General, was to reject the demand personally, arguing that the whole case was of

231

historical interest only, and there was no possibility of criminal prosecution because of the statute of limitations. If his concern was that any inquiry would raise more questions than were answered, then his political judgement would eventually prove correct. Yet, after substantial pressure, Smith was forced to reverse his stand and on 14 March 1983 he commissioned Allan Ryan to investigate America's relationship with Barbie. It would be the first time that the extremely sensitive post-war relationship between the western Allies and the defeated Nazis would be explored officially, and in public. Taken to its natural conclusion, an investigation would have shown that the intimate post-war relationship between the victors and the Nazi war criminals had been approved at the very highest levels of the American military and government establishments in Germany, usually in total disregard of the policy guidelines laid down in Washington. In the event, the Department of Justice report avoided that sensational conclusion by limiting the area of responsibility and so confining political repercussions.

The alternative would have provoked demands for innumerable further investigations with innumerable embarrassing disclosures.

Allan Ryan was head of the Justice Department's Office of Special Investigations. As the man leading a long, successful investigation into the presence of east European Nazis living illegally in the USA, he was ideally placed to discover and understand the available documentary evidence. His 218-page report, with a massive 680-page appendix of documents, was published on 16 August 1983. Superficially it seemed impressive. Here was the American government voluntarily declassifying literally hundreds of 'Top Secret' documents to prove that its servants had conspired not only to defeat justice but also to betray Barbie's victims and those who had fought and died to rid the world of the Nazi scourge. Adding to that self-inflicted wound, Ryan also recommended that the American government formally apologise to the French government for 'delaying the due process of the law'. Having suggested that the American government offer its help to the French prosecution, Ryan reported to the Attorney General: 'This is a matter of decency, and of honourable conduct. It should be, I believe, the final chapter by the United States in this case.' After initial State Department opposition, the White House formally announced that it had sent a formal note to the French government expressing 'the deep regrets' of the United States for the concealment of Barbie. It was magnanimous behaviour and proof that America, despite its contradictions, is an unique democracy. In contrast, when the British Foreign Office was asked whether they would allow Ryan to publish the British documents on British attempts to recruit Barbie, Richard Clarke, the FO spokesman just said, 'No comment.' The British have destroyed most of their archives concerning the occupation of Germany, a convenient excuse to conceal their own unsavoury dealings with the Nazis.

Yet, despite Ryan's achievement, his investigation suffers from a curious narrowness which suggests that he was anxious to present a completely unambiguous conclusion placing the exclusive blame for Barbie's concealment on the CIC.

It is a dubious conclusion, based on insufficient evidence; and because there is no apparent reason for that tactic, it produces more speculation.

For example, his blame of the CIC is preceded by a surprisingly generous explanation of the CIC's motives for hiring Barbie. After mentioning the mounting political and strategic problems facing the western Allies, Ryan summarises the opposing arguments facing the CIC in 1947 when considering whether Barbie should be recruited. For those in the CIC concerned about the future of Europe, says Ryan, the argument was that, 'If a Klaus Barbie was available and effective and loyal and reliable . . . his employment was in the best interests of the United States at the time.' The opposite argument, looking back to the past, would say, according to Ryan, that it was a 'grave misjudgement . . . incomprehensible and shameful' to employ anyone with a Gestapo record, regardless of his worth.

Ryan concludes that the 'conscientious and patriotic' CIC agents cannot be criticised for recruiting Barbie in their fight against the communists, because their motives were neither 'cynical nor corrupt'. His reasons are precise. The CROWCASS lists were uniformly disregarded because they were discredited; the French presented the evidence and demanded Barbie's return as a war criminal for the first time only in 1950; Barbie convincingly presented himself as an effective anti-Resistance and counter-intelligence agent and not a torturer; and had the CIC really known the man's record, they would not have agreed so readily to the French interrogations in 1948 and 1949: 'The decision to use Barbie was a defensible one, made in good faith by those who believed that they were advancing legitimate and important national security interests.'

The report's genuflexion to the CIC's predicament is not an expression of Ryan's benevolence. It is the direct result of his own approach. Until very late in the investigation Ryan and his advisers were very doubtful as to whether Barbie was actually head of Section IV, the Gestapo. In the absence of documentary proof, they were convinced that Barbie was in fact head of Section VI, Intelligence. They hoped to prove that Barbie was not 'the Butcher of Lyons'. What the investigators hoped to gain by pursuing that argument mystified the French when Ryan explained his thoughts during his visit in summer 1983. They could not understand why he discarded as unimportant evidence the UNWCC and CROWCASS 1945 listings of Barbie as a murderer. Many feared that he hoped to exculpate the Americans completely for any responsibility by pleading ignorance, and warned him of the consequences. But finally he split his own argument artificially and isolated the responsibility by entirely blaming the CIC – but only after 1949.

It was in May 1949 that the CIC received the newspaper cutting containing the French protest with the brief account of Barbie's crimes. According to Ryan, Browning's covering note to Region XII, that 'headquarters is inclined to believe that there is some element of truth in the allegations', changes the whole onus of responsibility. After that time, he argues, everyone in the CIC knew about the charges against Barbie but decided, on their own definition of 'national security interests', to ignore them. Thereafter, although Barbie was allegedly dropped, he was in truth more trusted than ever. It was a period of outright deception, primarily towards the French, but also according to Ryan, towards HICOG; the culprits were possibly EUCOM and definitely the CIC. Ryan condemns that deception and says that only the statute of limitations prevents the prosecution of those in the CIC who were solely responsible. It is a cosy argument because it limits the blame to a small, easily identifiable group of men who, operating at the lowest levels both then and now, possess neither the political power nor the prestige within the military establishment to upset the neat answer.

Ryan's report is wholly based on documents. Claiming that they provide infallible proof, he has deliberately ignored present-day explanations, saying that he suspects the accuracy of personal memories of events which happened more than thirty years ago – an argument which will not prevent Barbie's own trial. Ryan's approach would be less vulnerable if so many crucial documents were not missing, and if he had published all the documents which he had seen. In effect, he has excluded a mass of documents including those which reveal a grey area of both indecision and disagreement, and which suggest an inter-agency conspiracy. To corroborate his own conclusions, Ryan published low-level correspondence – for example, between Alan Lightner, who was an uninformed HICOG official, and an unimportant officer at the American embassy in Paris. This corroboration only establishes Lightner's ignorance, proving that the discussion within HICOG about the CIC's protection of Barbie took place elsewhere; the documents establishing those discussions are still classified.

The CIC did not operate in a vacuum. Had their military and political masters in EUCOM and HICOG been genuinely concerned about Barbie's presence, the records so far published would demonstrate something more than the evident institutional ignorance, disinterest and apathy. After all, no one was actually ordered to search for Barbie. Ryan does not criticise either HICOG or EUCOM for that failure. Despite the impressive volume of documents published, absolutely none are included from the highest levels of either EUCOM or HICOG. These were the crucial decision-making areas which were concerned with the Barbie question. If no documents have survived, it further weakens Ryan's exclusive dependence on documentary evidence.

Surviving CIC officers say that Ryan ignores the reality of the CIC operation. There were, they say, many intense internal disagreements but finally everyone had to obey the commander, Colonel Erskine. Yet the report implicitly blames individual officers such as Vidal, a civilian officer, and Browning, for decisions where the responsibility was not theirs to exercise. The overall result will be to fuel further demands for greater disclosure of the western Allies' relationship with Nazi war criminals.

The Klarsfelds are, however, satisfied with the results. Their allegations and long campaign have been entirely vindicated. When Serge Klarsfeld, representing the parents of the children of Izieu in the prosecution of Barbie, met his prey for the first time in the St Joseph prison, there was silence. 'Klarsfeld?' asked Barbie. 'Yes,' replied the lawyer with pride. His affirmation was answered by a long, hateful stare. Two actors on a vast stage, both casualties of the most monstrous crime in history.

As Barbie awaits trial, politicians, government officials and criminals in many countries have sought to distance themselves from the incriminating disclosures which they fear their former associate might release. Former SS officers, French collaborators, Western intelligence agents, drug dealers and arms merchants, all live in fear of betrayal. Many hope and believe that the French will now conspire to prevent his trial ever occurring, so silencing him forever. In this last wish they will be disappointed. Barbie's life is the triumph of evil over every semblance of justice. This ruthless, 'street-wise' individual will never cease to fight back.

NOTE ON SOURCES

Inevitably, there are many sources for this book – especially interviews with those who were directly involved either with Barbie himself or with his case, and classified government documents which were 'shown' to me. In both cases the source is clear in the text. The material on the postwar handling of Nazi war criminals is drawn from my previous book, *Blind Eye to Murder*. The history of France's Occupation and the Resistance is well covered in books listed below. Additional information on the Newtons' case was discovered by research in local and national Resistance archives. Details of Barbie's activities in 1944 during the sweeps against the Maquis, and of the SS's relationship with the Wehrmacht, are drawn from papers in the West German archives in Freiburg and Koblenz. The account of Barbie's employment by the Americans is the result of four months' research by Bob Fink, Margaret Jay and myself, and draws especially on the large appendix of documents published by the US Department of Justice special investigators. The major obstacle facing all researchers into Barbie's life in Bolivia is the disappearance of the official records and the natural reluctance of his accomplices to tell the truth. I have ignored any part of his life which is not verifiable from many different sources. The Klarsfelds have published several books containing government documents on Barbie's activities, and his life as an SS officer is partially chronicled in his SS file, reprinted by the Klarsfelds. Government officials in several countries have given me access to secret and confidential files. I have used them wherever appropriate. I have, naturally, read through all the newspaper cuttings on the subject; however, I found them to be often quite inaccurate and have only used them when more than two contemporary sources report the same incident, or where the quotation has been checked with the journalist himself.

Over the past ten years, Barbie has given several interviews about his life. All of them are flawed by his conceit and deliberate distortion. In 1979, General Karl Wolff, Himmler's wartime adjutant, travelled through South America visiting Nazi fugitives. He spent nearly a week with Barbie in La Paz. Flattered that an important SS general should visit him, Barbie told many untruths; but on some subjects he was more candid than on any other occasion. It was not until towards the end of the visit that Barbie realised that the German travelling with Wolff was the journalist Gerd Heidemann, who had tape-recorded their entire discussion. Heidemann continued to interview Barbie on tape after Wolff left. Although those conversations contain many unsubstantiated allegations and crucial omissions, there are several valuable insights into his life which he revealed innocently to his eminent guest. I have only used those parts of those conversations which either can be independently verified (and many have been confirmed by subsequent disclosures) or are so outrageous that, regardless of the truth, they are accurate revelations of Barbie's own thoughts.

BIBLIOGRAPHY

Amouroux, Henri, *Les Français sous l'Occupation* (Fayard, 1964).

Bernet, Philippe, *Roger Wybot et la Bataille pour la DST* (Presses de la Cité, 1975).

Bower, Tom, *Blind Eye to Murder* (Andre Deutsch, 1981).

Chavanet, Roger, *Histoire Vecue des Maquis de l'Azergues* (privately published).

Delarue, Jacques, *The History of the Gestapo* (Macdonald & Co., 1964).

Delperrie de Bayac, Jacques, *Histoire de la Milice, 1918–1945* (Fayard, 1969).

Ferreira, Dantas, *O Depoimento, do SS Altmann-Barbie* (Jose Olympio, 1972).

Foote, M. R. D., *SOE in France* (Her Majesty's Stationery Office, 1966).

Goldberg, Michel, *Namesake* (Yale University Press, 1982).

Guinguoin, Georges, *Quatre Ans de Lutte sur le Sol Limousin* (Hachette, 1974).

Hastings, Max, *Das Reich: Resistance and the March of the 2nd SS Panzer Division through France, June 1944* (Michael Joseph, 1981).

Heslop, Richard, *Xavier* (Mayflower Books Ltd, 1971).

Hohne, Heinz and Zolling, Hermann, *The General Was a Spy: The Truth about General Gehlen and His Spy Ring* (Pan Books, 1972).

Klarsfeld, Beate, *Wherever They May Be* (Vanguard Press, 1975).

Klarsfeld, Serge, *Vichy – Auschwitz: Le rôle de Vichy dans la solution finale de la question Juive en France, 1942* (Fayard, 1983).

Liddell Hart, Sir Basil, *History of the Second World War* (Pan Books, 1982).

Marrus, Michel R. and Paxton, Robert O., *Vichy France and the Jews* (Basic Books Inc., 1981).

Noguères, Henri, *Histoire de la Résistance en France* (five volumes, Robert Laffont, 1967).

239

Paxton, Robert O., *Vichy France: Old Guard and New Order, 1940–44* (Barrie and Jenkins, 1972).

Presser, Dr J., *Ashes in the Wind: The Destruction of the Dutch Jewry* (Souvenir Press, 1965).

Pryce-Jones, David, *Paris in the Third Reich: A History of the German Occupation, 1940–44* (Collins, 1981).

Rings, Werner, *Life with the Enemy: Collaboration and Resistance in Hitler's Europe, 1939–1945* (Weidenfeld & Nicholson, 1982).

Romans-Petit, Colonel Henri, *Les Maquis de l'Ain* (Hachette).

Ruby, Marcel, *La Résistance á Lyons* (three volumes, L'Hermes, 1981).

Rude, Fernand, *Libération de Lyons, et de sa région* (Hachette, 1974).

Schoenbrun, David, *The Story of the French Resistance* (New American Library, 1980).

Thomas, Jack, *No Banners: The Story of Alfred and Henry Newton* (W. H. Allen, 1955).

Trepper, Leopold, *The Great Game: Memoirs of a Master Spy* (Michael Joseph, 1977).

Vistel, Alban, *La Nuit sans Ombre: Histoire des Mouvements Unis de la Résistance, et leur rôle dans la libération du Sud-Est* (Fayard, 1970).

Vomécourt, Philippe de, *Who Lived to See the Day: France in Arms, 1940–44* (Hutchinson, 1961).

INDEX